Objective-C

A Problem-Solution Approach

Matthew Campbell

Apress®

Objective-C Recipes

ISBN-13 (pbk): 978-1-4302-4371-7

ISBN-13 (electronic): 978-1-4302-4372-4

President and Publisher: Paul Manning
Lead Editor: Steve Anglin
Developmental Editor: Matthew Moodie and Louise Corrigan
Technical Reviewer: Anselm Bradford
Editorial Board: Steve Anglin, Ewan Buckingham, Gary Cornell, Louise Corrigan, Morgan Ertel, Jonathan Gennick, Jonathan Hassell, Robert Hutchinson, Michelle Lowman, James Markham, Matthew Moodie, Jeff Olson, Jeffrey Pepper, Douglas Pundick, Ben Renow-Clarke, Dominic Shakeshaft, Gwenan Spearing, Matt Wade, Tom Welsh
Coordinating Editor: Corbin Collins
Copy Editor: Mary Behr
Compositor: Bytheway Publishing Services
Indexer: SPi Global
Artist: SPi Global
Cover Designer: Anna Ishchenko

Distributed to the book trade worldwide by Springer Science+Business Media New York, 233 Spring Street, 6th Floor, New York, NY 10013. Phone 1-800-SPRINGER, fax (201) 348-4505, e-mail orders-ny@springer-sbm.com, or visit www.springeronline.com.

For information on translations, please e-mail rights@apress.com, or visit www.apress.com.

Apress and friends of ED books may be purchased in bulk for academic, corporate, or promotional use. eBook versions and licenses are also available for most titles. For more information, reference our Special Bulk Sales–eBook Licensing web page at www.apress.com/bulk-sales.

Any source code or other supplementary materials referenced by the author in this text is available to readers at www.apress.com. For detailed information about how to locate your book's source code, go to www.apress.com/source-code/.

Contents at a Glance

Contents

About the Author

 **Matthew Campbell** has trained over 800 new iOS developers at the Mobile App Mastery Institute and iOS Code Camp. He also developed Tasting Notes, a universal app for wine lovers. Matt is the lead blogger for http://HowToMakeiPhoneApps.com, a blog about creating iPhone apps.

About the Technical Reviewer

 **Anselm Bradford** is a lecturer in digital media at the Auckland University of Technology (AUT) in New Zealand where he researches interactive media, web media, and visual communication. He has been a technical reviewer on several iOS-related books and is the lead author of *HTML5 Mastery* and a co-author of *CSS3 Solutions*. He may be found @anselmbradford on Twitter and occasionally blogs at AnselmBradford.com.

Acknowledgments

It's tempting to think that a book like this is the sole work of the person whose name is stamped on the front cover. Of course, that's not true, and this book never would have happened at all without the support and occasional ego massaging from the supportive editors at Apress.

In particular, I'd like to acknowledge Louise Corrigan, whose comments peppered throughout our shared documents encouraged me to finish each chapter. I'd also like to acknowledge our technical reviewer, Anselm Bradford, who helped me make sure that the code wasn't going horribly wrong and would work for you.

I'd like to acknowledge Corbin Collins, who helped keep us all on track. It is way too easy to miss a deadline or two without the occasional nudge to keep us all in line, and Corbin provided that.

Finally, I'd like to give a shout out to all the readers of the `http://HowToMakeiPhoneApps.com` blog and the Mobile App Mastery Institute students. Everything in this book is possible because of your generous support and attention throughout the years. I never would have written this book without your feedback and validation.

Preface

Today, learning programming is about learning how to shape our world. Objective-C programmers are in a unique position to create applications that people all over the world can use in their daily lives.

Objective-C is a delight to use. While other programming languages can feel clumsy at times, Objective-C will show you its power and reach with grace. Problems that seem intractable in other programming languages melt away in Objective-C.

At its core, this book is about exploring Objective-C in the language's natural environment. Objective-C has a story to tell in code that is about computer science and solving problems in an elegant way.

Application Development

This chapter covers some of the essentials involved with getting an Objective-C application set up from the command line and Xcode. You will see how to code command line Mac desktop apps and iOS apps for the iPhone and iPad.

The recipes in this chapter will show you how to:

- Compile an Objective-C program from the command line

- Code a custom class with properties and methods

- Implement both instance and class methods

- Extend existing classes using a category

- Code and compile a Mac command line application

- Use Xcode to set up a Mac application

- Use Xcode to set up an iOS application

- Add user controls to applications using Delegation and Target-Action patterns

---

NOTE: Most of this book assumes that you are using a Mac with Xcode 4.2, which you can obtain from the Mac App Store at `www.apple.com/mac/app-store/`.

1.1 Creating a Terminal Application

Problem

You want to use Terminal to build a simple Objective-C program that doesn't depend on the extra features that come with Xcode. Your program will use Objective-C to write out a message to the terminal console window on your Mac.

Solution

Use your favorite text editor to create a file in your home directory, which is at /Users/[yourusername]/. You can use the text editor vi from your terminal or the GUI-based TextEdit program that comes with your Mac. If you use TextEdit, make sure to save the file that you create as plain text.

In this file, you will add a main function (which, incidentally, would look the same if written in C), import the Foundation framework, and add Objective-C code to write out a Hello World message to the console.

To compile this program, you will use a tool called clang to create an executable file that you can run from your terminal screen.

How It Works

The code that Objective-C needs to start is always located in a function called main, which takes some arguments and returns an integer value. In the first line of code, you import Foundation, which is a framework necessary for working with Objective-C objects.

Inside of your main function you must set up an autorelease pool, which is used by Objective-C to manage memory. Once you do that, you can use the NSString class to build a Hello World string and NSLog to write this string to the console screen.

The terminal command that is used to compile code is called clang and it compiles Objective-C programs. Here are some options that you may set when using clang to compile your Objective-C programs:

- -fobj means that Objective-C is the programming language.
- -arc specifies Automatic Reference Counting.

- ▨ -framework is used to link to the Foundation framework.

- ▨ -o specifies the name of the executable file that will be created.

> **NOTE:** If your Mac is running OSX 10.7 or greater, then you can use Automatic Reference Counting (ARC). ARC is a new feature available in OSX 10.7 used for memory management and you can get it by adding –arc to the statement that you use to compile your program. If you aren't sure what version of OSX you are using just omit –arc for now. See Chapter 8 for more details on ARC and memory management in general.

The Code

This is what the code in your plain text file should look like:

```
#import <Foundation/Foundation.h>
int main (int argc, const char * argv[]){
        @autoreleasepool {
                NSString *helloString = @"Hello World";
                NSLog(@"%@", helloString);
        }
        return 0;
}
```

Usage

Open up your terminal and type in the following commands to compile your code. Make sure to navigate to the location where you placed your code file before compiling.

```
clang -fobjc -framework Foundation main.m -o maccommandlineapp
```

For this example, I'm assuming that the code was placed in a file named main.m and that the output file will be called maccommandlineapp.

Hit return to compile the code. Once the program is compiled, type in open maccommandlineapp and press return to run and test your work.

Another window should open up with output that looks like this:

```
Hello World
```

```
logout

[Process completed]
```

1.2 Writing to the Console

Problem

As you're testing code, you would like to be able to write out values to the console window. Objects and primitive type values can be reported but each requires specific string formatters to work with NSLog.

Solution

Substitute object and primitives values into NSLog to report the values of these variables to the console screen.

How It Works

Object and primitive type values may be reported to the console using NSLog. Each type has a different specifier that must be used as a placeholder for the value. You type out the string that you would like to appear in the console while putting in specifiers into the string where you would like to see values reported. You can put as many specifiers into the string as you like, but you must make sure to include each value in the call to NSLog.

For example, if you had an integer variable named myInteger and a character variable named myCharacter and you wanted to report each of these values to the console, you would do something like this:

```
NSLog(@"myCharacter = %c and myInteger = %i", myCharacter, myInteger);
```

> **WARNING:** Each specifier that you include in the NSLog string must have a corresponding value in the comma-separated list to the right or the compiler will throw an error more '%' conversions than data arguments at compile time.

There are a few more specifiers that you may use. See Table 1-1 for a list of commonly used format specifiers.

Table 1-1. *List of Specifiers Used with NSLog*

Specifier	Data Type
%@	Objective-C object (looks at description method)
%d, %D, %i	Int (signed 32-bit integer)
%u, %U	Unsigned int (unsigned 32-bit integer)
%f	Double (64-bit floating point number)
%e	Double (64-bit floating point number in scientific notation)
%c	Unsigned char (unsigned 8-bit character)
%C	Unichar (16-bit character)
%p	Pointer (printed in hexadecimal)
%%	Escape character so you can print the % sign

The Code

Here is how you report the values of various variables to the console using NSLog:

```
#import <Foundation/Foundation.h>
int main (int argc, const char * argv[]){
        @autoreleasepool {

                //To print out primitive types:
                int myInteger = 1;
                NSLog(@"myInteger = %i", myInteger);

                float myFloatingPointNumber = 2;
                NSLog(@"myFloatingPointNumber = %f", myFloatingPointNumber);
                NSLog(@"myFloatingPointNumber in scientific notation = %e",  ↵
                                                myFloatingPointNumber);


                char myCharacter = 'A';
                NSLog(@"myCharacter = %c", myCharacter);

                //To print out the % symbol
                NSLog(@"Percent Sign looks like %%");
```

```
            //To print out Objective-C objects:
            NSString *myString = @"My String";
            NSLog(@"myString = %@", myString);
            NSLog(@"myString's pointer = %p", myString);

            //To print out a series of values
            NSLog(@"myCharacter = %c and myInteger = %i", myCharacter, myInteger);

        }
        return 0;
}
```

Usage

To test this code, compile the files with clang as you did in Recipe 1-1.

```
clang -fobjc -framework Foundation main.m -o maccommandlineapp
```

Run the app by typing open maccommandlineapp in your terminal window and you should see output that looks like this:

```
myInteger = 1
myFloatingPointNumber = 2.000000
myFloatingPointNumber in scientific notation = 2.000000e+00
myCharacter = A
Percent Sign looks like %
myString = My String
myString's pointer = 0x105880110
myCharacter = A and myInteger = 1
logout

[Process completed]
```

> **NOTE:** In your output, the pointer for myString will have a different
> value than mine.

1.3 Creating a New Custom Class

Problem

Object-oriented programmers like to be able to encapsulate functionality in objects. To do this, you must be able to define a custom class with attributes and behaviors.

Solution

Classes in Objective-C need interface and implementation definitions. Although it's not absolutely required, you typically keep the interface and implementations in separate files. The file with the interface is named as same as the class itself but with the .**h** file extension. The file with the implementation also has the class name but with the .**m** file extension.

To use a custom class, you must import the class header file into the code file where you intend on using the class. Then you can instantiate an object from the class to use the functionality encapsulated in the class.

How It Works

The first step is to add two files where you will write your custom class code. You can use your text editor of choice to do this. Let's assume that you want a class to represent a car. In this case, you simply add two new files: Car.h and Car.m. Put these files in the same directory as your main.m file to make it easier later on to compile these together (see Listings 1-1 through 1-3 for the code).

In the Car.h file, you locate the interface for the Car class. A class interface must begin with the @interface keyword and end with the @end keyword. Everything in between these two keywords defines the properties and methods of the class. The following is the essential code needed to define a Car class:

```
#import <Foundation/Foundation.h>

@interface Car : NSObject

@end
```

Notice that in the Car class definition you are importing Foundation again and right after the name car you have : NSObject. This means that your car is a subclass of NSObject. In fact, NSObject is the root object in Objective-C and all other objects are either a subclass of NSObject or a subclass of another class that is a subclass of NSObject.

The Car.m file looks similar to the Car.h file. Here you first import the Car.h file and then use the @implementation keyword to declare that you are implementing your custom class. All the code you use to implement comes after the line of code where you declare that you are implementing Car. This is what the Car class implementation looks like so far:

```
#import "Car.h"

@implementation Car

@end
```

In order to use your class, you need to import Car.h and then instantiate an object from the class. To instantiate an object, you send two messages: alloc and init. Both of these messages come from the NSObject superclass.

```
Car *car = [[Car alloc] init];
```

The Code

Listing 1-1. *Car.h*

```
#import <Foundation/Foundation.h>

@interface Car : NSObject

@end
```

Listing 1-2. *Car.m*

```
#import "Car.h"

@implementation Car

@end
```

Listing 1-3. *main.m*

```
#import "Car.h"

int main (int argc, const char * argv[]){
        @autoreleasepool {
                Car *car = [[Car alloc] init];
                NSLog(@"car is %@", car);
```

```
        }
        return 0;
}
```

Usage

To use this code, compile your files as you did before, except that you need to include the code file for the Car class in addition to the main.m code file.

```
clang -fobjc -framework Foundation Car.m main.m -o maccommandlineapp
```

It may be included right before the main.m file in the command text. When you open the maccommandlineapp, you will see output that looks something like this:

```
car is <Car: 0x10c411cd0>
logout
```

```
[Process completed]
```

Of course, Car doesn't do much until you add your own custom properties and methods, which you'll see in the upcoming recipes.

1.4 Code Property Assessors

Problem

Custom classes need to represent the attributes of the entities they are modeling. You need to know how to define and implement properties in Objective-C to do this.

Solution

To implement properties for custom classes, you must declare properties in the class interface and implement these properties in the class implementation. Once you implement these properties, you can use them in your other code files by accessing these properties when you need them.

How It Works

The first place you go when adding properties to classes is the custom class header file. You need two things here: a local instance variable to hold the value of your property and a property declaration. Here is what an interface looks like:

```
#import <Foundation/Foundation.h>

@interface Car : NSObject{
@private
    NSString *name_;
}

@property(strong) NSString *name;

@end
```

Here the local instance is named name_ and the property declaration starts with the keyword @property. Notice that the property declaration has the word strong in parentheses right before the class name. This word is called a *property attribute*, and strong is only one of many property descriptors available to you. See Table 1-2 for a list of property attributes.

Table 1-2. *Property Attributes*

Attribute	Description
readwrite	The property needs both a getter and a setter (default).
readonly	The property only needs a getter (objects can't set this property).
strong	The property will have a strong relationship (the object will be retained).
weak	The property will be set to nil when the destination object is deallocated.
assign	The property will simply use assignment (used with primitive types).
copy	The property returns a copy and must implement the NSCopying protocol.
retain	A retain message will be sent in the setter method.
nonatomic	This specifies that the property is not atomic (not locked while being accessed).

The second place you need to go to implement a property is the implementation, which in your example would be located in Car.m. Here you need to code your so-called *getters* and *setters*.

```
#import "Car.h"

@implementation Car
```

```
-(void)setName:(NSString *)name{
    name_ = name;
}

-(NSString *) name{
    return name_;
}
```

@end

You can use properties like this with dot notation to set and get properties values:

```
car.name = @"Sports Car";
NSLog(@"car is %@", car.name);
```

Or you can use properties with standard Objective-C messaging:

```
[car setName:@"New Car Name"];
NSLog(@"car.name is %@", [car name]);
```

You will see both examples of accessing properties as you look at more Objective-C code. Dot notation (the first example) is a relatively new Objective-C feature that was added with Objective-C 2.0. Note that dot notation has the advantage of being more familiar to programmers who are used to other programming languages where dot notation is the standard practice. The second example, regular Objective-C messaging, is still used often. Choosing one method over another is mostly a matter of personal preference. See Listings 1-4 through 1-6 for the code.

The Code

Listing 1-4. *Car.h*

```
#import <Foundation/Foundation.h>

@interface Car : NSObject{
@private
    NSString *name_;
}

@property(strong) NSString *name;

@end
```

Listing 1-5. *Car.m*

```
#import "Car.h"

@implementation Car

-(void)setName:(NSString *)name{
    name_ = name;
}

-(NSString *) name{
    return name_;
}

@end
```

Listing 1-6. *main.m*

```
#import "Car.h"
int main (int argc, const char * argv[]){
        @autoreleasepool {
                Car *car = [[Car alloc] init];
                car.name = @"Sports Car";
                NSLog(@"car.name is %@", car.name);

                [car setName:@"New Car Name"];
                NSLog(@"car.name is %@", [car name]);

        }
        return 0;
}
```

Usage

To use this code, compile your files as you did before.

```
clang -fobjc-arc -framework Foundation Car.m main.m -o maccommandlineapp
```

When you open the `maccommandlineapp`, you will see output that looks something like this:

```
car.name is Sports Car
car.name is New Car Name
logout

[Process completed]
```

1.5 Code Property Assessors with @synthesize

Problem

Custom classes need to represent the attributes of the entities they are modeling. You need to know how to define and implement properties in Objective-C to do this. If you don't want to code your own getter and setter methods, you can use the @synthesize as an alternative.

Solution

To implement properties with @synthesize, you still need to declare properties in the class interface as you did in Recipe 1.4 and implement these properties in the class implementation. However, instead of writing your own assessor code, you can use the @synthesize keyword to direct the complier to fill in the code for you in the background during the compilation process.

How It Works

The first place you go when adding properties to classes is the custom class header file. All you need to do with this method is to declare a property. Here is what an interface looks like:

```
#import <Foundation/Foundation.h>

@interface Car : NSObject

@property(strong) NSString *name;

@end
```

The second file you need to go to implement a property is the implementation, which in your example is located in Car.m. All you need to do here is use the @synthesize keyword and include the property that you want to generate getters and setters for (after the @implementation keyword).

```
#import "Car.h"

@implementation Car
@synthesize name;

@end
```

You can use properties like this with dot notation to set and get properties values:

```
car.name = @"Sports Car";
NSLog(@"car is %@", car.name);
```

Or you can use properties with standard Objective-C messaging, like so:

```
[car setName:@"New Car Name"];
NSLog(@"car.name is %@", [car name]);
```

See Listings 1-7 through 1-9 for the code.

The Code

Listing 1-7. *Car.h*

```
#import <Foundation/Foundation.h>

@interface Car : NSObject

@property(strong) NSString *name;

@end
```

Listing 1-8. *Car.m*

```
#import "Car.h"

@implementation Car
@synthesize name;

@end
```

Listing 1-9. *main.m*

```
#import "Car.h"
int main (int argc, const char * argv[]){
        @autoreleasepool {
                Car *car = [[Car alloc] init];
                car.name = @"Sports Car";
                NSLog(@"car.name is %@", car.name);

                [car setName:@"New Car Name"];
                NSLog(@"car.name is %@", [car name]);

        }
        return 0;
}
```

Usage

To use this code, compile your files as you did before.

```
clang -fobjc -framework Foundation Car.m main.m -o maccommandlineapp
```

When you open the `maccommandlineapp`, you will see output that looks something like this:

```
car.name is Sports Car
car.name is New Car Name
logout

[Process completed]
```

1.6 Adding a Class Method to a Custom Class

Problem

In Objective-C, you can send messages to either classes or objects to get things done. If you want your custom class to be able to respond to a message, you must first code a class method.

Solution

To add a class method, you need to add forward declaration in your header file. Class methods start with + and a return type like (void), followed by a set of parameter descriptors (descriptive text that appears before a parameter), data types, and parameter names. Class methods are implemented in the implementation file after the @implementation keyword.

How It Works

The first place you go when adding class methods to a class is the custom class header file. Class methods have a + sign in front of the return type. Here is a forward declaration for a class method that prints out a description to the console that includes a date:

```
+(void)writeDescriptionToLogWithThisDate:(NSDate *)date;
```

To implement a class method, go to the implementation file for the class, and after the @implementation keyword, write out the code for the class method.

```
+(void)writeDescriptionToLogWithThisDate:(NSDate *)date{
        NSLog(@"Today's date is %@ and this class represents a car", date);
}
```

To use this method, you simply send a message to the Car class without worrying about instantiating an object first.

```
[Car writeDescriptionToLogWithThisDate:[NSDate date]];
```

See Listings 1-10 through 1-12 for the code.

The Code

Listing 1-10. *Car.h*

```
#import <Foundation/Foundation.h>
@interface Car : NSObject

@property(strong) NSString *name;

+(void)writeDescriptionToLogWithThisDate:(NSDate *)date;

@end
```

Listing 1-11. *Car.m*

```
#import "Car.h"

@implementation Car

@synthesize name;

+(void)writeDescriptionToLogWithThisDate:(NSDate *)date{
        NSLog(@"Today's date is %@ and this class represents a car", date);
}

@end
```

Listing 1-12. *main.m*

```
#import "Car.h"
int main (int argc, const char * argv[]){
        @autoreleasepool {
                [Car writeDescriptionToLogWithThisDate:[NSDate date]];
        }
        return 0;
}
```

Usage

When you work with class methods, you don't need to instantiate an object first. You simply send a message to the class to execute the code in the class method. To use this code, compile your files as you did before.

```
clang -fobjc -framework Foundation Car.m main.m -o maccommandlineapp
```

When you open the `maccommandlineapp`, you will see output that looks something like this:

```
Today's date is 2011-12-19 14:23:11 +0000 and this class represents a car
logout
```

```
[Process completed]
```

1.7 Adding an Instance Method to a Custom Class

Problem

In Objective-C, you can send messages to either classes or objects to get things done. If you want objects that have been instantiated from your custom class to be able to respond to a message, you must first code an instance method.

Solution

To add an instance method, you need to add forward declaration in your header file. Instance methods start with – and a return type like (`void`), followed by a set of parameter descriptors (descriptive text that appears before a parameter), data types, and parameter names. Instance methods are implemented in the implementation file after the `@implementation` keyword.

How It Works

The first place you go when adding instance methods to a class is the custom class header file. Instance methods have a - sign in front of the return type. Here is a forward declaration for a class method that prints out a description to the console that includes a date:

```
-(void)writeOutThisCarsState;
```

To implement a class method, go to the implementation file for the class, and after the @implementation keyword, write out the code for the class method.

```
-(void)writeOutThisCarsState{
        NSLog(@"This car is a %@", self.name);
}
```

Usage

To use this method, you need to first instantiate an object from your Car class and then set the name property. Then you can send the writeOutThisCarsState message to execute the code in the instance method.

```
Car *newCar = [[Car alloc] init];
newCar.name = @"My New Car";
[newCar writeOutThisCarsState];
```

To test this code, compile your files as you did before from Terminal.

```
clang -fobjc -framework Foundation Car.m main.m -o maccommandlineapp
```

When you open the maccommandlineapp, you will see output that looks something like this:

```
Today's date is 2011-12-19 14:23:11 +0000 and this car is a My New Car
logout

[Process completed]
```

1.8 Extending a Class with a Category

Problem

You would like to add methods and behavior to a class, but you would rather not create an entire new subclass.

Solution

In Objective-C, you can use categories to define and implement properties and methods that can later be attached to a class. To do this, you need two files: a header file to list your interface and an implementation file to list your implementation. When you are ready to use your category, you can import the category header file; any class that has the category applied to it will have those properties and methods available for use.

How It Works

The first thing you need is a header file. Let's assume that you want to extend the NSString class to add methods to help you create HTML text. A category header file has an interface that looks like this:

```
@interface NSString (HTMLTags)
```

The class name that comes right after the @interface keyword is the class that you are extending. This means that the category may only be applied to NSString (or a subclass of NSString). In the parentheses that come after the class name you put the name that you are giving to the category.

You locate all the properties and methods for this category after the interface but before the @end keyword (just like in a regular class interface).

The implementation follows a similar pattern.

```
@implementation NSString (HTMLTags)
```

When you want to apply this extended functionality that you define in the category, you simply import the category header file, and you will be able to use the additional properties and methods that you have coded. See Listings 1-13 through 1-15 for the code.

The Code

Listing 1-13. *HTMLTags.h*

```
#import <Foundation/Foundation.h>

@interface NSString (HTMLTags)

-(NSString *) encloseWithParagraphTags;

@end
```

Listing 1-14. *HTMLTags.m*

```
#import "HTMLTags.h"

@implementation NSString (HTMLTags)

-(NSString *) encloseWithParagraphTags{
        return [NSString stringWithFormat:@"<p>%@</p>",self];
}

@end
```

Listing 1-15. *main.m*

```
#import "HTMLTags.h"

int main (int argc, const char * argv[]){
        @autoreleasepool {
                NSString *webText = @"This is the first line of my blog post";

                //Print out the string like normal:
                NSLog(@"%@", webText);

                //Print out the string using the category function:
                NSLog(@"%@", [webText encloseWithParagraphTags]);
        }
        return 0;
}
```

Usage

Categories are typically used in situations where you want to avoid creating a complex inheritance hierarchy. That is, you would rather not have to rely on using custom classes that are more than three or four levels removed from the root class because you don't want to end up in a situation where making a change to a class has unintended implications in a class farther down in the inheritance hierarchy.

Categories also help your code remain readable. For instance, if you use a category to extend NSString in your projects, most of your code will be familiar to anyone who has used NSString. The alternative method of subclassing NSString (with something like NSHTMLString) could cause confusion.

To compile the code in the listings from the command line, make sure to compile the file with the category in addition to the main.m file.

```
clang -fobjc-arc -framework Foundation HTMLTags.m main.m -o maccommandlineapp
```

When you open the maccommandlineapp, you will see output that looks something like this:

```
This is the first line of my blog post
<p>This is the first line of my blog post</p>
logout

[Process completed]
```

1.9 Creating a Mac Window-Based Application from Terminal

Problem

You want to create a Mac application that has a user interface from the terminal. While Xcode is generally used to develop rich window-based applications on Mac, sometimes it's easier to see what is happening when you set up an application without the extra help that Xcode project templates insert into your code.

Solution

Mac apps need some key components to work. Namely, you need to use the NSApplication and NSWindow classes to manage the application itself and the initial user interface. You also need an app delegate class, which you can code in a separate file. The app delegate acts as a helper for the application by implementing key methods that the application needs to work.

How It Works

There are two steps to this solution.

App Delegate

Mac apps make use of a design pattern called **Delegatation**. When you want to implement Delegation, you designate one object (called the delegate) to act on behalf of another object. Your Mac application is going to need a helper object called the app delegate to work.

The app delegate is a class that needs it's own header and implementation file. Mac app delegates must import the Cocoa framework and implement the NSApplicationDelegate protocol. Protocols are a set of properties and methods that a class must implement in order to act as a delegate. The NSApplicationDelegate protocol is required for your class to be an app delegate.

Here is a an example of how you start to define an app delegate:

```
@interface AppDelegate : NSObject <NSApplicationDelegate>
```

You can see you are adopting the NSApplicationDelegate protocol here because you have this specified between the < and > symbols. The app delegate should have an NSWindow property and implement the delegate method - (void)applicationDidFinishLaunching:(NSNotification *)aNotification;.

The NSWindow property is the UI element where you put your user content. The delegate method is a notification that executes when the application is done launching to the desktop, which makes it a good place to set up the rest of the application.

Application

The Mac application itself is set up and launched from the main function as before. You will need to first get a reference to the NSApplication instance. NSApplication is a Cocoa class that is implemented using the Singleton design pattern. This means that you can only have once instance of NSApplication per application and that you must use a particular procedure to get a reference to the NSApplication object.

```
NSApplication *macApp = [NSApplication sharedApplication];
```

The sharedApplication function is a class method that will either instantiate and return an instance of NSApplication or simply return the instance that has already been created. Once you have a reference to the Mac application, you can create an app delegate and set this as macApp's delegate.

```
AppDelegate *appDelegate = [[AppDelegate alloc] init];
macApp.delegate = appDelegate;
```

This has the effect of saying that the app delegate will now act on behalf of your Mac application. Next, your application must have a window, so use the NSWindow class to instantiate a window and set this to the app delegate's NSWindow property.

```
int style = NSClosableWindowMask | NSResizableWindowMask | ↵
  NSTexturedBackgroundWindowMask | NSTitledWindowMask | ↵
NSMiniaturizableWindowMask;

 NSWindow *appWindow = [[NSWindow alloc] initWithContentRect:NSMakeRect(50, 50, 600, 400)
                                        styleMask:style
                                          backing:NSBackingStoreBuffered
                                            defer:NO];
appDelegate.window = appWindow;
```

Now that you are all set up and connected, you can present the window to the user and run the Mac application.

```
[appWindow makeKeyAndOrderFront:appWindow];
[macApp run];
```

See Listings 1-16 through 1-18 for the code.

The Code

Listing 1-16. *AppDelegate.h*

```
#import <Cocoa/Cocoa.h>

@interface AppDelegate : NSObject <NSApplicationDelegate>

@property (assign) NSWindow *window;

@end
```

Listing 1-17. *AppDelegate.m*

```
#import "AppDelegate.h"

@implementation AppDelegate

@synthesize window = _window;

- (void)applicationDidFinishLaunching:(NSNotification *)aNotification{
    NSLog(@"Mac app finished launching");
}

@end
```

Listing 1-18. *main.m*

```
#import "AppDelegate.h"

int main (int argc, char *argv[]){
    NSApplication *macApp = [NSApplication sharedApplication];
    AppDelegate *appDelegate = [[AppDelegate alloc] init];
    macApp.delegate = appDelegate;

    int style = NSClosableWindowMask | NSResizableWindowMask | ↵
    NSTexturedBackgroundWindowMask | NSTitledWindowMask | ↵
NSMiniaturizableWindowMask;

   NSWindow *appWindow = [[NSWindow alloc] initWithContentRect:NSMakeRect(50, 50, 600, 400)
                                               styleMask:style
                                                 backing:NSBackingStoreBuffered
                                                   defer:NO];
    appDelegate.window = appWindow;
```

```
                                    [appWindow makeKeyAndOrderFront:appWindow];
    [macApp run];
}
```

Usage

To compile the code from the command line, make sure to compile the file with the AppDelegate in addition to the `main.m` file. For this program, you must also link to the Cocoa framework since you are using Cocoa to manage your UI elements for your Mac app.

```
clang -fobjc -framework Cocoa AppDelegate.m main.m -o macwindowapp
```

When you open the `macwindowapp` file, you will see a blank window appear. It should look like Figure 1-1.

Figure 1-1. *Mac application window*

1.10 Adding a User Control to a Mac Application

Problem

Mac applications need to be able to receive and interpret user intentions. This is done with user controls like buttons and text fields that you make available for user input so you can take some action based on what the user wants. You want to add a button to your app and have something happen when the user clicks the button.

Solution

To add a button to a Mac app, simply add code to the `applicationDidFinishLaunching` delegate method to create the button, set the necessary button properties, set the action method (the code that executes in response to a user click), and then add the button to the window. You also want to code the action method that does something in response to a user click.

How It Works

In a simple Mac application like you coded in Recipe 1.9, you can add a button to the window to present this control to the user:

```
button = [[NSButton alloc] initWithFrame:NSMakeRect(230,200,140,40)];
[[self.window contentView] addSubview: button];
```

This is something that you would do in the app delegate's `didFinishLaunching` delegate method. You can also set up the button UI by setting properties in this method:

```
[button setTitle: @"Change Color"];
[button setButtonType:NSMomentaryLightButton];
[button setBezelStyle:NSTexturedSquareBezelStyle];
```

Buttons use the **Target-Action** design pattern to respond to user actions like a button click. Target-Action is a design pattern where the object has the information necessary to execute an action (a special sort of method). You need to tell the object which method contains the code that will execute in response to an action and where the method is located (the target).

```
[button setTarget:self];
[button setAction:@selector(changeBackgroundColor)];
```

Here the target is self (the app delegate) and the method is called changeBackgroundColor. In the action method where you located the code, you need to change the background color of the window.

```
-(void)changeBackgroundColor{
    self.window.backgroundColor = [NSColor blackColor];
}
```

See Listings 1-19 through 1-21 for the code.

The Code

Listing 1-19. *AppDelegate.h*

```
#import <Cocoa/Cocoa.h>

@interface AppDelegate : NSObject <NSApplicationDelegate>

@property (assign) NSWindow *window;

@end
```

Listing 1-20. *AppDelegate.m*

```
#import "AppDelegate.h"

@implementation AppDelegate

@synthesize window = _window;
NSButton *button;

-(void)changeBackgroundColor{
    self.window.backgroundColor = [NSColor blackColor];
}

- (void)applicationDidFinishLaunching:(NSNotification *)aNotification{
    NSLog(@"Mac app finished launching");

    button = [[NSButton alloc] initWithFrame:NSMakeRect(230,200,140,40)];
    [[self.window contentView] addSubview: button];
    [button setTitle: @"Change Color"];
    [button setButtonType:NSMomentaryLightButton];
    [button setBezelStyle:NSTexturedSquareBezelStyle];
    [button setTarget:self];
    [button setAction:@selector(changeBackgroundColor)];
}

@end
```

Listing 1-21. *main.m*

```
#import "AppDelegate.h"

int main(int argc, char *argv[]){
    NSApplication *macApp = [NSApplication sharedApplication];
    AppDelegate *appDelegate = [[AppDelegate alloc] init];
    macApp.delegate = appDelegate;

    int style = NSClosableWindowMask | NSResizableWindowMask |↵
    NSTexturedBackgroundWindowMask | NSTitledWindowMask | NSMiniaturizableWindowMask;

  NSWindow *appWindow = [[NSWindow alloc] initWithContentRect:NSMakeRect(50, 50, 600, 400)
                                                 styleMask:style
                                                   backing:NSBackingStoreBuffered
                                                     defer:NO];
    appDelegate.window = appWindow;
[appWindow makeKeyAndOrderFront:appWindow];
    [macApp run];
}
```

Usage

To compile this code from the command line, make sure to compile the file with the AppDelegate in addition to the main.m file. For this program, you must also link to the Cocoa framework since you are using Cocoa to manage your UI elements for your Mac app.

```
clang -fobjc -framework Cocoa AppDelegate.m main.m -o macwindowapp
```

When you open the macwindowapp file, you will see a window like the one in Figure 1-2.

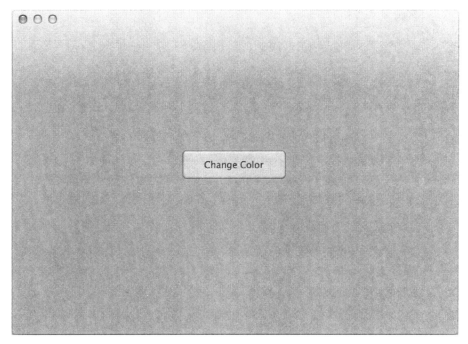

Figure 1-2. *Mac application window with button*

When you click the button, the action method will execute and turn the window's background color to black, as you can see in Figure 1-3.

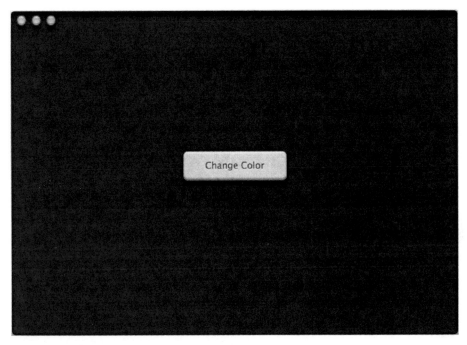

Figure 1-3. *Window after action method executed*

1.11 Creating a Mac Window-Based Application From Xcode

Problem

The recipes so far have simply been using the compiler from the command line to create Objective-C programs. However, if you want to develop a rich Mac application, you need to use Xcode to get it ready for the App Store.

> **NOTE:** The Mac App Store is a marketplace where developers can sell their software directly to users. You can see applications for sale by other developers by visiting www.apple.com/mac/app-store/.

Solution

Use Xcode to set up your Mac application. You can use Xcode to create command line apps or Cocoa apps; there are also other options.

> **NOTE:** Cocoa Mac applications have the user interface that consumers expect (the top menu items, familiar controls, and layouts). These types of applications require more frameworks, namely Cocoa, to work as expected. Command-line apps are simplier programs that are run from the Terminal application. Mac apps that you purchase from the Mac App Store are always Cocoa apps.

How It Works

Open Xcode and go to **File ➤ New ➤ New Project**. A dialog box will appear similar to the one in Figure 1-4.

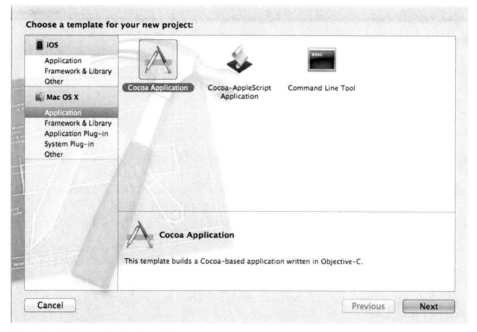

Figure 1-4. *Mac application templates*

Choose **Mac OS X ➤ Application ➤ Cocoa Application** to set up a Mac application. Click Next and you will be directed to another dialog box where you can specify some initial settings (see Figure 1-5).

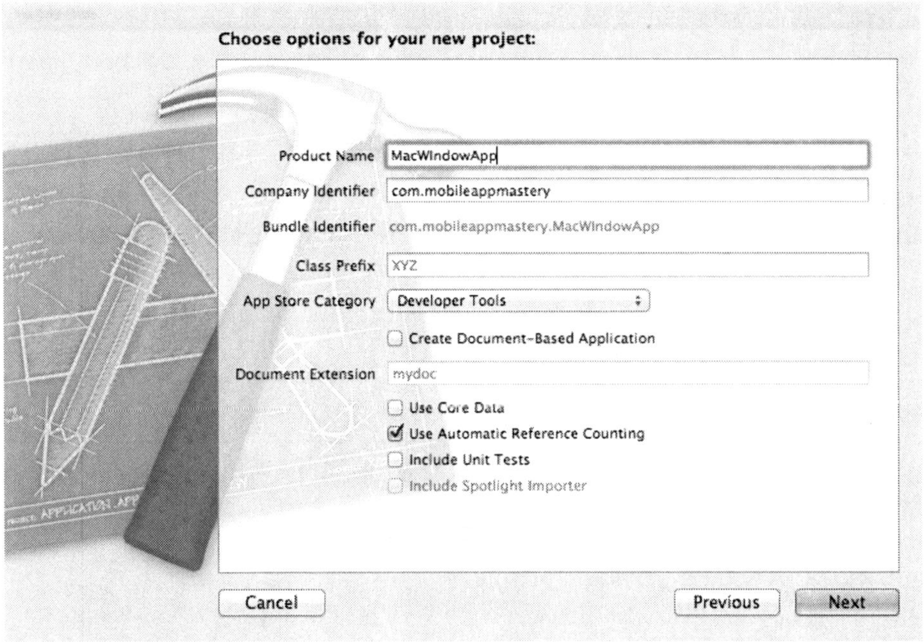

Figure 1-5. *Application settings*

See Table 1-3 for some more detail about all the options on this screen.

Table 1-3. *Property Attributes*

Option	Description
Product Name	The name of your Xcode project and the default name of your Mac app.
Company Identifier	Identifies your company (usually your domain name reversed).
Class Prefix	Xcode will automatically add a prefix to the file templates for this project.
App Store Category	Specifies the category for your app in the App Store.

Option	Description
Create Document-Based Application	Include the setup that you need to work with an NSDocument-based application.
Document Extension	Document extension associated with this app (for document-based apps).
Use Core Data	Automatically includes the Core Data Stack to be used for data persistence.
Use Automatic Reference Counting	Enables ARC for memory management. Use ARC unless you rather manage memory yourself.
Include Unit Test	Automatically includes setup that you need for unit testing your app.
Include Spotlight Importer	An option for document-based applications to allow the app's document files to be referenced by Spotlight.

After you choose your initial settings, click Next to choose your project location. Here you may choose to use the version control system Git locally.

Once you do all this, Xcode will automatically open with the files that you need all ready to go. Your code files and other resources will be located on the left. Click on any code file to see the code in the editor: the key code files will look similar to what you have worked on in previous recipes: AppDelegate.h, AppDelegate.m, and main.m (you can see that one by expanding the Supporting Files folder).

You will also find other resources used for application development like the MainMenu.xib file (used with Interface Builder), the Frameworks folder (linked frameworks), and your InfoPlist file (a keyed list of your app settings). See Listings 1-22 through 1-24 for the code.

The Code

Listing 1-22. *AppDelegate.h*

```
#import <Cocoa/Cocoa.h>

@interface AppDelegate : NSObject <NSApplicationDelegate>

@property (assign) IBOutlet NSWindow *window;

@end
```

Listing 1-23. *AppDelegate.m*

```
#import "AppDelegate.h"

@implementation AppDelegate

@synthesize window = _window;

- (void)applicationDidFinishLaunching:(NSNotification *)aNotification{
    // Insert code here to initialize your application
}

@end
```

Listing 1-24. *main.m*

```
#import <Cocoa/Cocoa.h>

int main(int argc, char *argv[]){
    return NSApplicationMain(argc, (const char **)argv);
}
```

Usage

You can test this initial setup by clicking the Run button in the top left hand corner of Xcode. Xcode will gather all your code and other resources, link them to the frameworks that you need, and then launch the application. The Mac app window will appear with a menu aready set up and ready for use.

You can add controls and other UI with Objective-C to a Mac app by following the example from Recipe 1.10 or you can use the tools that Xcode provides for creating the UI.

1.12 Creating an iOS Application from Xcode

Problem

You want to build an application that can run on the iPhone, the iPad, or both. These applications follow similar patterns as Mac apps but they require different frameworks for the user interface.

Solution

Use Xcode to set up your iOS application. You can use Xcode to create simple iOS apps with only one screen or richer applications with navigation, tabs, and page views. You can also specify whether your app will run on the iPhone, the iPad, or both. Xcode comes with templates for most of the situtations you will find.

How It Works

Open Xcode and go **File** ➤ **New** ➤ **New Project**. A dialog box will appear similar to the one in Figure 1-6.

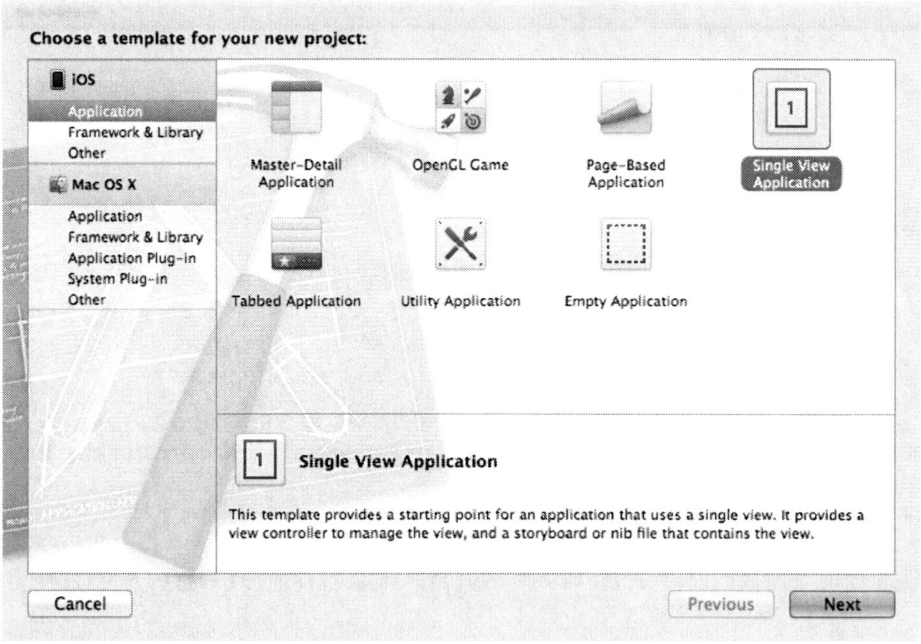

Figure 1-6. *iOS application templates*

Choose **iOS** ➤ **Application** ➤ **Single View Application** to set up an iOS application. Click Next and you will be directed to another dialog box where you can specify some initial settings (see Figure 1-7).

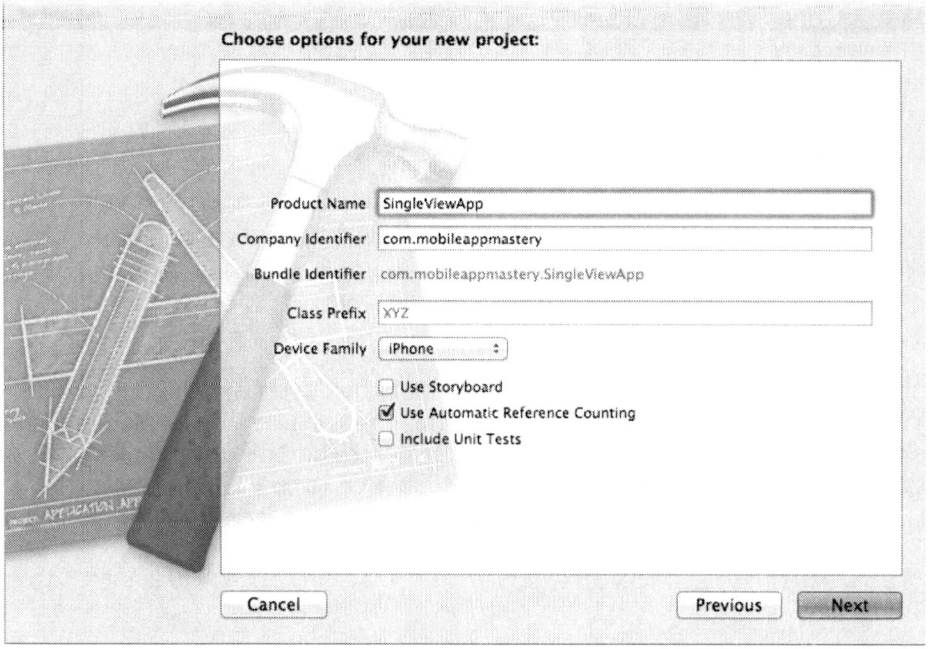

Figure 1-7. *iOS application settings*

See Table 1-4 for some more detail about all the options on this screen.

Table 1-4. *Property Attributes*

Option	Description
Product Name	The name of your Xcode project and the default name of your iOS app.
Company Identifier	Identifies your company (usually your domain name reversed).
Class Prefix	Xcode will automatically add a prefix to the file templates for this project.
Device Family	Set up project for iPhone, iPad, or Universal (both iPhone and iPad).
Use Automatic Reference Counting	Enables ARC for memory management. Use ARC unless you rather manage memory yourself.
Include Unit Tests	Automatically includes setup that you need for unit testing your app.

After you choose your initial settings, click Next to choose your project location. Here you may choose to use the version control system Git locally.

> **NOTE:** Git is a version control system that is now integrated with Xcode. If you choose to use version control, all the changes will be tracked and you will be able to compare all the versions of the code files that you create. Using Git version control is out of the scope of this book, but it can be a useful tool as you start to create production apps.

Once you do all this, you Xcode will automatically open up with the files that you need all ready to go. Your code files and other resources will be located on the left. Click on any code file to see the code in the editor. The key code files will look similar to what you have worked on in previous recipes: AppDelegate.h, AppDelegate.m, and main.m (you can see that one by expanding the Supporting Files folder). Since this is a single view application, you will also have code files for ViewController.h, ViewController.m, and ViewController.xib (an Interface Builder file).

iOS applications are set up in much the same way as Mac applications: they have an application class (called UIApplication for iOS) and an app delegate. The app delegate must adopt the UIApplicationDelegate protocol and have a window (called UIWindow for iOS). App delegates also have some delegate method that act as notifications for key events in the app lifecycle such as applicationDidFinishingLauchingWithOptions.

In the Single View Application template, the window and other user interface elements are set up in the app delegate's applicationDidFinishingLauchingWithOptions delegate method.

```
- (BOOL)application:(UIApplication *)application↩
didFinishLaunchingWithOptions:(NSDictionary *)launchOptions{
    self.window = [[UIWindow alloc] initWithFrame:[[UIScreen mainScreen] bounds]];
    self.viewController = [[ViewController alloc] initWithNibName:@"ViewController"↩
bundle:nil];
    self.window.rootViewController = self.viewController;
    [self.window makeKeyAndVisible];
    return YES;
}
```

This template is a little bit different than what you might remember from the Mac Cocoa Application template (Recipe 1.11). Namely, here you are using a class called ViewController (a subclass of UIViewController) and adding this to the window's rootViewController property.

This means that the screen that users see first is managed by this view controller. If you want to make changes to the app's user interface, you must do so in this view controller.

You will find other resources used for application development like the Frameworks folder (linked frameworks) and your InfoPlist file (a keyed list of your app settings). See Listings 1-25 through 1-29 for the code.

The Code

Listing 1-25. *AppDelegate.h*

```
#import <UIKit/UIKit.h>

@class ViewController;

@interface AppDelegate : UIResponder <UIApplicationDelegate>

@property (strong, nonatomic) UIWindow *window;
@property (strong, nonatomic) ViewController *viewController;

@end
```

Listing 1-26. *AppDelegate.m*

```
#import "AppDelegate.h"
#import "ViewController.h"

@implementation AppDelegate

@synthesize window = _window;
@synthesize viewController = _viewController;

- (BOOL)application:(UIApplication *)application↵
  didFinishLaunchingWithOptions:(NSDictionary *)launchOptions{
    self.window = [[UIWindow alloc] initWithFrame:[[UIScreen mainScreen] ↵
bounds]];
    self.viewController = [[ViewController alloc] ↵
initWithNibName:@"ViewController" bundle:nil];
    self.window.rootViewController = self.viewController;
    [self.window makeKeyAndVisible];
    return YES;
}

@end
```

Listing 1-27. *main.m*

```objc
#import <UIKit/UIKit.h>
#import "AppDelegate.h"

int main(int argc, char *argv[]){
    @autoreleasepool {
        return UIApplicationMain(argc, argv, nil, NSStringFromClass([AppDelegate↵
 class]));
    }
}
```

Listing 1-28. *ViewController.h*

```objc
#import <UIKit/UIKit.h>

@interface ViewController : UIViewController

@end
```

Listing 1-29. *ViewController.h*

```objc
#import "ViewController.h"

@implementation ViewController

-(void)viewDidLoad{
    [super viewDidLoad];
}

@end
```

Usage

You can test this initial setup by clicking the Run button in the top left hand corner of Xcode. Xcode will gather all your code and other resources, link them to the frameworks that you need, and then launch the application. The iOS app will appear in the iOS Simulator (a special program to test iOS apps on the Mac), as shown in Figure 1-8.

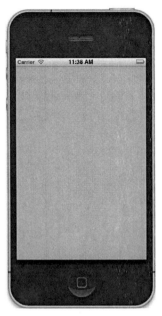

Figure 1-8. *iOS Simulator with single view application*

You can add controls and other UI with Objective-C to an iOS app (see recipes 1.13 and 1.14) or you can use the tools that Xcode provides for creating the UI.

1.13 Adding User Controls to an iOS Application with Target-Action

Problem

Now that you have an iOS application set up, you would like to add some user controls.

Solution

While you can add controls like buttons and labels to the window like you did with the Mac application in Recipe 1.11, it's more common to add controls to views, which are in turn presented in the application window. In this recipe, you are going to add a label and a button to the single view application from Recipe 1.12.

How It Works

Typically, you can think of the controls you want to use on a view controller as properties and follow the same rules as in Recipe 1.4. Then you instantiate these properties in the viewDidLoad view controller delegate method. Finally, you code any necessary action methods and then associated these action methods with the user controls using the Target-Action design pattern.

In this Recipe, you are going to add a UILabel and UIButton to the view controller that came with the Xcode template. This is what these property forward declarations look like:

```
#import <UIKit/UIKit.h>

@interface ViewController : UIViewController

@property(strong) UILabel *myLabel;
@property(strong) UIButton *myButton;

@end
```

In the implemenation, you use @synthesize to generate the getters and setters and set these controls to nil when the view is unloaded.

```
#import "ViewController.h"

@implementation ViewController
@synthesize myLabel, myButton;

- (void)viewDidLoad{
    [super viewDidLoad];

}

@end
```

The action method needs a forward declaration in the view controller header file.

```
#import <UIKit/UIKit.h>

@interface ViewController : UIViewController

@property(strong) UILabel *myLabel;
@property(strong) UIButton *myButton;

-(void)updateLabel;

@end
```

This action method can be implemented like this to update the label:

```
-(void)updateLabel{
    self.myLabel.text = @"The button was pressed...";
}
```

This is what you want to happen when the user presses the button. Finish the label and button by instantiating them, setting their properties, and adding them to the view. The button also needs to use Target-Action, so hook up the updateLabel action method to the button's touch up event. All of this happens in the view controllers viewDidLoad event.

```
- (void)viewDidLoad{
    [super viewDidLoad];

    //Create label
    self.myLabel = [[UILabel alloc] init];
    self.myLabel.frame = CGRectMake(20, 20, 280, 40);
    self.myLabel.textAlignment = UITextAlignmentCenter;
    self.myLabel.backgroundColor =[UIColor clearColor];
    self.myLabel.text = @"Press the button";
    [self.view addSubview:self.myLabel];

    //Create button
    self.myButton = [UIButton buttonWithType:UIButtonTypeRoundedRect];
    self.myButton.frame = CGRectMake(110, 200, 100, 50);

    //Add the pressButton action method
    [self.myButton addTarget:self
                      action:@selector(updateLabel)
            forControlEvents:UIControlEventTouchUpInside];
    [self.myButton setTitle:@"Press" forState:UIControlStateNormal];

    [self.view addSubview:self.myButton];

}
```

See Listings 1-30 and 1-31 for the code.

The Code

Listing 1-30. *ViewController.h*

```
#import <UIKit/UIKit.h>

@interface ViewController : UIViewController

@property(strong) UILabel *myLabel;
@property(strong) UIButton *myButton;

-(void)updateLabel;
```

@end

Listing 1-31. *ViewController.m*

```objc
#import "ViewController.h"

@implementation ViewController
@synthesize myLabel, myButton;

- (void)viewDidLoad{
    [super viewDidLoad];

    //Create label
    self.myLabel = [[UILabel alloc] init];
    self.myLabel.frame = CGRectMake(20, 20, 280, 40);
    self.myLabel.textAlignment = UITextAlignmentCenter;
    self.myLabel.backgroundColor =[UIColor clearColor];
    self.myLabel.text = @"Press the button";
    [self.view addSubview:self.myLabel];

    //Create button
    self.myButton = [UIButton buttonWithType:UIButtonTypeRoundedRect];
    self.myButton.frame = CGRectMake(110, 200, 100, 50);

    //Add the pressButton action method
    [self.myButton addTarget:self
                    action:@selector(updateLabel)
          forControlEvents:UIControlEventTouchUpInside];
    [self.myButton setTitle:@"Press" forState:UIControlStateNormal];
    [self.view addSubview:self.myButton];

}

-(void)updateLabel{
    self.myLabel.text = @"The button was pressed...";
}

@end
```

Usage

You can test this initial setup by clicking the Run button in the top left hand corner of Xcode. Xcode will gather all your code and other resources, link them to the frameworks that you need, and then launch the application. The iOS app will appear in the iOS Simulator (a special program to test iOS apps on the Mac), as shown in Figure 1-9.

Figure 1-9. *iOS Simulator with single view application with user controls*

When you touch the button, the action method will execute and update the label with the text "The button was pressed...".

1.14 Adding User Controls to an iOS Application with Delegation

Problem

While many user controls follow the Target-Action pattern in the same way as the button did in Recipe 1.13, other user controls use the Delegation design pattern. The procedure with working with controls like this is very different, so you would like to know how to do it.

Solution

Controls that use Delegation are added to the view controller just like the button and label, so you need properties to reference these controls. The control in this recipe that uses Delegation is the UIPickerView. This control presents a list of selections to users and requires a delegate, which is usually the view controller. The delegate is responsible for providing the content that appears on the picker view and taking action when the user makes a selection.

How It Works

Typically, you can think of the controls you want to use on a view controller as properties and follow the same rules as in Recipe 1.4. Then you instantiate these properties in the viewDidLoad view controller method.

Controls that use Delegation must use a delegate to adopt the required protocols. For this Recipe, you are using a UIPickerView, so your view controller needs to adopt two protocols: UIPickerViewDelegate and UIPickerViewDataSource.

The view controller needs to implement two required delegate methods that let the picker view know how many components (another name for columns) and rows to present.

```
- (NSInteger)numberOfComponentsInPickerView:(UIPickerView *)pickerView{
    return 1;
}

- (NSInteger)pickerView:(UIPickerView *)pickerView ↵
numberOfRowsInComponent:(NSInteger)component{
    return 3;
}
```

These two methods configure your picker view to present one component and three rows. When the picker view needs to know what content to put in each row, it asks its delegate for that information as well. Your view controller, as the delegate, answers with the delegate method titleForRow, like this:

```
-(NSString *)pickerView:(UIPickerView *)pickerView titleForRow:(NSInteger)row ↵
forComponent:(NSInteger)component{
    return [NSString stringWithFormat:@"row number %i", row];
}
```

This delegate method populates each row with text that differs slightly depending on the row. Finally, the delegate helps you out when a user makes a selection with the picker view via the didSelectRow delegate method.

```
- (void)pickerView:(UIPickerView *)pickerView didSelectRow:(NSInteger)row ↵
inComponent:(NSInteger)component{
    self.myLabel.text = [NSString stringWithFormat:@"row number %i", row];
}
```

Once these delegate methods are set up, you can instantiate the picker view, set the picker view' delegate property to the view controller, and then add the picker view to the view. This is the code where you do this:

```
self.myPickerView = [[UIPickerView alloc]initWithFrame:CGRectMake(0, 250, 325, 250)];

self.myPickerView.showsSelectionIndicator = YES;
self.myPickerView.delegate = self;

[self.view addSubview:self.myPickerView];
```

See Listings 1-32 and 1-33 for the code.

The Code

Listing 1-32. *ViewController.h*

```
#import <UIKit/UIKit.h>

@interface ViewController : UIViewController<UIPickerViewDelegate,↵
 UIPickerViewDataSource>

@property(strong) UILabel *myLabel;
@property(strong) UIPickerView *myPickerView;

@end
```

Listing 1-33. *ViewController.m*

```
#import "ViewController.h"

@implementation ViewController
@synthesize myLabel, myPickerView;

- (void)viewDidLoad{
    [super viewDidLoad];

    //Create label
    self.myLabel = [[UILabel alloc] init];
    self.myLabel.frame = CGRectMake(20, 20, 280, 40);
    self.myLabel.textAlignment = UITextAlignmentCenter;
    self.myLabel.backgroundColor =[UIColor clearColor];
    self.myLabel.text = @"Make a selection";
    [self.view addSubview:self.myLabel];
```

```
    //Create picker view
    self.myPickerView = [[UIPickerView alloc]initWithFrame:CGRectMake(0, 250, 325, 250)];

    self.myPickerView.showsSelectionIndicator = YES;
    self.myPickerView.delegate = self;

    [self.view addSubview:self.myPickerView];

}

- (NSInteger)numberOfComponentsInPickerView:(UIPickerView *)pickerView{
    return 1;
}

- (NSInteger)pickerView:(UIPickerView *)pickerView ↵
numberOfRowsInComponent:(NSInteger)component{
    return 3;
}

-(NSString *)pickerView:(UIPickerView *)pickerView titleForRow:(NSInteger)row ↵
forComponent:(NSInteger)component{
    return [NSString stringWithFormat:@"row number %i", row];
}

- (void)pickerView:(UIPickerView *)pickerView didSelectRow:(NSInteger)row ↵
inComponent:(NSInteger)component{
    self.myLabel.text = [NSString stringWithFormat:@"row number %i", row];
}

@end
```

Usage

You can test this initial setup by clicking the Run button in the top left hand corner of Xcode. Xcode will gather all your code and other resources, link them to the frameworks that you need, and then launch the application. The iOS app will appear in the iOS Simulator (a special program to test iOS apps on the Mac), as shown in Figure 1-10.

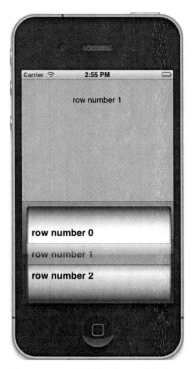

Figure 1-10. *iOS Simulator with single view application with a picker view*

All the content in the picker view comes from the delegate view controller. When you make a selection, the delegate is responsible for updating the view.

Chapter 2

Working With Strings and Numbers

This chapter covers how to work with strings and numbers using the Foundation framework with Objective-C.

The recipes in this chapter will show you how to:

- Create a string object using NSString
- Read strings from text files on Mac and iOS
- Write strings to text files on Mac and iOS
- Compare strings
- Manipulate strings
- Search through strings
- Create localized strings
- Convert between numbers and strings
- Format numbers for currency and other presentations

> **NOTE:** The recipes in this chapter may be used with any Mac or iOS app that links to the Foundation framework. Follow one of the recipes from Chapter 1, such as 1.1, to set up an app to test out the code in this chapter. Be sure to locate the code in the main function unless the recipe specifies another location for the code.

2.1 Creating a String Object

Problem

Most of your programs will need to represent strings, or arrays of characters. It's possible to use the C method of representing strings, but it's much easier to use an object-oriented approach to manage them. To get started using strings with Objective-C, you must first instantiate string objects.

Solution

Use the Foundation NSString class constructors to create string objects that you can use in your program. NSString comes with a set of constructors that starts with init and a set of functions that start with string and return string objects. You may use any of these to create string objects.

How It Works

Typically, you create strings by simply assigning an NSString object to a string that you typed out, preceded by the @ symbol. The @ symbol tells the compiler that this is an Objective-C entity; when the @ symbol is in front of quotes, the complier knows that this is an Objective-C NSString.

Here's an example of creating a string object:

```
NSString *myString1 = @"My String One";
```

At times you may need to instantiate a string object from a C array of UTF8-encoded bytes. NSString has a function that will return an instance of NSString given a string encoded in this way.

```
NSString *myString2 = [NSString stringWithUTF8String:"My String Two"];
```

As you work more with NSString, you will see that there are many functions that begin with the word string that return an NSString instance. There are also many NSString constructors that begin with init that have similar names to the string functions and basically do the same thing. For instance, you could get an NSString instance similar to the previous one using alloc and initWithUTF8String, like this:

```
NSString *myString3 = [[NSString alloc] initWithUTF8String:"My String Three"];
```

These two ways of returning NSString instances are helpful when you are managing memory manually. The functions that begin with the word string all return *autoreleased* objects, which means they should be treated as temporary. NSString objects return with alloc and init are retained; they must be released manually when you are finished with them. If you are using automatic reference counting (ARC), you don't need to worry about this; you may use these two methods interchangeably.

There are a few more constructors and functions that return string instances. One of the most useful is the stringWithFormat function. This function makes it really easy to compose a new string by substituting values into placeholders. You may use the same placeholders that you used in Recipe 1.2 to substitute values into the strings that were written to the console window. Here is an example of stringWithFormat:

```
int number = 4;
NSString *myString4 = [NSString stringWithFormat:@"My String %i", number];
```

The Code

Here are some examples of how you may experiment with NSString constructors in a simple Mac application:

```
#import <Foundation/Foundation.h>

int main (int argc, const char * argv[])
{

    @autoreleasepool {

        NSString *myString1 = @"My String One";
        NSLog(@"myString1 = %@", myString1);

        NSString *myString2 = [NSString stringWithUTF8String:"My String Two"];
        NSLog(@"myString2 = %@", myString2);

        NSString *myString3 = [[NSString alloc] initWithUTF8String:"My String Three"];
        NSLog(@"myString3 = %@", myString3);

        int number = 4;
        NSString *myString4 = [NSString stringWithFormat:@"My String %i", number];
        NSLog(@"myString4 = %@", myString4);


    }
    return 0;
}
```

Usage

To use this code, build and run your Mac app from Xcode. You can view the results of the strings in the console window.

```
myString1 = My String One
myString2 = My String Two
myString3 = My String Three
myString4 = My String 4
```

2.2 Reading Strings from Files on a Mac

Problem

You would like to use content stored on your file system to create and use string objects in your app.

Solution

To create string objects from text files, you need two things: an error object and the complete file path name of the text file. Once you have these in place, you may use the NSString function stringWithContentsOfFile:encoding:error: to return an NSString object filled with the contents of the text file.

How It Works

The NSString class will attempt to read the text file that you specify. If the operation is successful, a string object with the contents of the text file will be returned. If the operation is not successful, nil will be returned and an error object will be generated that you can inspect to find the problem.

The first thing you need is a reference to the file path name. This file path name is referencing a file named textfile.txt in the Shared folder on my Mac.

```
NSString *filePathName = @"/Users/Shared/textfile.txt";
```

> **NOTE:** Mac applications can work with the hardcoded file path names to access any file on your Mac. However, iOS applications are sandboxed and so only have access to files that come with their app bundle or are in the iOS app's documents directory (see Recipe 2.3).

Next, you want an error object to hold error reporting data that you'll need if the operation to read the file fails.

```
NSError *fileError;
```

The error object doesn't need to be instantiated here because you pass the error object to the function by reference, and the function will do all the necessary setup work on the error object for you.

Finally, you use the `NSString` function to return the string object to use, like so:

```
NSString *textFileContents = [NSString stringWithContentsOfFile:filePathName
                                        encoding:NSASCIIStringEncoding
                                        error:&fileError];
```

The string object will be either empty or filled with the contents of the text file. The first parameter is the file path name and the second requires you to specify how the file was encoded. The last parameter takes the error object. The & in front of `fileError` means that the object is being passed by reference so you can test the error object to make sure everything worked as expected.

Before you use the string, you should query the error object to make sure that an error did not occur. Test the error object's code property to see that the error code is 0. If it is, go ahead and use the string; otherwise you might want to report the error in some way or try an alternate file.

```
if(fileError.code == 0)
    NSLog(@"textfile.txt contents: %@", textFileContents);
else
    NSLog(@"error(%ld): %@", fileError.code, fileError.description);
```

The Code

```
#import <Foundation/Foundation.h>

int main (int argc, const char * argv[])
{

    @autoreleasepool {
        NSString *filePathName = @"/Users/Shared/textfile.txt";
        NSError *fileError;
```

```
        NSString *textFileContents = [NSString stringWithContentsOfFile:filePathName
                                              encoding:NSASCIIStringEncodin
                                              error:&fileError];
    if(fileError.code == 0)
        NSLog(@"textfile.txt contents: %@", textFileContents);
    else
        NSLog(@"error(%ld): %@", fileError.code, fileError.description);

    }

    return 0;
}
```

Usage

To use this code, build and run your Mac app from Xcode. You can view the text file content or the error object contents in the console window.

```
textfile.txt contents: This string comes from a local text file.
```

2.3 Reading Strings from Files on iOS

Problem

You would like to use content packaged with your iOS app to create and use string objects in your app.

Solution

iOS apps can't read text files from your Mac like Mac command line apps can. However, you can include text files in your iOS app bundle to make them available for use when your app runs. You can get references to any text files that you want in your app bundle or your app's documents directory.

How It Works

To include text files in iOS apps, you need to drag the text file into the Supporting Files folder in Xcode. When the dialog box pops up, check the box that says Copy items into destination group's folder (if needed). Doing this ensures that the text file will be included with the bundle that will be installed in the iOS Simulator and included in the App Store app.

The NSString class will attempt to read in the text file that you specify. If the operation is successful, a string object with the contents of the text file will be returned. If the operation is not successful, nil will be returned and an error object will be generated that you can inspect to locate the problem.

The first thing you need is a reference to the file path name. In iOS, you need to get a reference to the bundle folder. Since this is a dynamic folder path, you can't hardcode the folder pathname in advance. However, you can use [[NSBundle mainBundle] resourcePath] to get a reference to the folder where all the resources are included. Once you have that, you can use the stringWithFormat method to build a reference to your text file.

```
NSString *bundlePathName = [[NSBundle mainBundle] resourcePath];
NSString *filePathName = [NSString stringWithFormat:@"%@/textfile.txt", ⏎
bundlePathName];
```

The file path name here is referencing a file named textfile.txt in the bundle's resource folder in the iOS app.

You also need an error object to hold all error reporting data in case the operation to read the file fails.

```
NSError *fileError;
```

The error object doesn't need to be instantiated here because you pass the error object to the function by reference and the function does all the necessary setup work on the error object for you.

Finally, use the NSString function to return the string object to use, like so:

```
NSString *textFileContents = [NSString stringWithContentsOfFile:filePathName
                                    encoding:NSASCIIStringEncoding
                                      error:&fileError];
```

The string object will be either empty or filled with the contents of the text file. The first parameter is the file path name and the second requires you to specify how the file was encoded. The last parameter takes the error object. The & in front of fileError means that the object is being passed by reference so you can test the error object to make sure everything worked as expected.

Before you use the string, you should query the error object to find out if an error occurred. If the code property is 0, you are ok. If everything looks good, go ahead and use the string; otherwise, you might want to report the error in some way or try an alternate file.

```
if(fileError.code == 0)
    NSLog(@"textfile.txt contents: %@", textFileContents);
else
    NSLog(@"error(%ld): %@", fileError.code, fileError.description);
```

See Listing 2-1 for the code.

The Code

Listing 2-1. *AppDelegate.m*

```
#import "AppDelegate.h"

@implementation AppDelegate
@synthesize window = _window;

- (BOOL)application:(UIApplication *)application⏎
didFinishLaunchingWithOptions:(NSDictionary *)launchOptions{

    NSString *bundlePathName = [[NSBundle mainBundle] resourcePath];

    NSString *filePathName = [NSString stringWithFormat:@"%@/textfile.txt",⏎
bundlePathName];

    NSError *fileError;

    NSString *textFileContents = [NSString stringWithContentsOfFile:filePathName
                                            encoding:NSASCIIStringEncoding
                                               error:&fileError];

    if(fileError.code == 0)
       NSLog(@"textfile.txt contents: %@", textFileContents);
    else
       NSLog(@"error(%d): %@", fileError.code, fileError.description);

    self.window = [[UIWindow alloc] initWithFrame:[[UIScreen mainScreen] ⏎
bounds]];
    self.window.backgroundColor = [UIColor whiteColor];
    [self.window makeKeyAndVisible];
    return YES;
}

@end
```

Usage

To try this code out for yourself, you will need an iOS app; see Recipe 1.12 for instructions. The code in Listing 2-1 is what you should have in your app delegate code file. The applicationDidFinishLaunchingWithOptions delegate method is where the significant code is located for the purposes of this recipe.

Build and run your app with Xcode and view the console to see the contents of the text file printed to the log.

```
textfile.txt contents: This string comes from a local text file.
```

2.4 Writing Strings to Files on a Mac

Problem

You would like to be able to store text content generated from your Mac app on the file system to be used later or by other programs.

Solution

NSString comes with built-in methods to write the contents of string objects to your Mac's filesystem. Simply send the message `writeToFile:atomically:encoding:error:` to a string object and the file pathname to store the contents in the string object.

How It Works

You can send the message `writeToFile:atomically:encoding:error:` to save the contents of a string to the filesystem. If the operation isn't successful, an error object will be generated that you can inspect to locate the problem.

The first thing you need is a reference to the file path name. This file path name is referencing a file named `textfile.txt` in the Shared folder on my Mac.

```
NSString *filePathName = @"/Users/Shared/textfile.txt";
```

> **NOTE:** Mac applications can work with the hardcoded file path names to access any file on your Mac. However, iOS applications are sandboxed and so only have access to files that come with their app bundle or are in the iOS app's documents directory (see Recipe 2.3).

You also want an error object to hold all error reporting data that you'll need if the operation to read the file fails.

```
NSError *fileError;
```

The error object doesn't need to be instantiated here because you pass the error object to the function by reference and the function does all the necessary setup work on the error object for you.

You need some content in the string to save to the file that will look something like this:

```
NSString *textFileContents = @"Content generated from a Mac program.";
```

Finally, send the message writeToFile:atomically:encoding:error: to save the contents of a textFileContents to the filesystem.

```
[textFileContents writeToFile:filePathName
               atomically:YES
             encoding:NSStringEncodingConversionAllowLossy
               error:&fileError];
```

The first parameter in this message is the full name of the file where you want to store your string contents. The second parameter, atomically, refers to whether you would like to write out the contents to an auxiliary file first. When you pass YES, this auxiliary file is used and you're guaranteed that the data will not be corrupted even if the system crashes. The encoding parameter gives you some control over how the string is stored on the system and the error parameter is used to report back any errors that happen during the write.

Before you move on in your program, you should query the error object to make sure everything looks good. If its code is 0, the operation was successful. If so, go ahead and use the string; if not, you might want to report the error in some way or try an alternate file.

```
if(fileError.code == 0)
    NSLog(@"textfile.txt contents: %@", textFileContents);
else
    NSLog(@"error(%ld): %@", fileError.code, fileError.description);
```

See Listing 2-2 for the code.

The Code

Listing 2-2. *main.m*

```objc
#import <Foundation/Foundation.h>

int main (int argc, const char * argv[]){

    @autoreleasepool {
        NSString *filePathName = @"/Users/Shared/textfile.txt";
        NSError *fileError;
        NSString *textFileContents = @"Content generated from a Mac program.";

        [textFileContents writeToFile:filePathName
                           atomically:YES
                             encoding:NSStringEncodingConversionAllowLossy
                                error:&fileError];

        if(fileError.code == 0)
            NSLog(@"textfile.txt was written successfully with these contents: %@",↵
    textFileContents);
        else
            NSLog(@"error(%ld): %@", fileError.code, fileError.description);


    }
    return 0;
}
```

Usage

To use this code, build and run your Mac app from Xcode. You can view the text file contents or the error object contents in the console window. You should also be able to open the text file with any text editor to see the contents of the string object that you wrote out to the file system.

2.5 Writing Strings To Files On iOS

Problem

You would like to be able to store text content generated from your iOS app in the app's documents directory to be used later or by other programs.

Solution

iOS apps can't write text files to your Mac like Mac command line apps can. However, you don't get a sandboxed area in your iOS application where you can write to when needed. The place where you store your own content in iOS is called the documents directory, and you will need a reference to this dynamic directory to store your string objects.

> **NOTE:** While you may read text files from the bundle resource directory as discussed in Recipe 2.3, you can't write to any files in that directory. If you need to work on a file in your app, you must either copy the file to your documents directory or simply save the updated version in the documents directory.

How It Works

You may send the message writeToFile:atomically:encoding:error: to save the contents of a string to the documents directory. If the operation is not successful, an error object will be generated that you can inspect to locate the problem.

The first thing you need is the documents directory. It is dynamically generated for each app install so you can't hardcode it. However, you can use this function to get a reference to the documents directory:

```
NSString *documentsDirectory = [NSSearchPathForDirectoriesInDomains
(NSDocumentDirectory, NSUserDomainMask, YES) lastObject];
```

Next, you need to construct a reference to the file path name that you would like in the documents directory.

```
NSString *filePathName = [NSString stringWithFormat:@"%@/textfile.txt",
 documentsDirectory];
```

This file path name is referencing a file named textfile.txt in the iOS app's document directory.

You also want an error object to hold any error reporting data that you'll need in case the operation to read the file fails.

```
NSError *fileError;
```

The error object doesn't need to be instantiated here because you pass the error object to the function by reference and the function does all the necessary setup work on the error object for you.

You need some content in the string to save to the file that will look something like this:

```
NSString *textFileContents = @"Content generated from an iOS app.";
```

Finally, send the message writeToFile:atomically:encoding:error: to save the contents of a textFileContents to the filesystem.

```
[textFileContents writeToFile:filePathName
                   atomically:YES
                     encoding:NSStringEncodingConversionAllowLossy
                        error:&fileError];
```

The first parameter in this message is the full name of the file where you want to store your string contents. The second parameter, atomically, refers to whether you would like to write out the contents to an auxiliary file first. When you pass YES, this auxiliary file is used and you're guaranteed that the data will not be corrupted even if the system crashes. The encoding parameter gives you some control over how the string is stored on the system and the error parameter is used to report back any errors that happen during the write.

Before you move on in your program, you should query the error object. If its code is 0, the operation was successful. If everything looks good, go ahead and use the string; otherwise you might want to report the error in some way or try an alternate file.

```
if(fileError.code == 0)
    NSLog(@"textfile.txt was written successfully with these contents: %@",↵
 textFileContents);
else
    NSLog(@"error(%d): %@", fileError.code, fileError.description);
```

See Listing 2-3 for the code.

The Code

Listing 2-3. *AppDelegate.m*

```
#import "AppDelegate.h"

@implementation AppDelegate

@synthesize window = _window;
```

```
- (BOOL)application:(UIApplication *)application
didFinishLaunchingWithOptions:(NSDictionary *)launchOptions{

    NSString *documentsDirectory = [NSSearchPathForDirectoriesInDomains
(NSDocumentDirectory, NSUserDomainMask, YES) lastObject];

    NSString *filePathName = [NSString stringWithFormat:@"%@/textfile.txt",
documentsDirectory];

    NSError *fileError;

    NSString *textFileContents = @"Content generated from an iOS app.";

    [textFileContents writeToFile:filePathName
                        atomically:YES
                          encoding:NSStringEncodingConversionAllowLossy
                             error:&fileError];

    if(fileError.code == 0)
        NSLog(@"textfile.txt was written successfully with these contents: %@",
textFileContents);
    else
        NSLog(@"error(%d): %@", fileError.code, fileError.description);

    self.window = [[UIWindow alloc] initWithFrame:[[UIScreen mainScreen] bounds]];
    self.window.backgroundColor = [UIColor whiteColor];
    [self.window makeKeyAndVisible];
    return YES;
}

@end
```

Usage

Locate this code in your iOS app delegate in the
`applicationDidFinishLaunchingWithOptions` delegate method. Build and run
your app with Xcode and view the console to see the contents of the text file
printed to the log. If a problem occurred during the writing process, you will see
the details of the error reported to the log.

Your app now has the contents of the string object stored in the documents
directory and may be used later on by referencing the new text file in documents
directory.

2.6 Comparing Strings

Problem

You would like to be able to see if two strings have the same value, but you can't simply use the == comparison operator because strings are objects.

Solution

Use the NSString method isEqualToString: to get a Boolean value that indicates whether the string is the same as the string that you pass as a parameter. You may use this in if statements as needed.

How It Works

When you have two strings that you want to compare, send the isEqualToString: message to the first string and pass the second string as a parameter. A Boolean value will be returned that you can use to evaluate statements.

```
BOOL isEqual = [myString1 isEqualToString:myString2];
```

You can also find out if a string has a matching suffix or prefix. For instance, if you had a string "Mr. John Smith, MD" you could find out whether the string had the prefix "Mr" by sending the hasPrefix message to the string.

```
NSString *name = @"Mr. John Smith, MD";

BOOL hasMrPrefix = [name hasPrefix:@"Mr"];
```

Similarly, you can find out if the same string has the suffix "MD" by sending the hasSuffix message.

```
BOOL hasMDSuffix = [name hasSuffix:@"MD"];
```

Finally, you can compare a substring by using the NSRange composite type to define the starting point and length of the substring in question. You first use the NSRange information to return the substring and then use that to test if the strings are the same.

```
NSString *alphabet = @"ABCDEFGHIJKLMONPQRSTUVWXYZ";

NSRange range = NSMakeRange(2, 3);

BOOL lettersInRange = [[alphabet substringWithRange:range] isEqualToString:@"CDE"];
```

See Listing 2-4 for the code.

The Code

Listing 2-4. *main.m*

```
#import <Foundation/Foundation.h>

int main (int argc, const char * argv[]){

    @autoreleasepool {

        NSString *myString1 = @"A";
        NSString *myString2 = @"B";
        NSString *myString3 = @"A";

        BOOL isEqual = [myString1 isEqualToString:myString2];

        if(isEqual)
            NSLog(@"%@ is equal to %@", myString1, myString2);
        else
            NSLog(@"%@ is not equal to %@", myString1, myString2);

        if([myString1 isEqualToString:myString2])
            NSLog(@"%@ is equal to %@", myString1, myString2);
        else
            NSLog(@"%@ is not equal to %@", myString1, myString2);

        if([myString1 isEqualToString:myString3])
            NSLog(@"%@ is equal to %@", myString1, myString3);
        else
            NSLog(@"%@ is not equal to %@", myString1, myString3);

        NSString *name = @"Mr. John Smith, MD";

        BOOL hasMrPrefix = [name hasPrefix:@"Mr"];

        if(hasMrPrefix)
            NSLog(@"%@ has the Mr prefix", name);
        else
        NSLog(@"%@ doesn't have the Mr prefix", name);

        BOOL hasMDSuffix = [name hasSuffix:@"MD"];

        if(hasMDSuffix)
            NSLog(@"%@ has the MD suffix", name);
        else
            NSLog(@"%@ doesn't have the MD suffix", name);
```

```
    NSString *alphabet = @"ABCDEFGHIJKLMONPQRSTUVWXYZ";

    NSRange range = NSMakeRange(2, 3);

    BOOL lettersInRange = [[alphabet substringWithRange:range] ↵
isEqualToString:@"CDE"];

    if(lettersInRange)
        NSLog(@"The letters CDE are in alphabet starting at position 2");
    else
        NSLog(@"The letters CDE aren't in alphabet starting at position 2");

    }
    return 0;
}
```

Usage

To use this code, build and run your Mac app from Xcode. Check the console to see the results of the various comparisons. Your output should look like this:

```
A is not equal to B
A is not equal to B
A is equal to A
Mr. John Smith, MD has the Mr prefix
Mr. John Smith, MD has the MD suffix
The letters CDE are in alphabet starting at position 2
```

Change the various strings to see how these comparisons work. See if you can test correctly in the cases when the strings are not equal as well as equal.

2.7 Manipulating Strings

Problem

You would like your app to be able to make changes to your string content, but NSString objects are immutable and thus can't be altered in any way.

Solution

Use the NSMutableString class when you want to be able to change the contents of your string. NSMutableString is a subclass of NSString and so you can use it in the same way as NSString. However, when you work with NSMutableString you can append, insert, replace, and remove substrings.

How It Works

You can create an NSMutableString with the same constructors that you use for strings, but make sure to send the message to the NSMutableString class and not the NSString class. NSMutableString does come with one unique constructor that lets you set the initial capacity of the string.

```
NSMutableString *myString = [[NSMutableString alloc] initWithCapacity:26];
```

You are not limited to the number of characters based on this constructor; you are simply passing a hint to the compiler to help manage the string more efficiently. Once you have a mutable string, you can set the string content by sending the setString message to the mutable string.

```
[myString setString:@"ABCDEFGHIJKLMONPQRSTUVWXYZ"];
```

To append a string to your mutable string, send the appendString message.

```
[myString appendString:@", 0123456789"];
```

This will append the string to the end of your mutable string. However, if you want to insert characters into another location of your mutable string, you need to specify the location where the string will be inserted and use the insertString message.

```
[myString insertString:@"abcdefg, "
            atIndex:0];
```

You can also delete characters from your mutable string by sending the deleteCharactersInRange message with the range you would like to delete as a parameter. Use the NSMakeRange function to define a range with the starting location and length of the range of characters that you would like to delete.

```
NSRange range = NSMakeRange(9, 3);

[myString deleteCharactersInRange:range];
```

NSMutableString also comes with a built-in method to replace all the characters in a range with a different character. So, if you'd rather have the character "|" instead of "," appear in your string, you could replace all instances of "," with "|" by using the replaceOccurrencesOfString:withString:options:range: method.

```
NSRange rangeOfString = [myString rangeOfString:myString];
```

```
[myString replaceOccurrencesOfString:@", "
                       withString:@"|"
                          options:NSCaseInsensitiveSearch
                            range:rangeOfString];
```

Here the `rangeOfString` message was used to specify the entire string, but you can define any range that you would like to perform this action.

Another common type of string manipulation is replacing ranges of characters with other characters. To do this, use the `replaceCharactersInRange:withString:` method.

```
NSRange rangeToReplace = NSMakeRange(0, 4);

[myString replaceCharactersInRange:rangeToReplace
                        withString:@"MORE"];
```

This replaces the first four characters in the string with the word "MORE." See Listing 2-5 for the code.

The Code

Listing 2-5. *main.m*

```objc
#import <Foundation/Foundation.h>

int main (int argc, const char * argv[])
{

    @autoreleasepool {

        NSMutableString *myString = [[NSMutableString alloc] initWithCapacity:26];

        [myString setString:@"ABCDEFGHIJKLMONPQRSTUVWXYZ"];

        NSLog(@"%@", myString);

        [myString appendString:@", 0123456789"];

        NSLog(@"%@", myString);

        [myString insertString:@"abcdefg, "
                       atIndex:0];

        NSLog(@"%@", myString);

        NSRange range = NSMakeRange(9, 3);

        [myString deleteCharactersInRange:range];
```

```
        NSLog(@"%@", myString);
        NSRange rangeOfString = [myString rangeOfString:myString];

        [myString replaceOccurrencesOfString:@", "
                            withString:@"|"
                                options:NSCaseInsensitiveSearch
                                  range:rangeOfString];

        NSLog(@"%@", myString);


        NSRange rangeToReplace = NSMakeRange(0, 4);

        [myString replaceCharactersInRange:rangeToReplace
                          withString:@"MORE"];

        NSLog(@"%@", myString);
    }

    return 0;
}
```

Usage

To use this code, build and run your Mac app from Xcode. Check the console to see the how the string is manipulated.

```
ABCDEFGHIJKLMONPQRSTUVWXYZ
ABCDEFGHIJKLMONPQRSTUVWXYZ, 0123456789
abcdefg, ABCDEFGHIJKLMONPQRSTUVWXYZ, 0123456789
abcdefg, DEFGHIJKLMONPQRSTUVWXYZ, 0123456789
abcdefg|DEFGHIJKLMONPQRSTUVWXYZ|0123456789
MOREefg|DEFGHIJKLMONPQRSTUVWXYZ|0123456789
```

2.8 Searching Through Strings

Problem

You want know if the strings that you are working with contain key phrases that your app needs to know about.

Solution

To search a string for another string you can send the message
`rangeOfString:options:range:` to the string that you want to search. You must
specify the range where you will look along with a search option. This method
will return either `NSNotFound` and a length of 0 if nothing is found, or it will return
a range with the information you need to locate the string.

How It Works

To search through a string you can simply send the
`rangeOfString:options:range:` message. You need to specify the search
options that you would like to use and the range of the string that you would like
to search.

```
NSString *stringToSearch = @"This string is something that you can search.";

NSRange rangeToSearch = [stringToSearch rangeOfString:stringToSearch];

NSRange resultsRange = [stringToSearch rangeOfString:@"something"
                                             options:NSCaseInsensitiveSearch
                                               range:rangeToSearch];
```

When the search is complete you will have the information that you need
contained in the NSRange object that is returned to you. If the NSRange location
property is equal to `NSNotFound`, the search didn't turn up any results. Otherwise,
the NSRange object will have the location and length of the string that you are
looking for. You can later use this information as needed. See Listing 2-6 for the
code.

The Code

Listing 2-6. *main.m*

```
#import <Foundation/Foundation.h>

int main (int argc, const char * argv[])
{
    @autoreleasepool {

        NSString *stringToSearch = @"This string is something that you can search.";

        NSRange rangeToSearch = [stringToSearch rangeOfString:stringToSearch];
```

```
            NSRange resultsRange = [stringToSearch rangeOfString:@"something"
                                               options:NSCaseInsensitiveSearch
                                                 range:rangeToSearch];

        if(resultsRange.location != NSNotFound){

            NSLog(@"String found starting at location %lu with a length of %lu",
                    resultsRange.location, resultsRange.length);

            NSLog(@"%@", [stringToSearch substringWithRange:resultsRange]);
        }
        else
            NSLog(@"The search didn't turn up any results");

    }
    return 0;
}
```

Usage

To use this code, build and run your Mac app from Xcode. Check the console to see if the search string was found. Test this code further by searching for different strings and strings that you know are not there.

Here is the output that you would get after running the code as-is:

```
String found starting at location 15 with a length of 9
something
```

2.9 Localizing Strings

Problem

You would like to include string content that is appropriate for your audience language preferences. Hardcoding the string doesn't work because you can only include one language.

Solution

To include localized strings in your apps you must add a strings file for each language that you would like to support. A strings file contains keyed data, and the system picks which strings file to use depending on the language your user prefers. To include these localized strings you must use the `NSFoundation` function `NSLocalizedString`.

> **NOTE:** This method only works with iOS or Mac apps (not command line apps) since localizing strings requires the strings files to be located in an app's application bundle.

How It Works

Make sure that you have an iOS app (Recipe 1.12) or Mac app (Recipe 1.11) set up if you intend on following along with this recipe. The code is located in your app delegate.

First, add a strings file to your application. From Xcode go to **File ➤ New ➤ New File**. In the dialog box that appears, choose **Mac OS X ➤ Resource ➤ Strings File**. Name your strings file **Localizable.strings**.

Now you need to add localization to this file, so select the file and make sure that the identity tab is selected. To add localization to this file, click the + button in the localization pane and choose a language from the drop-down that appears (see Figure 2-1).

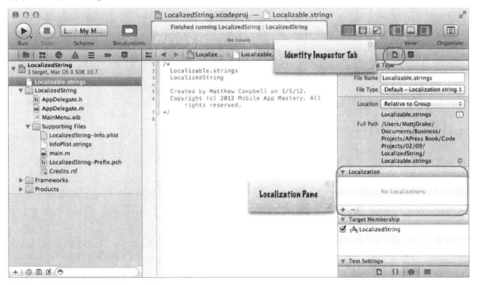

Figure 2-1. *Strings file identity options*

> **NOTE:** In Xcode 4.2, the first time you click the button, the Identity Inspector may automatically advance to the next file without giving you the option to choose a language first. If this happens, go back to the strings file in the Identity Inspector and add the remaining language support.

Each language that you intend on supporting will appear in the localization pane (see Figure 2-2). If you look closely at your strings file in Xcode, you will notice that you have a strings file for each language that you want to support (you may need to expand the group folder to see the files).

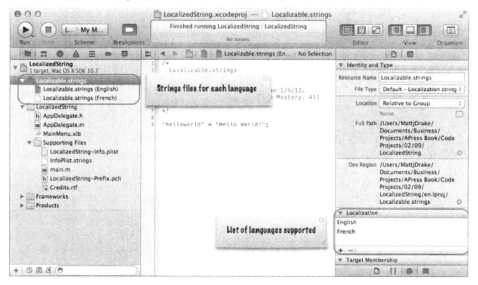

Figure 2-2. *Localized strings files*

To add content to each file, you need to specify a key (that you can use later to look up the content) and the string content itself. For instance, if you want to add a Hello World! string in French and English, you add this keyed data starting in the strings file for English (Localizable.strings (English)).

```
"helloworld" = "Hello World!";
```

Here helloworld is the key and the string content is included between the quotes. The line ends with a semicolon.

Next, add the same for the French strings file (Localizable.strings (French)).

```
"helloworld" = "Bonjour tout le monde!";
```

To get this string into your app, use the NSLocalizedString function to return the localized string based on the key that you provide.

```
NSString *localizedString = NSLocalizedString(@"helloworld", @"Hello world in ↵
localized languages");
```

In this example, English users will get "Hello World!" and French users will get "Bonjour tout le monde!" See Listing 2-7 for the code.

The Code

Listing 2-7. *AppDelegate.m*

```
#import "AppDelegate.h"

@implementation AppDelegate

@synthesize window = _window;

- (void)applicationDidFinishLaunching:(NSNotification *)aNotification{

    NSString *localizedString = NSLocalizedString(@"helloworld", @"Hello world ↵
in localized languages");

    NSLog(@"%@", localizedString);

}

@end
```

Usage

To use this code, build and run your Mac or iOS app from Xcode. Check the console to see what string was written out to the log. If you have your system preferences set to English, you will see "Hello World!" in your console.

If you are working with a Mac app and want to see the localized string for French, go to your Mac's system preferences, click on "Language and Text," and drag the word "Français" to the top of the list of languages. If you are working with an iOS app, use the iOS Simulator's or device's Settings app and then choose **General** ➤ **International** ➤ **Language** ➤ **Francais**. Then go back to Xcode, run your app, and look at the console to see the localized string appear.

2.10 Converting Numbers to Strings

Problem

You have numbers (either primitive types or NSNumber objects) that you would like to use as strings.

Solution

You work with numbers in two ways: as primitive types and NSNumber objects. To use a primitive type as a string, you need to create a new string using the stringWithFormat constructor and insert the value of the primitive type. Here you can use the same string formatters as you did in Recipe 1.2.

NSNumber objects can be inserted into new strings in the same way or you can use NSNumber's stringValue function to return the string version of a number directly.

How It Works

If you have a primitive type like a float that you would like to turn into a string, you need to create a new string with the stringWithFormat constructor.

```
float fNumber = 12;

NSString *floatToString = [NSString stringWithFormat:@"%f", fNumber];
```

If the number you want to convert is an NSNumber object, you can simply use the NSNumber object's stringValue function.

```
NSNumber *number = [NSNumber numberWithFloat:30];

NSString *numberToString = [number stringValue];
```

See Listing 2-8 for the code.

The Code

Listing 2-8. *main.m*

```
#import <Foundation/Foundation.h>

int main (int argc, const char * argv[])
```

```
{

    @autoreleasepool {

        float fNumber = 12;

        NSString *floatToString = [NSString stringWithFormat:@"%f", fNumber];

        NSLog(@"floatToString = %@", floatToString);

        NSNumber *number = [NSNumber numberWithFloat:30];

        NSString *numberToString = [number stringValue];

        NSLog(@"numberToString = %@", numberToString);

    }
    return 0;
}
```

Usage

To use this code, build and run your Mac app from Xcode. You can see that the new strings have been created and used based on the numbers that are present.

```
floatToString = 12.000000
numberToString = 30
```

2.11 Converting Strings to Numbers

Problem

In your app you have numbers that are stored as strings, but you need to use these numbers for math functions or to apply special formatting using NSNumber.

Solution

If you need to do any math functions like addition or subtraction, you need to convert any numbers stored as strings into primitive types like float or int. Happily, NSString comes with built-in functions that make this type of conversion really easy.

But, if you want to use the object-oriented features of NSNumber, then you need to use NSNumber. Using NSNumber requires that you construct new NSNumber objects for each number. Do this if you need to store these numbers in an array or if you want to use the other features built into NSNumber.

How It Works

If you have a number stored in a string that you want to use as a float primitive type, use the strings floatValue function to get this value.

```
NSString *aFloatValue = @"12.50";
float f = [aFloatValue floatValue];
```

If you prefer to convert this string to an NSNumber object, you need to use the floatValue function in the NSNumber constructer.

```
NSNumber *aFloatNumber = [NSNumber numberWithFloat:[aFloatValue floatValue]];
```

See Listing 2-9 for the code.

The Code

Listing 2-9. *main.m*

```
#import <Foundation/Foundation.h>

int main (int argc, const char * argv[])
{

    @autoreleasepool {

        NSString *aFloatValue = @"12.50";

        float f = [aFloatValue floatValue];

        float result = f * 2 + 45;

        NSLog(@"f = %f and result = %f", f, result);

        NSNumber *aFloatNumber = [NSNumber numberWithFloat:[aFloatValue floatValue]];

        NSLog(@"aFloatNumber = %@", aFloatNumber);

    }
    return 0;
}
```

Usage

To use this code, build and run your Mac app from Xcode. You can write the numbers out to the log, but you must use the correct string formatters for the primitive types and %@ for the NSNumber objects.

```
f = 12.500000 and result = 70.000000
aFloatNumber = 12.5
```

2.12 Formatting Numbers

Problem

You would like to present numbers to your users that are formatted in the way they expect. This includes situations when you want to present the number as currency, scientific notation, or spelled out.

Solution

Use the NSNumberFormatter class to format numbers. You need to instantiate an NSNumberFormatter object and set some properties to instruct it to display your number in the way that you would like.

How It Works

Let's assume that you have a number that you would like to display as currency.

```
NSNumber *numberToFormat = [NSNumber numberWithFloat:9.99];
```

First, instantiate a NSNumberFormatter object and set the object's numberStyle to present the currency style.

```
NSNumberFormatter *numberFormatter = [[NSNumberFormatter alloc] init];

numberFormatter.numberStyle = NSNumberFormatterCurrencyStyle;
```

When you are ready to present the number as a string formatted for currency, use the stringFromNumber function.

```
NSLog(@"Formatted for currency: %@", [numberFormatter
stringFromNumber:numberToFormat]);
```

This will present the number as currency for the system's set locale. In the United States you will see the dollar sign, and in the United Kingdom you will see the pound sign.

Currency is one of many possible number styles that you may apply to your numbers. See Table 2-1 for a complete list of number styles. See Listing 2-10 for the code.

Table 2-1. *Number Format Styles*

Format	Description
NSNumberFormatterNoStyle	Presents the number without formatting
NSNumberFormatterDecimalStyle	Presents the number as a decimal
NSNumberFormatterCurrencyStyle	Presents the number as currency
NSNumberFormatterPercentStyle	Presents the number as a percentage
NSNumberFormatterScientificStyle	Presents the number in scientific notation
NSNumberFormatterSpellOutStyle	Spells out the number in natural language

The Code

Listing 2-10. *main.m*

```
#import <Foundation/Foundation.h>

int main (int argc, const char * argv[])
{

    @autoreleasepool {

        NSNumber *numberToFormat = [NSNumber numberWithFloat:9.99];

        NSLog(@"numberToFormat = %@", numberToFormat);

        NSNumberFormatter *numberFormatter = [[NSNumberFormatter alloc] init];

        numberFormatter.numberStyle = NSNumberFormatterCurrencyStyle;

        NSLog(@"Formatted for currency: %@", [numberFormatter ↩
stringFromNumber:numberToFormat]);
```

```
    }
    return 0;
}
```

Usage

To use this code, build and run your Mac app from Xcode. You can see the formats applied in the console window.

```
numberToFormat = 9.99
Formatted for currency: $9.99
```

Working with Object Collections

This chapter will help you work with arrays and dictionaries using the Foundation framework with Objective-C.

The recipes in this chapter will show you how to:

- Create arrays using `NSArray` and `NSMutableArray`
- Add, remove, and insert objects into arrays
- Search and sort arrays
- Use different procedures to iterate through arrays
- Save array contents to the file system
- Create dictionaries using `NSDictionary` and `NSMutableDictionary`
- Add and remove objects from dictionaries
- Use different procedures to iterate through dictionaries
- Save dictionary contents to the file system
- Create sets using `NSSet` and `NSMutableSet`
- Compare sets based on their object contents
- Use different procedures to iterate through sets
- Add and remove objects from sets

> **NOTE:** There are three types of objects collections to work with in Objective-C: arrays, dictionaries, and sets. Your choice of collection will depend on the needs of your app.
>
> Arrays organize objects in lists that are indexed by integers.
>
> Dictionaries organize objects with keys; each object in a dictionary is associated with a string key that you can use later to retrieve the object.
>
> Sets contain objects, but don't assume that they will be in any order be indexed. Objects in sets also must be unique (no duplicates). Retrieving objects from sets is very fast because sets don't have the overhead of an index so you will see this used in situations where performance is a consideration.

3.1 Creating an Array

Problem

Your app requires you to group objects together in a list.

Solution

Objective-C has two Foundation classes named `NSArray` and `NSMutableArray` that you can use to create lists of objects. Use `NSArray` when you have a list that you know you won't need to change on the fly and `NSMutableArray` when you know you will need to add and remove objects from the array at a later time.

How It Works

Arrays are created in Objective-C like other objects: you use the `alloc` and `init` constructors or convenience functions like `arrayWithObjects` to create the array. If you use `NSArray` to create your array, you can't make any changes to the array once the array is created. Use `NSMutableArray` to create arrays that you can later modify.

Here is an example of creating an array of strings:

```
NSArray *listOfLetters = [NSArray arrayWithObjects:@"A", @"B", @"C", nil];
```

When you use `arrayWithObjects` to create your array, you must pass in the objects in a comma-separated list that ends with `nil`. This example used `NSString` objects but you can use any object that you like with `NSArray` and `NSMutableArray`, including objects instantiated from your custom classes.

If you choose to use `NSMutableArray`, you can use the same constructors to create your arrays (`NSMutableArray` is a subclass of `NSArray`). You can also create your `NSMutableArray` by using `alloc` and `init` since you will likely add objects to your array at some future point. See Table 3-1 for a complete list of available constructors for `NSArray` and `NSMutableArray` and Listing 3-1 for the code.

Table 3-1. *NSArray and NSMutableArray Constructors*

Constructor	Description
- (id)initWithObjects:(const id [])objects ↵ count:(NSUInteger)cnt;	Initializes an array with the specified objects and count
- (id)initWithObjects:(id)firstObj, ... ↵ NS_REQUIRES_NIL_TERMINATION;	Initializes an array with the specified nil-terminated list of objects
- (id)initWithArray:(NSArray *)array;	Initializes an array using another array
- (id)initWithArray:(NSArray *)array ↵ copyItems:(BOOL)flag;	Initializes an array using another array and creates new copies of each object
- (id)initWithContentsOfFile:(NSString ↵ *)path;	Initializes an array with the contents of a local file
- (id)initWithContentsOfURL:(NSURL *)url;	Initializes an array with the contents at a URL

The Code

Listing 3-1. *main.m*

```
#import <Foundation/Foundation.h>

int main (int argc, const char * argv[])
{
```

```
@autoreleasepool {

    NSArray *listOfLetters1 = [NSArray arrayWithObjects:@"A", @"B", @"C", nil];

    NSLog(@"listOfLetters1 = %@", listOfLetters1);

    NSNumber *number1 = [NSNumber numberWithInt:1];
    NSNumber *number2 = [NSNumber numberWithInt:2];
    NSNumber *number3 = [NSNumber numberWithInt:3];

    NSMutableArray *listOfNumbers1 = [[NSMutableArray alloc]↵
initWithObjects:number1, number2, number3, nil];

    NSLog(@"listOfNumbers1 = %@", listOfNumbers1);

    id list[3];
    list[0] = @"D";
    list[1] = @"E";
    list[2] = @"F";

    NSMutableArray *listOfLetters2 = [[NSMutableArray alloc] initWithObjects:list↵
count:3];

    NSLog(@"listOfLetters2 = %@", listOfLetters2);

}
return 0;
}
```

Usage

To use this code, build and run your Mac app from Xcode. Inspect the log to see the contents of each array. In the next recipe, you will see how to reference each of these array elements so you can print out their contents to the log or use them elsewhere in your programs.

3.2 Referencing Objects in Arrays

Problem

You would like to get references to the objects in your arrays to either access their properties or to send messages to the objects.

Solution

Use the `objectAtIndex:` method to get a reference to an object in the array that corresponds to an integer position. You may also get a reference to the last object in an array using the `lastObject` function.

How It Works

`NSArray` organizes objects in a list that is indexed by integers starting with the number 0. If you want to get a reference to an object in your array and know the position of the object, you can use the `objectAtIndex:` function to get a reference to that object.

```
NSString *stringObject1 = [listOfLetters objectAtIndex:0];
```

There is also a very convenient function named `lastObject` that you can use to quickly get a reference to the last object in your array.

```
NSString *stringObject2 = [listOfLetters lastObject];
```

Often, you won't know where in the array your object is located. If you already have a reference to the object in question, you can use the `indexOfObject:` function with the object reference as a parameter to find out where in the array the object is located.

```
NSUInteger position = [listOfLetters indexOfObject:@"B"];
```

See Listing 3-2 for the code.

The Code

Listing 3-2. *main.m*

```
#import <Foundation/Foundation.h>

int main (int argc, const char * argv[])
{
    @autoreleasepool {

        NSMutableArray *listOfLetters = [NSMutableArray arrayWithObjects:@"A", @"B",↩
@"C", nil];

        NSString *stringObject1 = [listOfLetters objectAtIndex:0];

        NSLog(@"stringObject1 = %@", stringObject1);
```

```
        NSString *stringObject2 = [listOfLetters lastObject];

        NSLog(@"stringObject2 = %@", stringObject2);

        NSUInteger position = [listOfLetters indexOfObject:@"B"];

        NSLog(@"position = %lu", position);


    }
    return 0;
}
```

Usage

To use this code, build and run your Mac app from Xcode. You can see that the objects were successfully referenced by the output written to the console.

```
stringObject1 = A
stringObject2 = C
position = 1
```

3.3 Obtaining the Array Count

Problem

Your app is working with the content in your arrays and you need to know how many elements are in the array in order to present your content appropriately.

Solution

NSArray objects have a count property that you can use to find out how many elements are in the array.

How It Works

To use the count property, you can use dot notation (listOfLetters.count) on any array object or you can send the count message ([listOfLetters count]) to find out how many elements are in the array. See Listing 3-3 for the code.

The Code

Listing 3-3. *main.m*

```
#import <Foundation/Foundation.h>

int main (int argc, const char * argv[])
{

    @autoreleasepool {

        NSMutableArray *listOfLetters = [NSMutableArray arrayWithObjects:@"A", @"B", ↵
 @"C", nil];

        NSLog(@"listOfLetters has %lu elements", listOfLetters.count);

    }
    return 0;
}
```

Usage

To use this code, build and run your Mac app from Xcode. The log message will present the number of elements.

```
listOfLetters has 3 elements
```

3.4 Iterating Through an Array

Problem

You have an array of objects and you would like to be able to send the same message or access the same property for every object in the array.

Solution

NSArray objects come with three built-in ways to iterate through a list of objects. Many people use a for-each loop to iterate through each element in the array. This structure gives you the ability to set up lines of code that will be applied to each element in the array.

You can also use a method named `makeObjectsPerformSelector:withObject:` where you can pass in the name of the method that you want each object to perform along with one parameter.

Finally, you now have the option of using blocks of code as a parameter that will be applied to each object in the array using the `enumerateObjectsUsingBlock:` method. This method gives you the same thing as a `for-each` loop, but you don't need to write the code for the loop itself and you get a parameter that will help you keep track of the current element's index.

How It Works

Since you need content to use as an example for this recipe, create three `NSMutableString` objects to put into a new array.

```
NSMutableString *string1 = [NSMutableString stringWithString:@"A"];
NSMutableString *string2 = [NSMutableString stringWithString:@"B"];
NSMutableString *string3 = [NSMutableString stringWithString:@"C"];

NSArray *listOfObjects = [NSArray arrayWithObjects:string1, string2, string3, nil];
```

To go through this array with a `for-each` loop, you need to set up the loop and provide a local variable that you can reference that will represent the current object within the array. You also need to add the code that will execute for each object in your list.

```
for(NSMutableString *s in listOfObjects){
    NSLog(@"This string in lowercase is %@", [s lowercaseString]);
}
```

In this `for-each` loop, you go through each mutable string in the array and write out a message to the log. The `lowercaseString` function is an `NSString` function that returns the string but in all lowercase letters.

You can send a message to each object in your array without using a `for-each` loop by sending the `makeObjectsPerformSelector:withObject:` message. You need to pass in the method by using the `@selector` keyword and the name of the method in parentheses. Pass in the parameter value after the property decoration `withObject:`.

```
[listOfObjects makeObjectsPerformSelector:@selector(appendString:)
                            withObject:@"-MORE"];
```

What you are doing here is sending the `appendString` message with the string parameter @"-MORE" to every mutable string in the array. So now each string has been changed to include the extra characters at the end.

> **WARNING:** Make sure that the objects in your array are capable of responding to the messages that you are trying to send. If you attempt to send a message to an object in your array that the object can't respond to, your program will crash and you will get an **unrecognized selector sent to instance** error message.

You can use blocks to define a block of code that you can apply to each object in the array. Blocks are a way to encapsulate code so that the code can be treated as an object and therefore passed to another object as a parameter. The NSArray method enumerateObjectsUsingBlock: gives you the ability to execute a block of code for each element in an array.

```
[listOfObjects enumerateObjectsUsingBlock:^(id obj, NSUInteger idx, BOOL *stop)
{
    NSLog(@"object(%lu)'s description is %@",idx, [obj description]);
}];
```

This essentially gives you the same thing as the for-each loop but you only need to use one line of code. Also, the block comes with built-in parameters for the object that you need to reference and an index to help you keep track of your position in the array. In this example, you are using blocks to write out a message to the log for each object in the list using the object's description function and the index parameter. See Listing 3-4 for the code.

The Code

Listing 3-4. *main.m*

```
#import <Foundation/Foundation.h>

int main (int argc, const char * argv[])
{

    @autoreleasepool {

        NSMutableString *string1 = [NSMutableString stringWithString:@"A"];
        NSMutableString *string2 = [NSMutableString stringWithString:@"B"];
        NSMutableString *string3 = [NSMutableString stringWithString:@"C"];

        NSArray *listOfObjects = [NSArray arrayWithObjects:string1, string2, string3,↩
nil];

        for(NSMutableString *s in listOfObjects){
```

```
        NSLog(@"This string in lowercase is %@", [s lowercaseString]);
    }

    [listOfObjects makeObjectsPerformSelector:@selector(appendString:)
                            withObject:@"-MORE"];

    [listOfObjects enumerateObjectsUsingBlock:^(id obj, NSUInteger idx,↩
BOOL *stop) {
        NSLog(@"object(%lu)'s description is %@",idx, [obj description]);
    }];

    }

    return 0;
}
```

Usage

To use this code, build and run your Mac app from Xcode. The log message will present the results of each way of iterating through the array that was created at the beginning.

```
This string in lowercase is a
This string in lowercase is b
This string in lowercase is c
object(0)'s description is A-MORE
object(1)'s description is B-MORE
object(2)'s description is C-MORE
```

3.5 Sorting an Array

Problem

You are using arrays to group your custom objects and you would like the objects to appear in lists sorted by the values of the object's properties.

Solution

Create one NSSortDescriptor object for each property that you want to use to sort your array. Put all these NSSortDescriptor objects into an array, which you will use as a parameter in the next step. Use the NSArray sortedArrayUsingDescriptors: method and pass the array of NSSortDescriptor objects as a parameter to return an array sorted by the properties that you specified.

How It Works

This recipe uses `Person` objects. See Listing 3-5 for the class definition of a `Person` object. While you can use this recipe to sort objects like strings or numbers, you can really see the power behind `NSSortDescriptor` when you use it with custom objects.

Your custom class is named `Person` and has three properties: `firstName`, `lastName`, and age. Your `Person` class also has two methods: `reportState` and `initWithFirstName:lastName:andAge`, which is a custom constructor.

First, create an array of `Person` objects.

```
//Instantiate Person objects and add them all to an array:
Person *p1 = [[Person alloc] initWithFirstName:@"Rebecca"
                                      lastName:@"Smith"
                                        andAge:33];
Person *p2 = [[Person alloc] initWithFirstName:@"Albert"
                                      lastName:@"Case"
                                        andAge:24];
Person *p3 = [[Person alloc] initWithFirstName:@"Anton"
                                      lastName:@"Belfey"
                                        andAge:45];
Person *p4 = [[Person alloc] initWithFirstName:@"Tom"
                                      lastName:@"Gun"
                                        andAge:17];
Person *p5 = [[Person alloc] initWithFirstName:@"Cindy"
                                      lastName:@"Lou"
                                        andAge:6];
Person *p6 = [[Person alloc] initWithFirstName:@"Yanno"
                                      lastName:@"Dirst"
                                        andAge:76];
```

```
NSArray *listOfObjects = [NSArray arrayWithObjects:p1, p2, p3, p4, p5, p6, nil];
```

If you print out each element in this array, the objects will appear in the order that you put them into the array. If you want to sort this array by each person's age, last name, and first name, you can use `NSSortDescriptor` objects. You need one sort descriptor for each `Person` property that you're using to sort.

```
//Create three sort descriptors and add to an array:
NSSortDescriptor *sd1 = [NSSortDescriptor sortDescriptorWithKey:@"age"
                                                      ascending:YES];
```

```
NSSortDescriptor *sd2 = [NSSortDescriptor sortDescriptorWithKey:@"lastName"
                                                      ascending:YES];

NSSortDescriptor *sd3 = [NSSortDescriptor sortDescriptorWithKey:@"firstName"
                                                      ascending:YES];

NSArray *sdArray1 = [NSArray arrayWithObjects:sd1, sd2, sd3, nil];
```

You must pass in the name of the property as a string and specify whether you want that property sorted ascending or descending. Finally, all the sort descriptors need to be in an array.

The position of each sort descriptor in the array determines the order in which the objects will be sorted. So, if you want the array sorted by age and then last name, make sure you add the sort descriptor corresponding to age before the sort descriptor corresponding to last name.

To get your sorted array, send the `sortedArrayUsingDescriptors` message to the array that you want to sort and pass the array of sort descriptors as a parameter.

```
NSArray *sortedArray1 = [listOfObjects sortedArrayUsingDescriptors:sdArray1];
```

To see the results, use the `makeObjectsPerformSelector` method to have each object in the sorted array report its state to the log.

```
[sortedArray1 makeObjectsPerformSelector:@selector(reportState)];
```

This will print out the details of each `Person` object to the log in the order that was specified by the sort descriptors (age, last name, first name). See Listings 3-5 through 3-7 for the code.

The Code

Listing 3-5. *Person.h*

```
#import <Foundation/Foundation.h>

@interface Person : NSObject

@property(strong) NSString *firstName;
@property(strong) NSString *lastName;
@property(assign) int age;

-(id)initWithFirstName:(NSString *)fName lastName:(NSString *)lName andAge:(int)a;

-(void)reportState;

@end
```

Listing 3-6. *Person.m*

```
#import "Person.h"

@implementation Person

@synthesize firstName, lastName, age;

-(id)initWithFirstName:(NSString *)fName lastName:(NSString *)lName andAge:(int)a{
    self = [super init];
    if (self) {
        self.firstName = fName;
        self.lastName = lName;
        self.age = a;
    }
    return self;
}

-(void)reportState{
    NSLog(@"This person's name is %@ %@ who is %i years old", firstName, lastName, age);
}

@end
```

Listing 3-7. *main.m*

```
#import <Foundation/Foundation.h>
#import "Person.h"

int main (int argc, const char * argv[])
{

    @autoreleasepool {

        //Instantiate Person objects and add them all to an array:
        Person *p1 = [[Person alloc] initWithFirstName:@"Rebecca"
                                              lastName:@"Smith"
                                                andAge:33];

        Person *p2 = [[Person alloc] initWithFirstName:@"Albert"
                                              lastName:@"Case"
                                                andAge:24];

        Person *p3 = [[Person alloc] initWithFirstName:@"Anton"
                                              lastName:@"Belfey"
                                                andAge:45];

        Person *p4 = [[Person alloc] initWithFirstName:@"Tom"
                                              lastName:@"Gun"
                                                andAge:17];
```

```objc
        Person *p5 = [[Person alloc] initWithFirstName:@"Cindy"
                                              lastName:@"Lou"
                                                andAge:6];

        Person *p6 = [[Person alloc] initWithFirstName:@"Yanno"
                                              lastName:@"Dirst"
                                                andAge:76];

        NSArray *listOfObjects = [NSArray arrayWithObjects:p1, p2, p3, p4, p5, p6,↵
nil];

        NSLog(@"PRINT OUT ARRAY UNSORTED");

        [listOfObjects makeObjectsPerformSelector:@selector(reportState)];

        //Create three sort descriptors and add to an array:
        NSSortDescriptor *sd1 = [NSSortDescriptor sortDescriptorWithKey:@"age"
                                                              ascending:YES];

        NSSortDescriptor *sd2 = [NSSortDescriptor sortDescriptorWithKey:@"lastName"
                                                              ascending:YES];


        NSSortDescriptor *sd3 = [NSSortDescriptor sortDescriptorWithKey:@"firstName"
                                                              ascending:YES];

        NSArray *sdArray1 = [NSArray arrayWithObjects:sd1, sd2, sd3, nil];

        NSLog(@"PRINT OUT SORTED ARRAY (AGE,LASTNAME,FIRSTNAME)");

        NSArray *sortedArray1 = [listOfObjects sortedArrayUsingDescriptors:sdArray1];

        [sortedArray1 makeObjectsPerformSelector:@selector(reportState)];

        NSArray *sdArray2 = [NSArray arrayWithObjects:sd2, sd1, sd3, nil];

        NSArray *sortedArray2 = [listOfObjects sortedArrayUsingDescriptors:sdArray2];

        NSLog(@"PRINT OUT SORTED ARRAY (LASTNAME,FIRSTNAME,AGE)");

        [sortedArray2 makeObjectsPerformSelector:@selector(reportState)];

    }
    return 0;
}
```

Usage

To use this code, you need to create a file for the `Person` class. This is an Objective-C class, and you may use the Xcode file templates to start it. The `Person` class must be imported into code located in `main.m` (for Mac command line apps). Build and run the project and then inspect the console log to see the results of the sorted arrays.

```
PRINT OUT ARRAY UNSORTED
This person's name is Rebecca Smith who is 33 years old
This person's name is Albert Case who is 24 years old
This person's name is Anton Belfey who is 45 years old
This person's name is Tom Gun who is 17 years old
This person's name is Cindy Lou who is 6 years old
This person's name is Yanno Dirst who is 76 years old
PRINT OUT SORTED ARRAY (AGE,LASTNAME,FIRSTNAME)
This person's name is Cindy Lou who is 6 years old
This person's name is Tom Gun who is 17 years old
This person's name is Albert Case who is 24 years old
This person's name is Rebecca Smith who is 33 years old
This person's name is Anton Belfey who is 45 years old
This person's name is Yanno Dirst who is 76 years old
PRINT OUT SORTED ARRAY (LASTNAME,FIRSTNAME,AGE)
This person's name is Anton Belfey who is 45 years old
This person's name is Albert Case who is 24 years old
This person's name is Yanno Dirst who is 76 years old
This person's name is Tom Gun who is 17 years old
This person's name is Cindy Lou who is 6 years old
This person's name is Rebecca Smith who is 33 years old
```

3.6 Querying an Array

Problem

You have a significant array full of objects and you would like to select a subset of this array based on some criteria to use in controls like the search bar in the table of an iOS app.

Solution

The first thing that you need is an `NSPredicate` object. `NSPredicate` is used to define a search query. Next, you can use the original array's filteredArrayUsingPredicate function to return a subset of the original array based on the specifications of the NSPredicate: object that you defined.

How It Works

For this recipe, use the same Person objects as you did in Recipe 3.5. You are going to define a predicate to return an array containing only Person objects with an age greater than 30.

```
NSPredicate *predicate = [NSPredicate predicateWithFormat:@"age > 30"];
```

Predicates require a logical expression to apply to the objects in the array. Here age is a property that must be part of the objects in the array that you are querying. You use the same comparison operators that you use in programming (see Table 3-2 for a complete list of NSPredicate operators).

Table 3-2. *NSPredicate Comparison Operators*

Basic Comparisons	Operators	Description
	=, ==	Left side is equal to the right side.
	>=, =>	Left side is greater than or equal to the right side.
	<=, =<	Left side is less than or equal to the right side.
	>	Left side is greater than the right side.
	<	Left side is less than the right side.
	!=, <>	Left side is not equal to the right side.
	BETWEEN	Left side is between the value specified on the right side.

Basic Comparisons	Operators	Description
Compound Predicates	AND, &&	Logical AND
	OR, ||	Logical OR
	NOT, !	Logical NOT
String Comparisons	BEGINSWITH	Left side begins with the right side expression.
	CONTAINS	Left side contains the right side expression.
	ENDSWITH	Left side ends with the right side expression.
	LIKE	Left side equals right side (? and * are allowed as wildcards).
	MATCHES	Left side matches right side using regex-style expression.
Aggregate Operations	ANY, SOME	Specifies any elements in the right side expression
	ALL	Specifies all elements in the right side expression
	NONE	Specifies none of the elements in the right side expression
	IN	Left side must appear in the collection specified by the right side.

Once you have your predicate set up, all you need to do is get the subset of the array by using the filteredArrayUsingPredicate: function while passing the NSPredicate object as a parameter.

```
NSArray *arraySubset = [listOfObjects filteredArrayUsingPredicate:predicate];
```

You will end up with another array that has only those objects that match the specifications that you coded in the NSPredicate object. See Listings 3-8 through 3-10 for the code.

The Code

Listing 3-8. *Person.h*

```objc
#import <Foundation/Foundation.h>

@interface Person : NSObject

@property(strong) NSString *firstName;
@property(strong) NSString *lastName;
@property(assign) int age;

-(id)initWithFirstName:(NSString *)fName lastName:(NSString *)lName andAge:(int)a;

-(void)reportState;

@end
```

Listing 3-9. *Person.m*

```objc
#import "Person.h"

@implementation Person

@synthesize firstName, lastName, age;

-(id)initWithFirstName:(NSString *)fName lastName:(NSString *)lName
andAge:(int)a{
    self = [super init];
    if (self) {
        self.firstName = fName;
        self.lastName = lName;
        self.age = a;
    }
    return self;
}

-(void)reportState{
    NSLog(@"This person's name is %@ %@ who is %i years old", firstName, lastName, age);
}

@end
```

Listing 3-10. *main.m*

```
#import <Foundation/Foundation.h>
#import "Person.h"

int main (int argc, const char * argv[])
{

    @autoreleasepool {
        //Instantiate Person objects and add them all to an array:
        Person *p1 = [[Person alloc] initWithFirstName:@"Rebecca"
                                              lastName:@"Smith"
                                                andAge:33];
        Person *p2 = [[Person alloc] initWithFirstName:@"Albert"
                                              lastName:@"Case"
                                                andAge:24];
        Person *p3 = [[Person alloc] initWithFirstName:@"Anton"
                                              lastName:@"Belfey"
                                                andAge:45];
        Person *p4 - [[Person alloc] initWithFirstNamc:@"Tom"
                                              lastName:@"Gun"
                                                andAge:17];
        Person *p5 = [[Person alloc] initWithFirstName:@"Cindy"
                                              lastName:@"Lou"
                                                andAge:6];
        Person *p6 = [[Person alloc] initWithFirstName:@"Yanno"
                                              lastName:@"Dirst"
                                                andAge:76];

    NSArray *listOfObjects = [NSArray arrayWithObjects:p1, p2, p3, p4, p5, p6,⏎
nil];

        NSPredicate *predicate = [NSPredicate predicateWithFormat:@"age > 30"];

        NSArray *arraySubset = [listOfObjects filteredArrayUsingPredicate:predicate];

        NSLog(@"PRINT OUT ARRAY SUBSET");

        [arraySubset makeObjectsPerformSelector:@selector(reportState)];


    }
    return 0;
}
```

Usage

To use this code, build and run your Mac app from Xcode. Check the console to see the results of the query made by the `NSPredicate` object.

```
PRINT OUT ARRAY SUBSET
This person's name is Rebecca Smith who is 33 years old
This person's name is Anton Belfey who is 45 years old
This person's name is Yanno Dirst who is 76 years old
```

3.7 Manipulating Array Contents

Problem

You want your array content to be more dynamic so that you or your users can add, remove, and insert objects into arrays. However, `NSArray` is an immutable class, so once you create an `NSArray` you can't make any changes to its contents.

Solution

If you know that your array needs to be dynamic, use `NSMutableArray`. `NSMutableArray` is a subclass of `NSArray`, so you can work with `NSMutableArray` as you would with `NSArray`. But `NSMutableArray` provides methods that let you add, remove, and insert objects into the array list.

How It Works

First, instantiate a `NSMutableArray` object. You can use any constructor to do this. To create a new empty `NSMutableArray`, you may simply use `alloc` and `init`.

```
NSMutableArray *listOfLetters = [[NSMutableArray alloc] init];
```

To add objects to this array, you must send the `addObject:` message to the array with the object that you are adding to the array as a parameter.

```
[listOfLetters addObject:@"A"];
```

```
[listOfLetters addObject:@"B"];
```

```
[listOfLetters addObject:@"C"];
```

When you use `addObject:` you are always adding objects to the end of the array list. If you would like to insert an object into another postion in the array, you need to use the `insertObject:atIndex:` method.

```
[listOfLetters insertObject:@"a"
                 atIndex:0];
```

This will insert the object into the first position in the array.

If you want to completely replace one object with another object at a particular index, you can use the `replaceObjectAtIndex:withObject:` method. Here is how to replace the string C with the lowercase c:

```
[listOfLetters replaceObjectAtIndex:2
                 withObject:@"c"];
```

To have two objects in the array exchange places, you can use the `exchangeObjectAtIndex:withObjectAtIndex:` method.

```
[listOfLetters exchangeObjectAtIndex:0
                 withObjectAtIndex:2];
```

When you need to remove objects from your array, you have a few different methods to choose from. You can remove an object at a specified index, you can remove the last object in the array, and you can remove all objects from the list. If you have a reference to the object on hand, you can also use that object reference to remove that object from the array. Here are some examples of removing objects:

```
[listOfLetters removeObject:@"A"];
```

```
[listOfLetters removeObjectAtIndex:1];
```

```
[listOfLetters removeLastObject];
```

```
[listOfLetters removeAllObjects];
```

See Listing 3-11 for the code.

The Code

Listing 3-11. *main.m*

```
#import <Foundation/Foundation.h>

int main (int argc, const char * argv[])
{

    @autoreleasepool {
```

```objc
NSMutableArray *listOfLetters = [[NSMutableArray alloc] init];

[listOfLetters addObject:@"A"];

[listOfLetters addObject:@"B"];

[listOfLetters addObject:@"C"];

NSLog(@"OBJECTS ADDED TO ARRAY: %@", listOfLetters);

[listOfLetters insertObject:@"a"
                    atIndex:0];

NSLog(@"OBJECT 'a' INSERTED INTO ARRAY: %@", listOfLetters);

[listOfLetters replaceObjectAtIndex:2
                         withObject:@"c"];

NSLog(@"OBJECT 'c' REPLACED 'C' IN ARRAY: %@", listOfLetters);

[listOfLetters exchangeObjectAtIndex:0
                   withObjectAtIndex:2];

NSLog(@"OBJECT AT INDEX 1 EXCHANGED WITH OBJECT AT INDEX 2 IN ARRAY: %@", ↵
listOfLetters);

[listOfLetters removeObject:@"A"];

 NSLog(@"OBJECT 'A' REMOVED IN ARRAY: %@", listOfLetters);

[listOfLetters removeObjectAtIndex:1];

 NSLog(@"OBJECT AT INDEX 1 REMOVED IN ARRAY: %@", listOfLetters);

[listOfLetters removeLastObject];

 NSLog(@"LAST OBJECT REMOVED IN ARRAY: %@", listOfLetters);

[listOfLetters removeAllObjects];

 NSLog(@"ALL OBJECTS REMOVED IN ARRAY: %@", listOfLetters);

    }
    return 0;
}
```

Usage

To use this code, build and run your Mac app from Xcode. Check the console to see what happens to the array after each operation is applied.

```
OBJECTS ADDED TO ARRAY: (
    A,
    B,
    C
)
OBJECT 'a' INSERTED INTO ARRAY: (
    a,
    A,
    B,
    C
)
OBJECT 'c' REPLACED 'C' IN ARRAY: (
    a,
    A,
    B,
    c
)
OBJECT AT INDEX 1 EXCHANGED WITH OBJECT AT INDEX 2 IN ARRAY: (
    B,
    A,
    a,
    c
)
OBJECT 'A' REMOVED IN ARRAY: (
    B,
    a,
    c
)
OBJECT AT INDEX 1 REMOVED IN ARRAY: (
    B,
    c
)
LAST OBJECT REMOVED IN ARRAY: (
    B
)
ALL OBJECTS REMOVED IN ARRAY: (
)
```

3.8 Saving Arrays to the File System

Problem

You want to save the objects in your array to the file system to be used later or by another program.

Solution

If your array contains lists of number or string objects, you can save all of these to your file system to be used later. Use the `writeToFile:atomically:` method to do this. Note that this does not work with custom objects. Custom objects require you to adopt the NSCoding protocol and use an archiving class (Chapter 9) or Core Data (Chapter 10).

How It Works

For this recipe, create an array filled up with strings and numbers.

```
NSArray *listOfObjects = [NSArray arrayWithObjects:@"A", @"B", @"C", [NSNumber ⏎
    numberWithInt:1], [NSNumber numberWithInt:2], [NSNumber numberWithInt:3],  nil];
```

To save this to the file system, you first need a file reference.

```
NSString *filePathName = @"/Users/Shared/array.txt";
```

> **NOTE:** This recipe assumes that you are trying this from a Mac app.
> iOS file references work differently; see Recipe 2.5 for examples of
> how to get iOS file references.

Now you can use the `writeToFile:atomically:` method to write the contents of this array to the Mac's file system.

```
[listOfObjects writeToFile:filePathName
            atomically:YES];
```

See Listing 3-12 for the code.

The Code

Listing 3-12. *main.m*

```objc
#import <Foundation/Foundation.h>

int main (int argc, const char * argv[])
{

    @autoreleasepool {

        NSArray *listOfObjects = [NSArray arrayWithObjects:@"A", @"B", @"C", [NSNumber↵
    numberWithInt:1], [NSNumber numberWithInt:2], [NSNumber numberWithInt:3],  nil];

        NSString *filePathName = @"/Users/Shared/array.txt";

        [listOfObjects writeToFile:filePathName
                        atomically:YES];

    }

    return 0;
}
```

Usage

To use this code, build and run your Mac app from Xcode. Use Finder to locate the file that was created, which will be at /Users/Shared/array.txt. Here is what the contents of the text file will look like:

```xml
<?xml version="1.0" encoding="UTF-8"?>
<!DOCTYPE plist PUBLIC "-//Apple//DTD PLIST 1.0//EN"↵
 "http://www.apple.com/DTDs/PropertyList-1.0.dtd">
<plist version="1.0">
<array>
        <string>A</string>
        <string>B</string>
        <string>C</string>
        <integer>1</integer>
        <integer>2</integer>
        <integer>3</integer>
</array>
</plist>
```

The data is organized in XML format as a property list (an Objective-C format to store keyed data).

3.9 Reading Arrays from the File System

Problem

You have files available to your app that contain content organized like an array and you want to use this content in your application.

Solution

If you have a file from an array that was saved using the writeToFile:atomically: method, use the initWithContentsOfFile: constructor to instantiate a new array populated with the contents from the file.

How It Works

For this recipe, use the file from Recipe 3.8 where you saved the contents of an array to the file system. So, use the same file path name here:

```
NSString *filePathName = @"/Users/Shared/array.txt";
```

> **NOTE:** This recipe assumes that you are trying this from a Mac app. iOS file references work differently; see Recipe 2.5 for examples of how to get iOS file references.

Once you have that, you can use the initWithContentsOfFile: constructor to create a new array populated with the content from the file.

```
NSArray *listOfObjects = [[NSArray alloc] initWithContentsOfFile:filePathName];
```

See Listing 3-13 for the code.

The Code

Listing 3-13. *main.m*

```
#import <Foundation/Foundation.h>

int main (int argc, const char * argv[])
{

    @autoreleasepool {
```

```
        NSString *filePathName = @"/Users/Shared/array.txt";

        NSArray *listOfObjects = [[NSArray alloc] initWithContentsOfFile:filePathName];

        NSLog(@"%@", listOfObjects);

    }
    return 0;
}
```

Usage

To use this code, build and run your Mac app from Xcode. Inspect the log to see the contents of the array.

```
(
    A,
    B,
    C,
    1,
    2,
    3
)
```

3.10 Creating a Dictionary

Problem

Your app requires you to group objects together in a list and you want to be able to reference the objects using a key.

Solution

Objective-C has two Foundation classes named NSDictionary and NSMutableDictionary that you can use to create lists of objects with keys. Use NSDictionary when you want a list that you know you won't need to change on the fly and NSMutableDictionary when you know you will need to add and remove objects from the dictionary later.

How It Works

Dictionaries are created in Objective-C like other objects: you can use the `alloc` and `init` constructors or convenience functions like `dictionaryWithObjects:forKeys:` to create the dictionary. If you use `NSDictionary` to create your dictionary, you can't make any changes to the dictionary once the dictionary is created. Use `NSMutableDictionary` to create dictionaries that you can later modify.

Here is an example of creating a dictionary that contains `Hello World` in different languages. Each version of the phrase is keyed to its language.

```
NSArray *listOfObjects = [NSArray arrayWithObjects:@"Hello World", @"Bonjour tout le
 monde", @"Hola Mundo", nil];

NSArray *listOfKeys = [NSArray arrayWithObjects:@"english", @"french", @"spanish", nil];

NSDictionary *dictionary2 = [NSDictionary dictionaryWithObjects:listOfObjects
                                                 forKeys:listOfKeys];
```

The `NSDictionary` constructor `arrayWithObjects:forKeys:` requires two arrays as parameters. The first array must contain the objects to be stored while the second array must contain the keys associated with the objects.

If you choose to use `NSMutableDictionary`, you can use the same constructors to create your arrays (`NSMutableDictionary` is a subclass of `NSDictionary`). You can also create your `NSMutableDictionary` by using `alloc` and `init` since you will likely add objects to your array at some future point. See Table 3-3 for a complete list of available constructors for `NSDictionary` and `NSMutableDictionary` and Listing 3-14 for the code.

Table 3-3. *NSDictionary and NSMutableDictionary Constructors*

Constructor	Description
`- (id)initWithObjects:(const id [])objects forKeys:(const id [])keys count:(NSUInteger)cnt;`	Initializes a dictionary with the specified objects, keys, and count
`- (id)initWithObjectsAndKeys:(id)firstObject, NS_REQUIRES_NIL_TERMINATION;`	Initializes a dictionary with the specified nil-terminated list of paired objects and keys
`- (id)initWithDictionary:(NSDictionary *)otherDictionary;`	Initializes a dictionary using another dictionary

Constructor	Description
- (id)initWithDictionary:(NSDictionary ↵ *)otherDictionary copyItems:(BOOL)flag;	Initializes a dictionary using another dictionary and optionally creates new copies of each object
- (id)initWithObjects:(NSArray *)objects ↵ forKeys:(NSArray *)keys;	Initializes a dictionary with the specified objects and keys
- (id)initWithContentsOfFile:(NSString *)path;	Initializes a dictionary with the contents of a local file
- (id)initWithContentsOfURL:(NSURL *)url;	Initializes a dictionary with the contents at a URL

The Code

Listing 3-14. *main.m*

```objc
#import <Foundation/Foundation.h>

int main (int argc, const char * argv[])
{

    @autoreleasepool {

        NSDictionary *dictionary1 = [[NSDictionary alloc] init];

        NSArray *listOfObjects = [NSArray arrayWithObjects:@"Hello World",  ↵
@"Bonjour tout le monde",  @"Hola Mundo", nil];

        NSArray *listOfKeys = [NSArray arrayWithObjects:@"english", @"french",↵
@"spanish", nil];

        NSDictionary *dictionary2 = [NSDictionary dictionaryWithObjects:listOfObject
                                                   forKeys:listOfKeys];

        NSLog(@"dictionary2 = %@", dictionary2);

    }
    return 0;
}
```

Usage

To use this code, build and run your Mac app from Xcode. You can set a breakpoint and use the Xcode debugger to inspect the contents of these dictionaries. In the next recipe, you will see how to reference each of these dictionary elements so you can print out their contents to the log or use them elsewhere in your programs. You can see the entire contents of the dictionary printed out in your log.

```
dictionary2 = {
    english = "Hello World";
    french = "Bonjour tout le monde";
    spanish = "Hola Mundo";
}
```

3.11 Referencing Objects in Arrays

Problem

You would like to get references to the objects in your dictionaries to either access their properties or to send messages to the objects.

Solution

Use the objectForKey: method to get a reference to the object referenced by the key that you supply.

How It Works

NSDictionary objects keep lists of objects organized based on the keys that you provide. This makes it very easy and fast to look up any object of interest. Simply use objectForKey: and provide the key for the object that you want to look up to get the reference that you need.

```
NSString *helloWorld = [dictionary objectForKey:@"english"];
```

See Listing 3-15 for the code.

The Code

Listing 3-15. *main.m*

```objc
#import <Foundation/Foundation.h>

int main (int argc, const char * argv[])
{

    @autoreleasepool {

        NSArray *listOfObjects = [NSArray arrayWithObjects:@"Hello World", ↵
@"Bonjour tout le monde", @"Hola Mundo", nil];

        NSArray *listOfKeys = [NSArray arrayWithObjects:@"english", @"french",↵
 @"spanish", nil];

        NSDictionary *dictionary = [NSDictionary dictionaryWithObjects:listOfObjects
                                                forKeys:listOfKeys];

        NSString *helloWorld = [dictionary objectForKey:@"english"];

        NSLog(@"%@", helloWorld);

    }
    return 0;
}
```

Usage

To use this code, build and run your Mac app from Xcode. The `hello world` message that prints out is the one keyed to English.

```
Hello World
```

To see the hello world message in French, add this code to your application:

```objc
helloWorld = [dictionary objectForKey:@"french"];

NSLog(@"%@", helloWorld);
```

Run the app again and take a look at the last console message to see the French hello world message. You can do the same for Spanish as well.

3.12 Obtaining the Dictionary Count

Problem

Your app is working with the content in your dictionaries and you need to know how many elements are in the dictionary to present your content appropriately.

Solution

NSDictionary objects have a count property that you can use to find out how many elements are in the dictionary.

How It Works

To use the count property, you can use dot notation (dictionary.count) on any dictionary object or you can send the count message ([dictionary count]) to find out how many elements are in the dictionary. See Listing 3-16 for the code.

The Code

Listing 3-16. *main.m*

```
#import <Foundation/Foundation.h>

int main (int argc, const char * argv[])
{

    @autoreleasepool {

        NSArray *listOfObjects = [NSArray arrayWithObjects:@"Hello World", ⏎
@"Bonjour tout le monde", @"Hola Mundo", nil];

        NSArray *listOfKeys = [NSArray arrayWithObjects:@"english", @"french",⏎
@"spanish", nil];

        NSDictionary *dictionary = [NSDictionary dictionaryWithObjects:listOfObjects
                                                    forKeys:listOfKeys];
        NSUInteger count = dictionary.count;

        NSLog(@"The dictionary contains %lu items", count);

    }
```

```
    return 0;
}
```

Usage

To use this code, build and run your Mac app from Xcode. The log message will present the number of elements.

```
The dictionary contains 3 items
```

3.13 Iterating Through a Dictionary

Problem

You have a dictionary of objects and you would like to be able to send the same message or access the same property for every object in the dictionary.

Solution

Use the `allValues` `NSDictionary` function to convert the dictionary to an array that you can use with a `for-each` loop. Or use `enumerateKeysAndObjectsUsingBlock:` to work with each object in the dictionary.

How It Works

`NSDictionary` objects come with one built-in way to iterate through a list of objects. However, you can temporarily convert the dictionary key and object contents to arrays if you would rather use the methods described in Recipe 3.4. For instance, to iterate through the objects in a dictionary using a `for-each` loop, you could do something like this:

```
for (NSString *s in [dictionary allValues]) {
    NSLog(@"value: %@", s);
}
```

The `allValues` `NSDictionary` function is what gives you the objects organized like an array instead of a dictionary. There is also an `allKeys` function that gives you all the key values as an array.

```
for (NSString *s in [dictionary allKeys]) {
    NSLog(@"key: %@", s);
}
```

You can also use blocks to execute code for each object in a dictionary by using the enumerateKeysAndObjectsUsingBlock: method. You can use this to define a block of code that will be applied to each object in the dictionary without setting up a for-each loop or getting references to the array version of the dictionary.

```
[dictionary enumerateKeysAndObjectsUsingBlock:^(id key, id obj, BOOL *stop) {
    NSLog(@"key = %@ and obj = %@", key, obj);
}];
```

See Listing 3-17 for the code.

The Code

Listing 3-17. *main.m*

```
#import <Foundation/Foundation.h>

int main (int argc, const char * argv[])
{

    @autoreleasepool {

        NSArray *listOfObjects = [NSArray arrayWithObjects:@"Hello World", ↩
@"Bonjour tout le monde", @"Hola Mundo", nil];

        NSArray *listOfKeys = [NSArray arrayWithObjects:@"english", @"french",↩
@"spanish", nil];

        NSDictionary *dictionary = [NSDictionary dictionaryWithObjects:listOfObjects
                                                               forKeys:listOfKeys];

        for (NSString *s in [dictionary allValues]) {
            NSLog(@"value: %@", s);
        }

        for (NSString *s in [dictionary allKeys]) {
            NSLog(@"key: %@", s);
        }

        [dictionary enumerateKeysAndObjectsUsingBlock:^(id key, id obj, BOOL *stop) {
            NSLog(@"key = %@ and obj = %@", key, obj);
        }];
```

```
    }
    return 0;
}
```

Usage

To use this code, build and run your Mac app from Xcode. The log message will present the results of each way of iterating through the dictionary.

```
value: Hello World
value: Bonjour tout le monde
value: Hola Mundo
key: english
key: french
key: spanish
key = english and obj = Hello World
key = french and obj = Bonjour tout le monde
key = spanish and obj = Hola Mundo
```

3.14 Manipulating Dictionary Contents

Problem

You want your dictionary content to be more dynamic so that you or users can add, remove, and insert objects into dictionaries. However, NSDictionary is an immutable class, so once you create an NSDictionary you can't make any changes to its contents.

Solution

When you know that your dictionary needs to be dynamic, use NSMutableDictionary. It is a subclass of NSDictionary, which means that you can work with NSMutableDictionary as you would with NSDictionary. But NSMutableDictionary gives you methods that let you add, remove, and insert objects into the dictionary.

How It Works

First, you must instantiate an NSMutableDictionary object. You can use any constructor to do this. To create a new empty NSMutableDictionary, you may simply use alloc and init.

```
NSMutableDictionary *dictionary = [[NSMutableDictionary alloc] init];
```

To add objects to this array, you must send the `setObject:forKey:` message to the dictionary with the object that you are adding and the key that goes with the object.

```
[dictionary setObject:@"Hello World"
            forKey:@"english"];

[dictionary setObject:@"Bonjour tout le monde"
            forKey:@"french"];

[dictionary setObject:@"Hola Mundo
            forKey:@"spanish"];
```

When you use `setObject:forKey` you are always adding objects to the dictionary indexed by the key that you provide.

To remove an object from a dictionary, you must have the key that is matched to the object. If you have the key, you can use the `removeObjectForKey:` method to remove an object.

```
[dictionary removeObjectForKey:@"french"];
```

Finally, you can remove all the objects from the dictionary at once by using the `removeAllObjects` method. See Listing 3-18 for the code.

The Code

Listing 3-18. *main.m*

```
#import <Foundation/Foundation.h>

int main (int argc, const char * argv[])
{

    @autoreleasepool {

        NSMutableDictionary *dictionary = [[NSMutableDictionary alloc] init];

        [dictionary setObject:@"Hello World"
                    forKey:@"english"];

        [dictionary setObject:@"Bonjour tout le monde"
                    forKey:@"french"];

        [dictionary setObject:@"Hola Mundo"
                    forKey:@"spanish"];
```

```
    NSLog(@"OBJECTS ADDED TO DICTIONARY: %@", dictionary);

    [dictionary removeObjectForKey:@"french"];

    NSLog(@"OBJECT REMOVED FROM DICTIONARY: %@", dictionary);

    [dictionary removeAllObjects];

    NSLog(@"ALL OBJECTS REMOVED FROM DICTIONARY: %@", dictionary);

    }
    return 0;
}
```

Usage

To use this code, build and run your Mac app from Xcode. Check the log console to see what happens to the dictionary after each operation is applied.

```
OBJECTS ADDED TO DICTIONARY: {
    english = "Hello World";
    french = "Bonjour tout le monde";
    spanish = "Hola Mundo";
}
OBJECT REMOVED FROM DICTIONARY: {
    english = "Hello World";
    spanish = "Hola Mundo";
}
ALL OBJECTS REMOVED FROM DICTIONARY: {
}
```

3.15 Saving Dictionaries to the File System

Problem

You want to save the objects in your dictionary to the file system to be used later on or by another program.

Solution

If your dictionary contains lists of number or string objects, you can save all of these to your file system to be used later. Use the writeToFile:atomically: method to do this. Note that this does not work with custom objects.

How It Works

For this recipe, set up a dictionary with phrases matched to keys.

```
NSArray *listOfObjects = [NSArray arrayWithObjects:@"Hello World", ↵
@"Bonjour tout le monde", @"Hola Mundo", nil];

NSArray *listOfKeys = [NSArray arrayWithObjects:@"english", @"french", @"spanish", nil];

NSDictionary *dictionary = [NSDictionary dictionaryWithObjects:listOfObjects
                                                      forKeys:listOfKeys];
```

To save this to the file system, you first need a file reference.

```
NSString *filePathName = @"/Users/Shared/dictionary.txt";
```

> **NOTE:** This recipe assumes that you are trying this from a Mac app. iOS file references work differently; see Recipe 2.5 for examples of how to get iOS file references.

Now you can use the `writeToFile:atomically:` method to write the contents of this dictionary to the Mac's file system.

```
[dictionary writeToFile:filePathName
               atomically:YES];
```

See Listing 3-19 for the code.

The Code

Listing 3-19. *main.m*

```
#import <Foundation/Foundation.h>

int main (int argc, const char * argv[])
{

    @autoreleasepool {

        NSArray *listOfObjects = [NSArray arrayWithObjects:@"Hello World", ↵
        @"Bonjour tout le monde", @"Hola Mundo", nil];

        NSArray *listOfKeys = [NSArray arrayWithObjects:@"english", @"french",↵
@"spanish", nil];
```

```
    NSDictionary *dictionary = [NSDictionary dictionaryWithObjects:listOfObjects
                                                          forKeys:listOfKeys];

    NSString *filePathName = @"/Users/Shared/dictionary.txt";

    [dictionary writeToFile:filePathName
                 atomically:YES];

    }
    return 0;
}
```

Usage

To use this code, build and run your Mac app from Xcode. Use Finder to locate the file that was created (which will be at /Users/Shared/dictionary.txt). Here is what the contents of the text file will look like:

```
<?xml version="1.0" encoding="UTF-8"?>
<!DOCTYPE plist PUBLIC "-//Apple//DTD PLIST 1.0//EN"↩
 "http://www.apple.com/DTDs/PropertyList-1.0.dtd">
<plist version="1.0">
<dict>
        <key>english</key>
        <string>Hello World</string>
        <key>french</key>
        <string>Bonjour tout le monde</string>
        <key>spanish</key>
        <string>Hola Mundo</string>
</dict>
</plist>
```

The data is organized in XML format as a property list (an Objective-C format to store keyed data).

3.16 Reading Dictionaries from the File System

Problem

You have files available to your app that contain content organized like a dictionary and you want to use this content in your application.

Solution

If you have a file from a dictionary that was saved using the
writeToFile:atomically: method, use the initWithContentsOfFile:
constructor to instantiate a new dictionary populated with the contents from the
file.

How It Works

For this recipe, use the file from Recipe 3.15 with the contents of that dictionary
on the file system. So, you can use the same file path name here:

```
NSString *filePathName = @"/Users/Shared/dictionary.txt";
```

> **NOTE:** This recipe assumes that you are trying this from a Mac app.
> iOS file references work differently; see Recipe 2.5 for examples of
> how to get iOS file references.

Once you have that, you can use the initWithContentsOfFile: constructor to
create a new dictionary populated with the content from the file.

```
NSDictionary *dictionary = [[NSDictionary alloc]
initWithContentsOfFile:filePathName];
```

See Listing 3-20 for the code.

The Code

Listing 3-20. *main.m*

```objc
#import <Foundation/Foundation.h>

int main (int argc, const char * argv[])
{

    @autoreleasepool {

        NSString *filePathName = @"/Users/Shared/dictionary.txt";

        NSDictionary *dictionary = [[NSDictionary alloc]↵
    initWithContentsOfFile:filePathName];

        NSLog(@"dictionary: %@", dictionary);
```

```
    }
    return 0;
}
```

Usage

To use this code, build and run your Mac app from Xcode. Inspect the log to see the contents of the dictionary.

```
dictionary: {
    english = "Hello World";
    french = "Bonjour tout le monde";
    spanish = "Hola Mundo";
}
```

3.17 Creating a Set

Problem

Your app requires you to group objects together in an unordered collection or a set.

Solution

Objective-C has two Foundation classes named NSSet and NSMutableSet that you can use to create sets. Use NSSet when you have a set that you know you won't need to change on the fly and NSMutableSet when you know you will need to add and remove objects from the set later.

How It Works

Sets are created in Objective-C like other objects: use the alloc and init constructors or convenience functions like setWithObjects: to create the set. If you use NSSet to create your set, you can't make any changes to the dictionary once the set is created. Use NSMutableSet to create sets that you can later modify.

Here is an example of creating a set that contains `Hello World` in different languages:

```
NSSet *set = [NSSet setWithObjects:@"Hello World", @"Bonjour tout le monde", @"Hola↵
    Mundo", nil];
```

The `NSSet` constructor `setWithObjects:` requires a nil-terminated array with the objects that will appear in the set.

If you choose to use `NSMutableSet`, you can use the same constructors to create your sets (`NSMutableSet` is a subclass of `NSSet`). You can also create your `NSMutableSet` by using `alloc` and `init` since you will likely add objects to your set at some future point. See Table 3-4 for a complete list of available constructors for `NSSet` and `NSMutableSet` and Listing 3-21 for the code.

Table 3-4. *NSSet and NSMutableSet Constructors*

Constructor	Description
`- (id)initWithObjects:(const id *)objects` ↵ `count:(NSUInteger)cnt;`	Initializes a set with the specified objects and count
`- (id)initWithObjects:(id)firstObj, ...` ↵ `NS_REQUIRES_NIL_TERMINATION;`	Initializes a set with the specified nil-terminated list of objects
`- (id)initWithSet:(NSSet *)set;`	Initializes a set using another set
`- (id)initWithSet:(NSSet *)set` ↵ `copyItems:(BOOL)flag;`	Initializes a set using another set and optionally creates new copies of each object
`- (id)initWithArray:(NSArray *)array;`	Initializes a set with the specified objects

The Code

Listing 3-21. *main.m*

```
#import <Foundation/Foundation.h>

int main (int argc, const char * argv[])
{

    @autoreleasepool {

        NSSet *set = [NSSet setWithObjects:@"Hello World", @"Bonjour tout le monde", ↵
```

```
@"Hola Mundo", nil];

      NSLog(@"set: %@",set);

  }
  return 0;
}
```

Usage

To use this code, build and run your Mac app from Xcode. In your log you can see the entire contents of the set printed out.

```
set: {(
    "Bonjour tout le monde",
    "Hello World",
    "Hola Mundo"
)}
```

3.18 Obtaining the Set Count

Problem

Your app is working with the content in your sets and you need to know how many elements are in the set to present your content appropriately.

Solution

NSSet objects have a count property that you can use to find out how many elements are in the set.

How It Works

To use the count property, you can use dot notation (set.count) on any set object or you can send the count message ([set count]) to find out how many elements are in the set. See Listing 3-22 for the code.

The Code

Listing 3-22. *main.m*

```
#import <Foundation/Foundation.h>

int main (int argc, const char * argv[])
{

    @autoreleasepool {

        NSSet *set = [NSSet setWithObjects:@"Hello World", @"Bonjour tout le monde", ⏎
@"Hola Mundo", nil];

        NSUInteger count = set.count;

        NSLog(@"The set contains %lu items", count);

    }
    return 0;
}
```

Usage

To use this code, build and run your Mac app from Xcode. The log message will present the number of elements.

```
The set contains 3 items
```

3.19 Comparing Sets

Problem

You work with many sets in your app and you would like to find out more information about each set and what objects are in each of your sets.

Solution

NSSet comes with some built-in methods that you can use to compare sets. You can find out if two sets intercept (they have some elements in common). You can find out if one set is a subset of another (one set is composed of objects that are entirely in another set). You can also find out if one set is equal to another or if an object is already in a set.

How It Works

For this recipe, you need two sets. These sets should simply have string objects for letters in the alphabet.

```
NSSet *set1 = [NSSet setWithObjects:@"A", @"B", @"C", @"D", @"E", nil];

NSSet *set2 = [NSSet setWithObjects:@"D", @"E", @"F", @"G", @"H", nil];
```

If you want to see if these sets have objects that overlap (the sets intersect), you can use the intersectsSet: function to return a BOOL.

```
BOOL setsIntersect = [set1 intersectsSet:set2];
```

To find out if one set contains objects that are entirely in another set, use the isSubsetOfSet: function.

```
BOOL set2IsSubset = [set2 isSubsetOfSet:set1];
```

To test whether two sets are identical, use the isEqualToSet: function.

```
BOOL set1IsEqualToSet2 = [set1 isEqualToSet:set2];
```

Finally, if you want to know whether an object is already in a set, use containsObject: to find out.

```
BOOL set1ContainsD = [set1 containsObject:@"D"];
```

See Listing 3-23 for the code.

The Code

Listing 3-23. *main.m*

```
#import <Foundation/Foundation.h>

int main (int argc, const char * argv[])
{

    @autoreleasepool {

        NSSet *set1 = [NSSet setWithObjects:@"A", @"B", @"C", @"D", @"E", nil];

        NSSet *set2 = [NSSet setWithObjects:@"D", @"E", @"F", @"G", @"H", nil];

        NSLog(@"set1 contains:%@", set1);
```

```
        NSLog(@"set2 contains:%@", set2);

        BOOL setsIntersect = [set1 intersectsSet:set2];

        BOOL set2IsSubset = [set2 isSubsetOfSet:set1];

        BOOL set1IsEqualToSet2 = [set1 isEqualToSet:set2];

        BOOL set1ContainsD = [set1 containsObject:@"D"];

        NSLog(@"setsIntersect = %i, set2IsSubset = %i, set1IsEqualToSet2 = %i,↵
    set1ContainsD = %i", setsIntersect, set2IsSubset, set1IsEqualToSet2, set1ContainsD);


    }
    return 0;
}
```

Usage

To use this code, build and run your Mac app from Xcode. The log message will present the sets and the results of the various tests. The log will print out 1 when a BOOL is YES and 0 when a BOOL is NO.

```
set1 contains:{(
    A,
    D,
    B,
    E,
    C
)}
set2 contains:{(
    H,
    F,
    D,
    G,
    E
)}
setsIntersect = 1, set2IsSubset = 0, set1IsEqualToSet2 = 0, set1ContainsD = 1
```

3.20 Iterating Through a Set

Problem

You have a set of objects and you would like to be able to send the same message or access the same property for every object in the set.

Solution

Use the `allObjects` NSSet function to convert the set to an array and then you can use a `for-each` loop. Or use `enumerateObjectsUsingBlock:` to work with each object in the set. NSSet also supports `makeObjectsPerformSelector:`, which is great when you specifically want each object to execute just one method.

How It Works

You can temporarily convert the set contents to an array if you would like to use the methods described in Recipe 3.4. For instance, to iterate through the objects in a set using a `for-each` loop, you could do something like this:

```
for (NSString *s in [set allObjects]) {
    NSLog(@"value: %@", s);
}
```

You can also use blocks to execute code for each object in a set by using the `enumerateObjectsUsingBlock:` method. You can use this to define a block of code that will be applied to each object in the dictionary without setting up a `for-each` loop or getting references to the array version of the set.

```
[set enumerateObjectsUsingBlock:^(id obj, BOOL *stop) {
    NSLog(@"obj = %@", obj);
}];
```

If you want to simply perform one action on each object and that action is a method coded in the object's class definition, you can use `makeObjectsPerformSelector:`.

```
[set makeObjectsPerformSelector:@selector(description)];
```

See Listing 3-24 for the code.

The Code

Listing 3-24. *main.m*

```
#import <Foundation/Foundation.h>

int main (int argc, const char * argv[])
{

    @autoreleasepool {

        NSSet *set = [NSSet setWithObjects:@"Hello World", @"Bonjour tout le monde", ↵
@"Hola Mundo", nil];

        for (NSString *s in [set allObjects]) {
            NSLog(@"value: %@", s);
        }

        [set enumerateObjectsUsingBlock:^(id obj, BOOL *stop) {
            NSLog(@"obj = %@", obj);
        }];

        [set makeObjectsPerformSelector:@selector(description)];

    }
    return 0;
}
```

Usage

To use this code, build and run your Mac app from Xcode. The log message will present the results of each way of iterating through the set.

```
value: Bonjour tout le monde
value: Hello World
value: Hola Mundo
obj = Bonjour tout le monde
obj = Hello World
obj = Hola Mundo
```

3.21 Manipulating Set Contents

Problem

You want your set contents to be more dynamic so that you or your users can add objects to sets and remove objects from sets. However, NSSet is an immutable class, so once you create an NSSet you can't make any changes to its contents.

Solution

When you know that your set needs to be dynamic, use NSMutableSet. It is a subclass of NSSet and so you can work with NSMutableArray as you would with NSSet. But NSMutableSet provides methods to add and remove objects.

How It Works

First, instantiate a NSMutableSet object. You can use any constructor to do this. To create a new empty NSMutableSet, you can use alloc and init.

```
NSMutableSet *set = [[NSMutableSet alloc] init];
```

To add objects to this set, you must send the addObject: message to the set with the object that you are adding as a parameter.

```
[set addObject:@"Hello World"];
```

```
[set addObject:@"Bonjour tout le monde"];
```

```
[set addObject:@"Hola Mundo"];
```

To remove an object from a set, you must already have a reference to the object. If you have this, then you can use removeObject.

```
[set removeObject:@"Bonjour tout le monde"];
```

Finally, you can remove all the objects from the set at once by using the removeAllObjects method. See Listing 3-25 for the code.

The Code

Listing 3-25. *main.m*

```objc
#import <Foundation/Foundation.h>

int main (int argc, const char * argv[])
{

    @autoreleasepool {

        NSMutableSet *set = [[NSMutableSet alloc] init];

        [set addObject:@"Hello World"];

        [set addObject:@"Bonjour tout le monde"];

        [set addObject:@"Hola Mundo"];

        NSLog(@"Objects added to set:%@", set);

        [set removeObject:@"Bonjour tout le monde"];

        NSLog(@"Object removed from set:%@", set);

        [set removeAllObjects];

        NSLog(@"All objects removed from set:%@", set);

    }
    return 0;
}
```

Usage

To use this code, build and run your Mac app from Xcode. Check the console to
see what happens to the set after each operation is applied.

```
Objects added to set:{(
    "Bonjour tout le monde",
    "Hello World",
    "Hola Mundo"
)}
Object removed from set:{(
    "Hello World",
    "Hola Mundo"
)}
All objects removed from set:{(
)}
```

File System

This chapter covers working with the file system on Mac and iOS.

The recipes in this chapter will show you how to:

- Get a reference to the file manager
- Reference key directories for Mac and iOS
- Discover and change a file's attributes
- Get a listing of files in a given directory
- Manage files and directories
- Use delegation with file manager
- Work with data using the NSData class
- Manage caching objects that take up lots of memory

4.1 Referencing and Using the File Manager

Problem

You need to work with your app's file system.

Solution

Get a reference to your app's NSFileManager to work with the file system.

How It Works

NSFileManager is an Objective-C singleton object (see the note below for an explanation of singleton) that you use to deal with the file system. You can use NSFileManager in both iOS and Mac applications, but be aware that folder locations in iOS apps are restricted to the iOS app's documents directory because iOS apps are sandboxed. Mac apps may reference any folder on the user's computer.

> **NOTE:** Singleton is a design pattern that restricts a class to only one instantiation. Singleton is seen in a few places in Objective-C, including UIApplication and NSApplication.

To work with the file system using NSFileManager, you first need to get a reference to the file manager for this application. You can use the defaultManager function to get this reference.

```
NSFileManager *fileManager = [NSFileManager defaultManager];
```

Once you have this reference, you can perform the operations that you expect. For instance, to find out the current directory, you can access the currentDirectoryPath property of the file manager.

```
NSString *currentDirectoryPath = [fileManager currentDirectoryPath];
```

To change the current directory, send the changeCurrentDirectoryPath message to the file manager.

```
[fileManager changeCurrentDirectoryPath:@"/Users/Shared"];
```

This line of code will change the current directory path to the Mac's shared folder. See Listing 4-1 for the code.

The Code

Listing 4-1. *main.m*

```
#import <Foundation/Foundation.h>

int main (int argc, const char * argv[])
{

    @autoreleasepool {

        NSFileManager *fileManager = [NSFileManager defaultManager];
```

```
        NSString *currentDirectoryPath = [fileManager currentDirectoryPath];

        NSLog(@"currentDirectoryPath = %@", currentDirectoryPath);

        [fileManager changeCurrentDirectoryPath:@"/Users/Shared"];

        currentDirectoryPath = [fileManager currentDirectoryPath];

        NSLog(@"currentDirectoryPath = %@", currentDirectoryPath);

    }
    return 0;
}
```

Usage

To use this code, build and run your Mac app from Xcode. View the log to see
the current directory before and after the current directory was changed.

```
currentDirectoryPath = /Users/[YOUR-USER-NAME]/Library/Developer/Xcode⮠
/DerivedData/GetFileManagerReference-
bdycvqvpjxccqqfvchrjapqmvgpj/Build/Products/Debug

currentDirectoryPath = /Users/Shared
```

4.2 Getting Mac System Directory References

Problem

Your Mac application needs to reference key directories such as the user's
documents and downloads directories.

Solution

Use NSSearchPathForDirectoriesInDomains to get the information your app
needs to reference your user's key directories. Use NSBundle to get a reference
to the application bundle, which is where you include files that will be distributed
with your applications.

How It Works

To get a reference to your application's bundle, you can use the main bundle's bundlePath function.

```
NSString *bundlePath = [[NSBundle mainBundle] bundlePath];
```

The main bundle is a singleton that you can get by using the NSBundle function mainBundle.

NSSearchPathForDirectoriesInDomains is a function that returns back a directory reference based on three parameters: the directory that you are interested in, the domain (user, machine, network, all), and a BOOL indicating whether you want the tilde expanded.

For instance, if you want to find the location of the user's documents directory, you do this:

```
NSString *directoryPathName = [NSSearchPathForDirectoriesInDomains↩
(NSDocumentDirectory,  NSAllDomainsMask, YES) lastObject];
```

The first parameter specifies the directory in which you are interested. See Table 4-1 for a listing of the directory constants you can use here.

Table 4-1. *Mac System Directory Constants*

Directory Constant	Description
NSApplicationDirectory	Applications directory
NSDemoApplicationDirectory	Demos directory
NSAdminApplicationDirectory	System applications
NSLibraryDirectory	Documentation directory
NSUserDirectory	The user's directory
NSDocumentDirectory	The user's documents directory
NSAutosavedInformationDirectory	Directory of auto-saved documents
NSDesktopDirectory	The user's desktop
NSCachesDirectory	Directory for temporary cache files
NSDownloadsDirectory	The user's downloads directory

Directory Constant	Description
NSMoviesDirectory	The user's movies directory
NSMusicDirectory	The user's music directory
NSPicturesDirectory	The user's pictures directory
NSSharedPublicDirectory	The user's public sharing directory

The second parameter is used to specify what domain that you want included in the search. See Table 4-2 for a listing of the domains that you can search on. The last parameter gives you the option to expand the tilde character (~).

Table 4-2. *Available Domain Masks*

Domain Mask	Description
NSUserDomainMask	The user's home directory
NSLocalDomainMask	The machine's directory (for all users)
NSNetworkDomainMask	Publically available location on network
NSSystemDomainMask	Apple's system directories
NSAllDomainsMask	All of the aforementioned domains

NSSearchPathForDirectoriesInDomains returns an array. Listing 4-2 uses the NSArray lastObject function to return the last object in the array and assign this to the string.

The Code

Listing 4-2. *main.m*

```
#import <Foundation/Foundation.h>

int main (int argc, const char * argv[])
{

    @autoreleasepool {

        NSString *bundlePath = [[NSBundle mainBundle] bundlePath];
```

```
        NSLog(@"bundlePath = %@", bundlePath);

        NSString *directoryPathName = [NSSearchPathForDirectoriesInDomains⏎
(NSDocumentDirectory, NSAllDomainsMask, YES) lastObject];

        NSLog(@"directoryPathName = %@", directoryPathName);

    }
    return 0;
}
```

Usage

To use this code, build and run your Mac app from Xcode. You can see the
location of the documents directory and the application bundle reflected in the
console log.

```
bundlePath = /Users/[YOUR-USER-NAME]/Library/Developer/Xcode⏎
/DerivedData/GetKeyMacFolderReferences-
belypecqtyqdumeenpjlbpeeaxun/Build/Products/Debug

directoryPathName = /Users/[YOUR-USER-NAME]/Documents
```

4.3 Getting Key iOS Directory References

Problem

Your iOS application needs to reference key directories like the app documents
directory and the bundle directory.

Solution

Your application bundle contains the resources that you include with your app.
Use NSBundle to get a reference to this directory so that you can extract your
resources as needed. To get references to iOS directories designated for
documents, libraries, and caches, use NSSearchPathForDirectoriesInDomains,
as in Recipe 4.2.

> **NOTE:** iOS apps can't reference all your Mac directories because iOS apps can only run in the iOS Simulator or on an iOS device and therefore can only access the simulator's or device's directories.

How It Works

To get a reference to your application's bundle, you can use the main bundle's bundlePath function.

```
NSString *bundlePath = [[NSBundle mainBundle] bundlePath];
```

The main bundle is a singleton that you can get by using the NSBundle function mainBundle. If you look up this directory in Finder, you will find your app name with the .app extension. Control+click this app name and choose "Show Package Contents" to see your app executable and the supporting files (including any that you added yourself). This package is what ultimately gets posted to the app store.

> **NOTE:** iOS app bundle directories are read-only so you must copy any files from the app bundle and place them into a writeable directory in the app sandbox before modifying the files.

NSSearchPathForDirectoriesInDomains returns back a directory reference based on three parameters: the directory that you are interested in, the domain (user, machine, network, all), and a BOOL indicating whether you want the tilde expanded.

For instance, if you want to find the location of the user's documents directory, you do this:

```
NSString *documentsDirectory = [NSSearchPathForDirectoriesInDomains↵
(NSDocumentDirectory, NSUserDomainMask, YES) lastObject];
```

See Table 4-3 for a list of the directories that you can reference with this function and Listing 4-3 for the code.

Table 4-3. *iOS System Directories*

NSSearchPathDirectory	Usage
NSDocumentDirectory	Location for user-generated content (read-write, backed up)
NSLibraryDirectory	The app's library directory (read-write, backed up)
NSCachesDirectory	A directory for cached files (read-write, not backed up)

Apple provides automatic backup with both iTunes and iCloud for some of these directories. Generally, you use the documents directory for user-generated content that you want backed up, the library directory to store information that your app needs as a reference, and the cache directory to store temporary files (the cache is not backed up).

The Code

Listing 4-3. *main.m*

```objc
#import "AppDelegate.h"

@implementation AppDelegate

@synthesize window = _window;

- (BOOL)application:(UIApplication *)application ↩
didFinishLaunchingWithOptions:(NSDictionary  *)launchOptions{

    //app bundle not backed up, readonly
    NSString *bundlePath = [[NSBundle mainBundle] bundlePath];

    NSLog(@"bundlePath = %@", bundlePath);

    //documents directory is backed up
    NSString *documentsDirectory = [NSSearchPathForDirectoriesInDomains↩
(NSDocumentDirectory, NSUserDomainMask, YES) lastObject];

    NSLog(@"documentsDirectory = %@", documentsDirectory);

    //Library directory is backed up
    NSString *libraryDirectory = [NSSearchPathForDirectoriesInDomains↩
(NSLibraryDirectory, NSUserDomainMask, YES) lastObject];

    NSLog(@"libraryDirectory = %@", libraryDirectory);
```

```
    //Cache directory is not backe up
    NSString *cacheDirectory = [NSSearchPathForDirectoriesInDomains↵
(NSCachesDirectory, NSUserDomainMask, YES) lastObject];

    NSLog(@"cacheDirectory = %@", cacheDirectory);

    self.window = [[UIWindow alloc] initWithFrame:[[UIScreen mainScreen] bounds]];

    self.window.backgroundColor = [UIColor whiteColor];
    [self.window makeKeyAndVisible];
    return YES;
}

@end
```

Usage

This code must be located in an iOS app to work as expected; I put the code into the app delegate's didFinishLaunchingWithOptions: method. Build your app to see the directory strings being written out to your log.

```
bundlePath = /Users/[YOUR-USER-NAME]/Library/Application Support/iPhone ↵
Simulator/5.0/Applications/18AF23E1-9CAB-4FA6-9D5D-
39994AD355D7/GetiOSDirectories.app

documentsDirectory = /Users/[YOUR-USER-NAME]/Library/Application Support/iPhone ↵
Simulator/5.0/Applications/18AF23E1-9CAB-4FA6-9D5D-39994AD355D7/Documents

libraryDirectory = /Users/[YOUR-USER-NAME]/Library/Application Support/iPhone ↵
Simulator/5.0/Applications/18AF23E1-9CAB-4FA6-9D5D-39994AD355D7/Library

cacheDirectory = /Users/[YOUR-USER-NAME]/Library/Application Support/iPhone ↵
Simulator/5.0/Applications/18AF23E1-9CAB-4FA6-9D5D-39994AD355D7/Library/Caches
```

You can also copy and paste these directory strings into Finder to be directed to the location on your Mac that iOS Simulator temporarily used for these directories. For instance, copy and paste the app bundle pathname from your log, go to **Finder ➤ Go ➤ Go to Folder**, and then paste the pathname into the dialog box and click Go. You will see all the temporary directories that the iOS Simulator created for your app here.

4.4 Getting File Attributes

Problem

Your application needs information about files and folders such as creation date, modification date, and file type.

Solution

Use the `NSFileManager attributesOfItemAtPath:error:` function to return a dictionary listing all the attributes for the file or folder of interest.

How It Works

This recipe assumes that you have a file reference handy that you can inspect. You will need a reference to the file manager and the file (or folder) to follow along.

```
NSFileManager *fileManager = [NSFileManager defaultManager];

NSString *filePathName = @"/Users/Shared/textfile.txt";
```

Next you need an error object. You will find that when you are working with the file system it often pays to use an error object. This gives your app a good chance to recover from common problems like wrong filenames.

```
NSError *error = nil;
```

Now you need a dictionary, which you can get by using the file manager's `attributesOfItemAtPath:error:` function. You need to give this function the file path name and a reference to the error object. The reference to the error object requires the & to indicate that the error object is being passed by reference (so you can test it later to see if an error occurred).

```
NSDictionary *fileAttributes = [fileManager attributesOfItemAtPath:filePathName
                                                             error:&error];
```

In the next step, you check to make sure there is no error and then use a key to retrieve the desired information from the dictionary that you just retrieved.

```
if(!error){

    NSDate *dateFileCreated = [fileAttributes valueForKey:NSFileCreationDate];

    NSString *fileType = [fileAttributes valueForKey:NSFileType];
```

}

You look up the file creation date as well as the file type. See Table 4-4 for a list of file attribute keys and Listing 4-4 for the code.

Table 4-4. *File Attribute Keys*

Directory Constant	Description
NSFileType	File type
NSFileSize	File size in bytes
NSFileModificationDate	Last time file was modified
NSFileReferenceCount	File's reference count
NSFileDeviceIdentifier	Identifier of the device where file is located
NSFileOwnerAccountName	File owner's name
NSFileGroupOwnerAccountName	Group name of the file owner
NSFilePosixPermissions	File's POSIX permissions
NSFileSystemNumber	Directory for temporary cache files
NSFileSystemFileNumber	File's file system number
NSFileExtensionHidden	File's extension is hidden
NSFileHFSCreatorCode	File's HFS creator code
NSFileHFSTypeCode	File's HFS type code
NSFileImmutable	Indicates if file is immutable
NSFileAppendOnly	File is read-only
NSFileCreationDate	Date file was created
NSFileOwnerAccountID	File owner's account ID
NSFileGroupOwnerAccountID	File group ID

Directory Constant	Description
NSFileBusy	File is busy

The Code

Listing 4-4. *main.m*

```objc
#import <Foundation/Foundation.h>

int main (int argc, const char * argv[])
{

    @autoreleasepool {
        NSFileManager *fileManager = [NSFileManager defaultManager];

        NSString *filePathName = @"/Users/Shared/textfile.txt";

        NSError *error = nil;

        NSDictionary *fileAttributes = [fileManager attributesOfItemAtPath:filePathName
                                                        error:&error];

        if(!error){

            NSDate *dateFileCreated = [fileAttributes valueForKey:NSFileCreationDate];
            NSString *fileType = [fileAttributes valueForKey:NSFileType];

            NSLog(@"This %@ file was created on %@",fileType, dateFileCreated);

        }

    }
    return 0;
}
```

Usage

To use this code, replace the file reference that I used with one from your own Mac. Then build and run your Mac app from Xcode. View the log to see the file attributes.

```
This NSFileTypeRegular file was created on 2012-01-03 15:21:47 +0000
```

4.5 Getting the List of Files and Sub-Directories in a Directory

Problem

You want to find out what files and folders are in a given directory.

Solution

Use the NSFileManager contentsOfDirectoryAtPath:error: to get an array of all the file and folder path names contained in a directory. To get a listing of all the files and folders in a directory and all subdirectories, use NSFileManager subpathsOfDirectoryAtPath: function.

How It Works

This recipe assumes that you have a directory reference handy that you can inspect. You will need a reference to the file manager and a directory to follow along.

```
NSFileManager *fileManager = [NSFileManager defaultManager];

NSString *sharedDirectory = @"/Users/Shared";
```

To simply get a listing of all the contents in a directory, you can use contentsOfDirectoryAtPath:error: to get an array of file path names. Note that you will get path names for all the files in the directory as well as all the sub-directories in the directory.

```
NSError *error = nil;

NSArray *listOfFiles = [fileManager contentsOfDirectoryAtPath:sharedDirectory
                                                        error:&error];
```

As with most file system operations, you should use an NSError object, which you should test before working on the results of a file system operation. This function just provides files and directory paths for the top level of the directory that you specified.

To recursively get all the file and directory path names starting from the directory that you specify, you can use subpathsOfDirectoryAtPath:error.

```
NSArray *listOfSubPaths = [fileManager subpathsOfDirectoryAtPath:sharedDirectory
                                                           error:&error];
```

See Listing 4-5 for the code.

The Code

Listing 4-5. *main.m*

```
#import <Foundation/Foundation.h>

int main (int argc, const char * argv[])
{

    @autoreleasepool {

        NSFileManager *fileManager = [NSFileManager defaultManager];

        NSString *sharedDirectory = @"/Users/Shared";

        NSError *error = nil;

        NSArray *listOfFiles = [fileManagercontentsOfDirectoryAtPath:sharedDirectory
                                                               error:&error];

        if(!error)
            NSLog(@"Contents of shared directory: %@", listOfFiles);

        NSArray *listOfSubPaths = [fileManager subpathsOfDirectoryAtPath:sharedDirectory
                                                                   error:&error];

        if(!error)
            NSLog(@"Sub Paths of shared directory": %@", listOfSubPaths);

    }
    return 0;
}
```

Usage

To use this code, replace the directory reference that I used with one from your own Mac. Then build and run your Mac app from Xcode. Here is the output from my run; I edited out some of the sub-directories because the listing became very long.

```
Contents of shared directory: (
```

```
     "array.txt",
     "dictionary.txt",
     "textfile.txt"
         [EDITED SUB-DIRECTORIES OUT]
)
Sub Paths of shared directory: (
     ".DS_Store",
     ".ioSharedDefaults.W80152WTAGV",
     ".ioSharedDefaults.W8815GRBOPO",
     ".localized",
     ".localized (from old Mac)",
     ".SharedUserDB",
     "array.txt",

         [EDITED SUB-DIRECTORIES OUT]

     subversion,
     "subversion/.DS_Store",
     "subversion/HelloWorld",

         [EDITED SUB-DIRECTORIES OUT]

     "textfile.txt"
)
```

> **NOTE:** Be careful when recursively getting these pathnames of every subdirectory. Complex directory hierarchies can make this an expensive proposition.

4.6 Managing Directories

Problem

Your application needs to add, move, copy, and remove directories.

Solution

Use the NSFileManager createDirectoryAtPath:withIntermediateDirectories:attributes:error: to create a new directory, moveItemAtPath:toPath:error: to move a directory,

`removeItemAtPath:error:` to remove a directory, and
`copyItemAtPath:toPath:error:` to copy a directory.

How It Works

You will need a reference to the file manager and the directory that you want to create to follow along.

`NSFileManager *fileManager = [NSFileManager defaultManager];`

`NSString *sharedDirectory = @"/Users/Shared/NewDirectory1/NewSubDirectory1";`

As with most of the `NSFileManager` functions, you need an error object.

`NSError *error = nil;`

Use `createDirectoryAtPath:withIntermediateDirectories:attributes:error:` to create a new directory. This function needs the new directory path name to create, a `BOOL` indicating whether you want to create any intermediate directories in the path name that do not yet exist, a dictionary of attributes to be applied to the new directory, and an error object reference.

```
BOOL directoryCreated = [fileManager createDirectoryAtPath:newDirectory
                            withIntermediateDirectories:YES
                                         attributes:nil
                                             error:&error];
```

The function returns a `BOOL`, which tells you whether the operation was successful, but you should use the error object to test it just to be safe. In this recipe, I left the attributes parameter as nil but you can supply an `NSDictionary` object filled with file attributes here if need. See Table 4-4 (in Recipe 4.4) for a list of file attributes that you can use here.

You can also move a directory with the `moveItemAtPath:toPath:error` function. You need to specify the old and new directory locations along with an error object reference.

`NSString *directoryMovedTo = @"/Users/Shared/NewSubDirectory1";`

```
BOOL directoryMoved = [fileManager moveItemAtPath:newDirectory
                                   toPath:directoryMovedTo
                                    error:&error];
```

To remove a directory, use the file manager's `removeItemAtPath:error` function. Pass the directory to be removed along with a reference to an error object.

`NSString *directoryToRemove = @"/Users/Shared/NewDirectory1";`

```
BOOL directoryRemoved =[fileManager removeItemAtPath:directoryToRemove
                                          error:&error];
```

To copy a directory, use `copyItemAtPath:toPath:error:` from your file manager.

```
NSString *directoryToCopy = @"/Users/Shared/NewSubDirectory1";
NSString *directoryToCopyTo = @"/Users/Shared/CopiedDirectory";

BOOL directoryCopied =[fileManager copyItemAtPath:directoryToCopy
                                      toPath:directoryToCopyTo
                                       error:&error];
```

See Listing 4-6 for the code.

The Code

Listing 4-6. *main.m*

```
#import <Foundation/Foundation.h>

int main (int argc, const char * argv[])
{

    @autoreleasepool {

        NSFileManager *fileManager = [NSFileManager defaultManager];

        NSString *newDirectory =
@"/Users/Shared/NewDirectory1/NewSubDirectory1";

        NSError *error = nil;

        BOOL directoryCreated = [fileManager createDirectoryAtPath:newDirectory
                                    withIntermediateDirectories:YES
                                                     attributes:nil
                                                          error:&error];
        if(!error)
            NSLog(@"directoryCreated = %i with no error", directoryCreated);
        else
            NSLog(@"directoryCreated = %i with error %@", directoryCreated, error);


        NSString *directoryMovedTo = @"/Users/Shared/NewSubDirectory1";

        BOOL directoryMoved = [fileManager moveItemAtPath:newDirectory
                                              toPath:directoryMovedTo
                                               error:&error];

        if(!error)
```

```
            NSLog(@"directoryMoved = %i with no error", directoryMoved);
        else
            NSLog(@"directoryMoved = %i with error %@", directoryMoved, error);


    NSString *directoryToRemove = @"/Users/Shared/NewDirectory1";

    BOOL directoryRemoved =[fileManager removeItemAtPath:directoryToRemove
                                               error:&error];



    if(!error)
        NSLog(@"directoryRemoved = %i with no error", directoryRemoved);
    else
        NSLog(@"directoryRemoved = %i with error %@", directoryRemoved, error);

    NSString *directoryToCopy = @"/Users/Shared/NewSubDirectory1";
    NSString *directoryToCopyTo = @"/Users/Shared/CopiedDirectory";

    BOOL directoryCopied =[fileManager copyItemAtPath:directoryToCopy
                                             toPath:directoryToCopyTo
                                              error:&error];

    if(!error)
        NSLog(@"directoryCopied = %i with no error", directoryCopied);
    else
        NSLog(@"directoryCopied = %i with error %@", directoryCopied, error);
    }
    return 0;
}
```

Usage

To use this code, replace the directory reference that I used with one from your own Mac. Then build and run your Mac app from Xcode. Use Finder to see if your directories modified in the way you expected. You can also view the console log output to see if the operations were successful.

```
directoryCreated = 1 with no error
directoryMoved = 1 with no error
directoryRemoved = 1 with no error
directoryCopied = 1 with no error
```

4.7 Managing Files

Problem

Your application needs to add, move, copy, and remove files.

Solution

Use the `NSFileManager` `createFileAtPath:contents:attributes:` to create a new file, `moveItemAtPath:toPath:error:` to move a file, `removeItemAtPath:error:` to remove a file, and `copyItemAtPath:toPath:error:` to copy a file.

How It Works

You will need a reference to the file manager before you can do anything else.

```
NSFileManager *fileManager = [NSFileManager defaultManager];
```

To create a file, you need to use `NSData`, which is used to work with data and content. For this recipe, I'm going to use `NSData` to get a picture from my blog. To do this, I need to start with `NSURL` so I can reference this resource.

```
NSURL *url = [NSURL URLWithString:@"http://howtomakeiphoneapps.com/wp- ↵
content/uploads/2012/01/apples-oranges.jpg"];
```

Once I have the `NSURL` object, I can use the `NSData` function `dataWithContentsOfURL` to download the content directly into my app.

```
NSData *dataObject = [NSData dataWithContentsOfURL:url];
```

With this data object set up for use, I can now use the file manager function `createFileAtPath:contents:attributes:` to create the file on the Mac's file system.

```
NSString *newFile = @"/Users/Shared/apples-oranges.jpg";

BOOL fileCreated = [fileManager createFileAtPath:newFile
                                        contents:dataObject
                                      attributes:nil];
```

This function uses the data stored in the `NSData` object along with any attributes that you would like to specify and stores the data as a file.

You can also move a file with the `moveItemAtPath:toPath:error` function. You need to specify the old and new file path names along with an error object reference.

```
NSError *error = nil;

NSString *fileMovedTo = @"/Users/Shared/apples-oranges-moved.jpg";

BOOL fileMoved = [fileManager moveItemAtPath:newFile
                                      toPath:fileMovedTo
                                       error:&error];
```

To remove a file, use the file manager's `removeItemAtPath:error` function. Pass the file to be removed along with a reference to an error object.

```
NSString *fileToRemove = @"/Users/Shared/apples-oranges-moved.jpg";

BOOL fileRemoved =[fileManager removeItemAtPath:fileToRemove
                                          error:&error];
```

To copy a file, use `copyItemAtPath:toPath:error:` from your file manager.

```
NSString *fileToCopy = @"/Users/Shared/apples-oranges-moved.jpg";
NSString *copiedFileName = @"/Users/Shared/apples-oranges-backup-copy.jpg";

BOOL fileCopied = [fileManager copyItemAtPath:fileToCopy
                                       toPath:copiedFileName
                                        error:&error];
```

See Listing 4-7 for the code.

The Code

Listing 4-7. *main.m*

```
#import <Foundation/Foundation.h>

int main (int argc, const char * argv[])
{

    @autoreleasepool {

        NSFileManager *fileManager = [NSFileManager defaultManager];

        NSURL *url = [NSURL URLWithString:@"http://howtomakeiphoneapps.com/wp-↵
content/uploads/2012/01/apples-oranges.jpg"];

        NSData *dataObject = [NSData dataWithContentsOfURL:url];
```

```
        NSString *newFile = @"/Users/Shared/apples-oranges.jpg";

        BOOL fileCreated = [fileManager createFileAtPath:newFile
                                                contents:dataObject
                                              attributes:nil];

        NSLog(@"fileCreated = %i with no error", fileCreated);

        NSError *error = nil;

        NSString *fileMovedTo = @"/Users/Shared/apples-oranges-moved.jpg";

        BOOL fileMoved = [fileManager moveItemAtPath:newFile
                                              toPath:fileMovedTo
                                               error:&error];

        if(!error)
            NSLog(@"fileMoved = %i with no error", fileMoved);
        else
            NSLog(@"fileMoved = %i with error %@", fileMoved, error);

        NSString *fileToCopy = @"/Users/Shared/apples-oranges-moved.jpg";
        NSString *copiedFileName = @"/Users/Shared/apples-oranges-backup-copy.jpg";

        BOOL fileCopied = [fileManager copyItemAtPath:fileToCopy
                                               toPath:copiedFileName
                                                error:&error];

        if(!error)
            NSLog(@"fileCopied = %i with no error", fileCopied);
        else
            NSLog(@"fileCopied = %i with error %@", fileCopied, error);


        NSString *fileToRemove = @"/Users/Shared/apples-oranges-moved.jpg";

        BOOL fileRemoved =[fileManager removeItemAtPath:fileToRemove
                                                  error:&error];

        if(!error)
            NSLog(@"fileRemoved = %i with no error", fileRemoved);
        else
            NSLog(@"fileRemoved = %i with error %@", fileRemoved, error);


    }
    return 0;
}
```

Usage

To use this code, replace the directory reference with the file that I used with a directory that will work from your own Mac. Then build and run your Mac app from Xcode. Use Finder to see if your directories modified in the way you expected. You can also view the console log output to see if the operations were successful.

```
fileCreated = 1 with no error
fileMoved = 1 with no error
fileCopied = 1 with no error
fileRemoved = 1 with no error
```

4.8 Checking File Status

Problem

You want to know if the file you're interested in is writeable or if it even exists at all before you attempt to work on it.

Solution

Use the appropriate NSFileManager functions to test for various states of interest. Each of these functions returns a BOOL indicating the state of the file in question:

- fileExistsAtPath:
- isReadableFileAtPath:
- isWritableFileAtPath:
- isExecutableFileAtPath:
- isDeletableFileAtPath:.

> **NOTE:** Be careful if you are using these functions to predicate the behavior of your app based solely on the results of these functions. In Apple's documentation, it's recommended that you use these in conjunction with the proper error handling with NSError. You will find examples of NSError in Recipes 4.6 and 4.7.

How It Works

To follow this recipe, you will need a reference to a file on your Mac, like the one I'm using below. You also need a reference to the file manager.

```
NSFileManager *fileManager = [NSFileManager defaultManager];

NSString *filePathName = @"/Users/Shared/textfile.txt";
```

The first thing that you are going to test is whether the file exists at this location. Use the fileExistsAtPath: function and assign the results to a BOOL variable that you can later use to test.

```
BOOL fileExists = [fileManager fileExistsAtPath:filePathName];
```

To find out if the file can be read, use isReadableFileAtPath:.

```
BOOL fileIsReadable = [fileManager isReadableFileAtPath:filePathName];
```

Follow the same pattern to find out if the file can be written to using isWriteableFileAtPath:.

```
BOOL fileIsWriteable = [fileManager isWritableFileAtPath:filePathName];
```

To find out if the file is an executable, use the function isExecutableFileAtPath:.

Finally, to figure out whether you can delete the file, use the isDeletableFileAtPath: function and follow the same pattern as before.

```
BOOL fileIsDeleteable = [fileManager isDeletableFileAtPath:filePathName];
```

See Listing 4-8 for the code.

The Code

Listing 4-8. *main.m*

```
#import <Foundation/Foundation.h>
```

```
int main (int argc, const char * argv[])
{

    @autoreleasepool {

        NSFileManager *fileManager = [NSFileManager defaultManager];

        NSString *filePathName = @"/Users/Shared/textfile.txt";

        BOOL fileExists = [fileManager fileExistsAtPath:filePathName];

        if(fileExists)
            NSLog(@"%@ exists", filePathName);
        else
            NSLog(@"%@ doesn't exist", filePathName);

        BOOL fileIsReadable = [fileManager isReadableFileAtPath:filePathName];

        if(fileIsReadable)
            NSLog(@"%@ is readable", filePathName);
        else
            NSLog(@"%@ isn't readable", filePathName);

        BOOL fileIsWriteable = [fileManager isWritableFileAtPath:filePathName];

        if(fileIsWriteable)
            NSLog(@"%@ is writable", filePathName);
        else
            NSLog(@"%@ isn't writable", filePathName);

        BOOL fileIsExecutable = [fileManager isExecutableFileAtPath:filePathName];

        if(fileIsExecutable)
            NSLog(@"%@ is an executable", filePathName);
        else
            NSLog(@"%@ isn't an executable", filePathName);

        BOOL fileIsDeleteable = [fileManager isDeletableFileAtPath:filePathName];

        if(fileIsDeleteable)
            NSLog(@"%@ is deletable", filePathName);
        else
            NSLog(@"%@ isn't an deletable", filePathName);

    }
    return 0;
}
```

Usage

Build and run this code from a Mac command line app to test. Each test of the file status has a corresponding log entry printed out based on the results of the test. Here is my output:

```
/Users/Shared/textfile.txt exists
/Users/Shared/textfile.txt is readable
/Users/Shared/textfile.txt is writable
/Users/Shared/textfile.txt isn't an executable
/Users/Shared/textfile.txt is deletable
```

4.9 Changing File Attributes

Problem

Your application needs to change a file's attributes.

Solution

Use the file manager's `setAttributes:ofItemAtPath:error:` function to change the attributes of a file or directory.

How It Works

You will need a reference to the file manager, a file, and an error object.

```
NSFileManager *fileManager = [NSFileManager defaultManager];

NSString *filePathName = @"/Users/Shared/textfile.txt";

NSError *error = nil;
```

The first step is to set up a dictionary with the file attributes that you want to apply to the file. See Table 4-4 (in Recipe 4.4) for a list of file attributes.

```
NSMutableDictionary *attributes = [[NSMutableDictionary alloc] init];

[attributes setObject:[NSDate date] forKey:NSFileModificationDate];
```

For this recipe, you are going to change just the file modification date. Use the `NSFileManager` function `setAttributes:ofItemPath:error:` and pass the dictionary, file path name, and error object as parameters.

```
BOOL attributeChanged = [fileManager setAttributes:attributes
                                      ofItemAtPath:filePathName
                                             error:&error];
```

Make sure to check the error object and returned BOOL value when you use this function. See Listing 4-9 for the code.

The Code

Listing 4-9. *main.m*

```objc
#import <Foundation/Foundation.h>

int main (int argc, const char * argv[])
{

    @autoreleasepool {

        NSFileManager *fileManager = [NSFileManager defaultManager];

        NSString *filePathName = @"/Users/Shared/textfile.txt";

        NSError *error = nil;

        //Get the file attributes so you can compare later on:
        NSDictionary *fileAttributes = [fileManager attributesOfItemAtPath:filePathName
                                                                     error:&error];

        if(!error)
            NSLog(@"%@ file attributes (before): %@",filePathName, fileAttributes);

        NSMutableDictionary *attributes = [[NSMutableDictionary alloc] init];

        [attributes setObject:[NSDate date] forKey:NSFileModificationDate];

        BOOL attributeChanged = [fileManager setAttributes:attributes
                                              ofItemAtPath:filePathName
                                                     error:&error];

        if(error)
            NSLog(@"There was an error: %@", error);
        else{
            NSLog(@"attributeChanged = %i", attributeChanged);

            //Get the file attributes to see the change:
            NSDictionary *fileAttributes = [fileManager ↵
```

```
attributesOfItemAtPath:filePathName
                error:&error];

        if(!error)
            NSLog(@"%@ file attributes (after): %@",filePathName, fileAttributes);
    }

  }
  return 0;
}
```

Usage

Build and run this code from a Mac command line app to test. View the log output to see if an error occurred and to see if the file attribute was changed in the way that you expected.

```
/Users/Shared/textfile.txt file attributes (before): {
        NSFileCreationDate = "2012-01-26 14:17:04 +0000";
    NSFileExtensionHidden = 0;
    NSFileGroupOwnerAccountID = 0;
    NSFileGroupOwnerAccountName = wheel;
    NSFileHFSCreatorCode = 0;
    NSFileHFSTypeCode = 0;
    NSFileModificationDate = "2012-01-07 13:09:03 +0000";
    NSFileOwnerAccountID = 502;
    NSFileOwnerAccountName = [YOUR-USER-NAME];
    NSFilePosixPermissions = 511;
    NSFileReferenceCount = 1;
    NSFileSize = 37;
    NSFileSystemFileNumber = 40320513;
    NSFileSystemNumber = 234881026;
    NSFileType = NSFileTypeRegular;
}
attributeChanged = 1
/Users/Shared/textfile.txt file attributes (after): {
        NSFileCreationDate = "2012-01-26 14:17:04 +0000";
    NSFileExtensionHidden = 0;
    NSFileGroupOwnerAccountID = 0;
    NSFileGroupOwnerAccountName = wheel;
    NSFileHFSCreatorCode = 0;
    NSFileHFSTypeCode = 0;
    NSFileModificationDate = "2012-01-26 15:03:18 +0000";
    NSFileOwnerAccountID = 502;
    NSFileOwnerAccountName = [YOUR-USER-NAME];
    NSFilePosixPermissions = 511;
    NSFileReferenceCount = 1;
    NSFileSize = 37;
```

```
    NSFileSystemFileNumber = 40320513;
    NSFileSystemNumber = 234881026;
    NSFileType = NSFileTypeRegular;
}
```

4.10 Using Delegation with NSFileManager

Problem

You want more control over file system operations like copying and moving files and directories, and you need to make an additional action when a file is about to be copied or moved.

Solution

Create your own instance of NSFileManager instead of using the default file manager that is associated with your process. You must set your file manager's delegate to an object that has been instantiated from a class that implements the NSFileManagerDelegate protocol. Implement the delegate methods in the class that has adopted the NSFileManagerDelegate protocol to get more control over copy, move, and remove operations.

How It Works

Using NSFileManager in this way requires you to have a class available that can adopt the NSFileManagerDelegate protocol because you will be using the Delegation design pattern. This means that you need an object that will act on behalf of the file manager. Often this is simply a view controller or other class that you are using already. But, since you are only using a command line Mac app in this recipe, you need to add a custom class just for the file manager.

For the purposes of this recipe, let's assume that your application needs more control over the copy operation than you get from the NSFileManager's copyItemAtPath:toPath:error: function. You're going to intercept this operation and test to make sure you are not copying into your "protected" directory.

The first step is to add a new class to the application that has a file manager property (see Recipe 1.3 for more details on how to add custom classes). The header for such a class looks like this:

```
#import <Foundation/Foundation.h>
```

```
@interface MyFileManager : NSObject

@property(strong)NSFileManager *fileManager;

@end
```

The implementation for this class looks like this:

```
#import "MyFileManager.h"

@implementation MyFileManager
@synthesize fileManager;

@end
```

Note that your class is called MyFileManager and is acting mostly as a container for a file manager.

Now you want to adopt the NSFileManagerDelegate protocol so that this class can act on behalf of the file manager. You do this in the interface located in the header file.

```
#import <Foundation/Foundation.h>

@interface MyFileManager : NSObject<NSFileManagerDelegate>

@property(strong)NSFileManager *fileManager;

@end
```

The code <NSFileManagerDelegate> above means that this class is adopting the NSFileManagerDelegate protocol and objects instantiated from this class may act on behalf of NSFileManager objects. This protocol has no required methods, but there is an optional method that you want to implement because you are interested in getting a little bit more control over the copy operation.

So, implement the delegate method fileManager:shouldCopyItemAtPath:toPath:. This delegate method executes right before the file is copied, which gives you a chance to test to see if the copy operation should happen. From within this function you can return a BOOL indicating whether it's ok to go through with the copy operation or not.

This code belongs in the implementation file for MyFileManager.

```
- (BOOL)fileManager:(NSFileManager *)fileManager shouldCopyItemAtPath:↵
 (NSString *)srcPath  toPath:(NSString *)dstPath{

    if([dstPath hasPrefix:@"/Users/Shared/Book/Protected"]){
```

```
        NSLog(@"We cannot copy files into the protected folder and so this file was
    not copied");

        return NO;
    }
    else{

        NSLog(@"We just copied a file successfully");

        return YES;
    }
}
```

What you're doing here is testing to see if the destination directory matches the protected directory by using the NSString function hasPrefix (see Recipe 2.6). Based on these findings, the function returns YES or NO and writes out a message to the log.

You can override the MyFileManager init method to add your custom initialization code so you can instantiate a new file manager here and set the file manager's delegate to MyFileManager using the self keyword.

Of course, this also belongs in MyFileManager's implementation.

```
- (id)init {
    self = [super init];
    if (self) {
        self.fileManager = [[NSFileManager alloc] init];
        self.fileManager.delegate = self;
    }
    return self;
}
```

> **NOTE:** I suggest that you look over Listings 4-10 through 4-12. It will
> be much clearer to see the code in context once you understand the
> general pattern I'm following here.

What you've done so far is essentially wrap up a file manager in your own custom class that supports the delegation pattern that you require. Now you can move on to main.m and use the class you just created.

```
#import <Foundation/Foundation.h>
#import "MyFileManager.h"

int main (int argc, const char * argv[])
{
```

```
@autoreleasepool {
    MyFileManager *myFileManager = [[MyFileManager alloc] init];

    NSString *protectedDirectory = @"/Users/Shared/Book/Protected";

    NSString *cacheDirectory = @"/Users/Shared/Book/Cache";

    NSString *fileSource = @"/Users/Shared/Book/textfile.txt";

    NSString *fileDestination1 = @"/Users/Shared/Book/Protected/textfile.txt";

    NSString *fileDestination2 = @"/Users/Shared/Book/Cache/textfile.txt";

    NSError *error = nil;

}
return 0;
}
```

The key points in this code are the import statement for `myFileManager` and the instantiation of the `myFileManager` object. The rest of the code is simply file and directory references as well as the error object you always need when using the file manager.

Now, instead of using the default file manager directly, you will be using your own file manager that you can reference via `myFileManager`.

```
BOOL fileCopied1 = [myFileManager.fileManager copyItemAtPath:fileSource
                                                      toPath:fileDestination1
                                                       error:&error];
```

As you can see, you use the same file manager functions as in the other recipes. But you now reference the file manager property `myFileManager` and you can expect the corresponding delegate method that you just implemented to execute right before the item is copied.

> **NOTE:** This method clearly is more labor intensive than simply using the default file manager, but it does give a tad more control over the process as well as error handling.

The Code

Listing 4-10. *MyFileManager.h*

```objc
#import <Foundation/Foundation.h>

@interface MyFileManager : NSObject<NSFileManagerDelegate>

@property(strong)NSFileManager *fileManager;

@end
```

Listing 4.11. *MyFileManager.m*

```objc
#import "MyFileManager.h"

@implementation MyFileManager
@synthesize fileManager;

- (id)init {
    self = [super init];
    if (self) {
        self.fileManager = [[NSFileManager alloc] init];
        self.fileManager.delegate = self;
    }
    return self;
}

- (BOOL)fileManager:(NSFileManager *)fileManager shouldCopyItemAtPath: ↵
(NSString *)srcPath toPath:(NSString *)dstPath{

    if([dstPath hasPrefix:@"/Users/Shared/Book/Protected"]){

        NSLog(@"We cannot copy files into the protected folder and so this file was ↵
not copied");

        return NO;
    }
    else{

        NSLog(@"We just copied a file successfully");

        return YES;
    }
}

@end
```

Listing 4-12. *main.m*

```objc
#import <Foundation/Foundation.h>
#import "MyFileManager.h"

int main (int argc, const char * argv[])
{

    @autoreleasepool {
        MyFileManager *myFileManager = [[MyFileManager alloc] init];

        NSString *protectedDirectory = @"/Users/Shared/Book/Protected";

        NSString *cacheDirectory = @"/Users/Shared/Book/Cache";

        NSString *fileSource = @"/Users/Shared/Book/textfile.txt";

        NSString *fileDestination1 =
@"/Users/Shared/Book/Protected/textfile.txt";

        NSString *fileDestination2 = @"/Users/Shared/Book/Cache/textfile.txt";

        NSError *error = nil;

        NSArray *listOfFiles;

        NSLog(@"Look at directories BEFORE attempting to copy");

        listOfFiles = [myFileManager.fileManager ↵
contentsOfDirectoryAtPath:protectedDirectory
                    error:&error];

        NSLog(@"List of files in protected directory (before):%@", listOfFiles);

        listOfFiles = [myFileManager.fileManager ↵
contentsOfDirectoryAtPath:cacheDirectory
                    error:&error];

        NSLog(@"List of files in cache directory (before):%@", listOfFiles);


        //Attempt to copy into protected folder:
        BOOL fileCopied1 = [myFileManager.fileManager copyItemAtPath:fileSource
                                                toPath:fileDestination1
                                                  error:&error];

        if(error)
            NSLog(@"There was an error, %@.  fileCopied1 = %i", error, fileCopied1);

        //Attempt to copy into cache folder:
```

```
        BOOL fileCopied2 = [myFileManager.fileManager copyItemAtPath:fileSource
                                                  toPath:fileDestination2
                                                  error:&error];

        if(error)
            NSLog(@"There was an error, %@.  fileCopied2 = %i", error, fileCopied2);

        NSLog(@"Look at directories AFTER attempting to copy");

        listOfFiles = [myFileManager.fileManager ↵
contentsOfDirectoryAtPath:protectedDirectory
                error:&error];

        NSLog(@"List of files in protected directory (after):%@", listOfFiles);

        listOfFiles = [myFileManager.fileManager ↵
contentsOfDirectoryAtPath:cacheDirectory
                error:&error];

        NSLog(@"List of files in cache directory (after):%@", listOfFiles);


    }
    return 0;
}
```

Usage

Build and run this code from a Mac command line app to test. View the log output to see the log messages that print out the before and after directory listings to see if and when the file was copied. Also note the log entries that print out from the delegate method located in the MyFileManager implementation.

```
Look at directories BEFORE attempting to copy

List of files in protected directory (before):(
    ".DS_Store",
    "AAAA.txt"
)

List of files in cache directory (before):(
    ".DS_Store",
    "1.txt",
    "2.txt"
)


We cannot copy files into the protected folder and so this file was not copied
```

```
We just copied a file successfully

Look at directories AFTER attempting to copy

List of files in protected directory (after):(
    ".DS_Store",
    "AAAA.txt"
)

List of files in cache directory (after):(
    ".DS_Store",
    "1.txt",
    "2.txt",
    "textfile.txt"
)
```

4.11 Working with Data Using NSData

Problem

You need to work with data from files and other sources from within your application.

Solution

Use NSData and NSMutableData to work data from many sources. NSData brings data into your app via files, URLs, bytes, and other NSData objects. You can use NSMutableData to modify data, and you can save NSData objects back to the file system. NSData is also used with many other Foundation classes.

How It Works

This recipe demonstrates using NSData and NSMutableData by using these classes to combine two character arrays together and then saving them as a file to the file system.

The first thing you need is two arrays that you can use as your data source.

```
NSUInteger length = 3;

char bytes1[length];
```

```
bytes1[0] = 'A';
bytes1[1] = 'B';
bytes1[2] = 'C';

char bytes2[length];
bytes2[0] = 'D';
bytes2[1] = 'E';
bytes2[2] = 'F';
```

> **NOTE:** These arrays are both things are you would code in regular C.
> Don't confuse the arrays here with the NSArray and NSMutableArray
> Foundation classes, which are both object-oriented collections that
> work with objects only. The byte1 and byte2 arrays here only work
> with primitive types. You can do this because Objective-C is a
> superset of the C programming language, and you can use C code in
> conjunction with Objective-C code at any time.

Now that you have data, you're ready to start using a data object. For this
recipe, you use NSMutableData because you want to be able to modify the data.

```
NSMutableData *mutableData = [[NSMutableData alloc] init];
```

NSData and NSMutableData have other constructors that you will find helpful as
you work with different data sources. See Table 4-5 for a complete list.

Table 4-5. *List of NSData Constructors*

Constructor	Description
- (id)initWithBytes:(const void *)bytes ↵ length:(NSUInteger)length;	Creates NSData object with the provided bytes with a specified length
- (id)initWithBytesNoCopy:(void *)bytes ↵ length:(NSUInteger)length;	Creates NSData object with the provided bytes with a specified length without copying
- (id)initWithBytesNoCopy:(void *)bytes ↵ length:(NSUInteger)length ↵ freeWhenDone:(BOOL)flag;	Creates NSData object with the provided bytes with a specified length without copying and freeing memory when finished

Constructor	Description
- (id)initWithContentsOfFile:(NSString *)path ↵ options:(NSDataReadingOptions)readOptionsMask ↵ error:(NSError **)errorPtr;	Creates NSData object from a file with the specified options
- (id)initWithContentsOfURL:(NSURL *)url ↵ options:(NSDataReadingOptions)readOptionsMask ↵ error:(NSError **)errorPtr;	Creates NSData object from a URL with the specified options
- (id)initWithContentsOfFile:(NSString *)path;	Creates NSData object from a file
- (id)initWithContentsOfURL:(NSURL *)url;	Creates NSData object from a URL
- (id)initWithData:(NSData *)data;	Creates NSData object from another NSData object

Now you can move on to modifying the data object. Use the NSMutableData function appendBytes:length: to add the first byte array to the data object.

```
[mutableData appendBytes:bytes1
                length:length];
```

This adds the characters A, B, C to the data object. To add the remaining characters, repeat the process with the next byte array.

```
[mutableData appendBytes:bytes2
                length:length];
```

At this point, the data object contains both byte arrays. Appending bytes is one way of modifying a data object, but there are more things you can do to modify data with mutable data objects. See Table 4-6 for complete list.

Table 4-6. *NSMutableData Mutation Methods*

Method	Description
- (void)appendBytes:(const void *)bytes ↵ length:(NSUInteger)length;	Appends bytes to the data object
- (void)appendData:(NSData *)other;	Appends a data object to the data object
- (void)increaseLengthBy:(NSUInteger)extraLength;	Adds to the length of the data object

Method	Description
- (void)replaceBytesInRange:(NSRange)range ↵ withBytes:(const void *)bytes;	Replaces a byte array in the given range
- (void)resetBytesInRange:(NSRange)range;	Resets a byte array in the given range
- (void)setData:(NSData *)data;	Sets the state of the data object
- (void)replaceBytesInRange:(NSRange)range ↵ withBytes:(const void *)replacementBytes ↵ length:(NSUInteger)replacementLength;	Replaces bytes in a range with a specified range

If you need to use the new array in your application, you can retrieve the new array using the NSData byte function.

```
char *bytesFromData = (char *)[mutableData bytes];
```

To save the contents of the data object to the file system, you can use the writeToFile:options:error: function and supply a file path name, an options parameter, and an error object.

```
NSError *error = nil;

BOOL dataSaved = [mutableData writeToFile:@"/Users/Shared/Book/datadump.txt"
                                  options:NSDataWritingAtomic
                                    error:&error];
```

See Listing 4-13 for the code.

The Code

Listing 4-13. *main.m*

```
#import <Foundation/Foundation.h>

int main (int argc, const char * argv[])
{

    @autoreleasepool {

        NSUInteger length = 3;

        char bytes1[length];
        bytes1[0] = 'A';
        bytes1[1] = 'B';
```

```
        bytes1[2] = 'C';

        for (int i=0;i<sizeof(bytes1);i++)
            NSLog(@"bytes1[%i] = %c", i, bytes1[i]);

        char bytes2[length];
        bytes2[0] = 'D';
        bytes2[1] = 'E';
        bytes2[2] = 'F';

        for (int i=0;i<sizeof(bytes2);i++)
            NSLog(@"bytes2[%i] = %c", i, bytes2[i]);

        NSMutableData *mutableData = [[NSMutableData alloc] init];

        [mutableData appendBytes:bytes1
                          length:length];

        [mutableData appendBytes:bytes2
                          length:length];

        NSLog(@"mutableData = %@", mutableData);

        char *bytesFromData = (char *)[mutableData bytes];

        for (int i=0;i<length*2;i++)
            NSLog(@"bytesFromData[%i] = %c", i, bytesFromData[i]);

        NSError *error = nil;

        BOOL dataSaved = [mutableData writeToFile:@"/Users/Shared/datadump.txt"
                                         options:NSDataWritingAtomic
                                           error:&error];

    if(dataSaved)
        NSLog(@"mutableData successfully wrote contents to file system");
    else
        NSLog(@"mutableData was unsuccesful in writing out data because of ↵
%@", error);

    }
    return 0;
}
```

Usage

Build and run this code from a Mac command line app to test. View the log
output to see the log messages to view the contents of the various data objects.

Use a text editor to inspect the file that was created to see the content written to the file system.

```
bytes1[0] = A
bytes1[1] = B
bytes1[2] = C
bytes2[0] = D
bytes2[1] = E
bytes2[2] = F

mutableData = <41424344 4546>

bytesFromData[0] = A
bytesFromData[1] = B
bytesFromData[2] = C
bytesFromData[3] = D
bytesFromData[4] = E
bytesFromData[5] = F

mutableData successfully wrote contents to file system
```

4.12 Caching Content with NSCache

Problem

Your application has to operate in limited memory conditions so you need to be able to cache content.

Solution

Use NSCache to maintain a collection of objects that may be cached in memory. When used with NSPurgeableData, NSCache will keep an object in memory until the device or desktop application needs to reclaim the memory.

How It Works

NSCache works like NSDictionary in that NSCache stores objects that are indexed with keys. What is different about NSCache is that NSCache will get rid of objects when certain conditions are met. Usually, NSCache will react to low memory conditions but you can define other conditions if desired.

> **NOTE:** The behavior described here only works when the objects in the cache adopt the NSDiscardableContent protocol. The easiest way to make sure that a class adopts this protocol is to use the NSPurgeableData class, which adopts this protocol and can be used like NSData.

What makes NSCache very useful is that while it will get rid of objects smartly, it will also keep the key to the object in place. This gives you a chance to attempt to retrieve the object and then test to see if a nil value came back (indicating that an object has either been removed or not created yet). If the return value is nil, then you have the opportunity to recreate or reload the object.

> **NOTE:** When using NSCache to retrieve objects, make sure to test to see if the object is still cached. If the object is not cached anymore, then include code to recreate the object and insert the object back into the cache.

This recipe assumes that you have an iOS app set up with a view controller. See Listings 4-14 through 4-17 to see exactly how the user interface was set up. To get more information on how to set up iOS apps and user controls, see Recipes 1.12 and 1.13. For now, take a look at the view controller header file so you can see that the NSCache object is included as a property.

```
#import <UIKit/UIKit.h>

@interface ViewController : UIViewController

@property (strong) NSCache *cache;
@property (assign) BOOL regularLogo;
@property (strong) UIImageView *myImageView;
@property (strong) UIButton *loadImageButton;

- (void)presentImage;

@end
```

First, you need to instantiate the NSCache object itself. Here, you do this in the view controller viewDidLoad delegate method.

```
#import "ViewController.h"

@implementation ViewController
```

```
-(void)viewDidLoad{
    [super viewDidLoad];

    //set up the cache
    self.cache = [[NSCache alloc] init];

}

@end
```

> **NOTE:** You may locate your NSCache object anywhere in your
> application. One popular location is the app delegate because you can
> get a reference to the app delegate anywhere in your app so it's easy
> to share the cache. To keep this recipe as simple as possible, the
> cache is simply located in the view controllers as a property.

Putting the cache in the view controller as a property and instantiating the cache
in viewDidLoad means that you can use the cache as long as the view controller
is active.

Now you can retrieve an object from the cache. You need a key, which can be a
string, and you can use this key with the cache's objectForKey: function to
attempt to retrieve the object.

```
NSString *key = @"regular-logo";
NSPurgeableData *data = [cache objectForKey:key];
```

Here you are trying to retrieve an NSPurgeableData object from the cache. In the
next step, you must immediately test the object that comes back to see if a nil
value was returned. You use an if statement to do this.

```
if(!data){

}
```

!data means that the data object is equal to nil. If the object is nil, you can
recreate the object in the code that is between the curly braces. The data that
you want to retrieve here is an image that is stored in the app bundle. So, you
need to reference the app bundle (see Recipe 4.3 for more on this) and to
construct the image file's path name.

```
NSString *key = @"regular-logo";
NSPurgeableData *data = [cache objectForKey:key];
if(!data){
    NSString *bundlePath = [[NSBundle mainBundle] bundlePath];
```

```
    NSString *imagePath = [NSString stringWithFormat:@"%@/MobileAppMastery-Log.png", ⏎
bundlePath];
```

}

Once you have the file path reference, you can use it to instantiate an NSPurgeableData object with the contents of the file. Then you insert that object into the cache.

```
NSString *key = @"regular-logo";
NSPurgeableData *data = [cache objectForKey:key];
if(!data){
    NSString *bundlePath = [[NSBundle mainBundle] bundlePath];
    NSString *imagePath = [NSString stringWithFormat:@"%@/MobileAppMastery-Log.png", ⏎
bundlePath];

    data = [NSPurgeableData dataWithContentsOfFile:imagePath];
    [cache setObject:data forKey:key];
}
```

Now the object is cached and available to be used again whenever you ask for it with the key. If something happens and the object needs to be purged, you can still ask for the object with the key but you will get a nil result so you have to repeat the object creation process again.

The Code

Listing 4-14. *AppDelegate.h*

```
#import <UIKit/UIKit.h>

@class ViewController;

@interface AppDelegate : UIResponder <UIApplicationDelegate>

@property (strong, nonatomic) UIWindow *window;

@property (strong, nonatomic) ViewController *viewController;

@end
```

Listing 4-15. *AppDelegate.m*

```
#import "AppDelegate.h"

#import "ViewController.h"

@implementation AppDelegate
```

```objc
@synthesize window = _window;
@synthesize viewController = _viewController;

- (BOOL)application:(UIApplication *)application ↵
didFinishLaunchingWithOptions:(NSDictionary *)launchOptions
{
    self.window = [[UIWindow alloc] initWithFrame:[[UIScreen mainScreen] bounds]];
    // Override point for customization after application launch.
    self.viewController = [[ViewController alloc]
initWithNibName:@"ViewController"↵
 bundle:nil];
    self.window.rootViewController = self.viewController;
    [self.window makeKeyAndVisible];
    return YES;
}

@end
```

Listing 4-16. *ViewController.h*

```objc
#import <UIKit/UIKit.h>

@interface ViewController : UIViewController

@property (strong) NSCache *cache;
@property (assign) BOOL regularLogo;
@property (strong) UIImageView *myImageView;
@property (strong) UIButton *loadImageButton;

- (void)presentImage;

@end
```

Listing 4-17. *ViewController.m*

```objc
#import "ViewController.h"

@implementation ViewController
@synthesize cache, regularLogo, myImageView, loadImageButton;

-(void)viewDidLoad{
    [super viewDidLoad];

    //Change the view's background color to white
    self.view.backgroundColor = [UIColor whiteColor];

    //Load the regular logo first
    self.regularLogo = YES;
```

```objc
    //set up the cache
    self.cache = [[NSCache alloc] init];

    //Setup the button
    self.loadImageButton = [UIButton buttonWithType:UIButtonTypeRoundedRect];
    self.loadImageButton.frame = CGRectMake(20, 415, 280, 37);
    [self.loadImageButton addTarget:self
                             action:@selector(presentImage)
                  forControlEvents:UIControlEventTouchUpInside];
    [loadImageButton setTitle:@"Present Image" forState:UIControlStateNormal];
    [self.view addSubview:loadImageButton];

    //Setup the UIImageView
    self.myImageView = [[UIImageView alloc] init];
    self.myImageView.frame = CGRectMake(0, 0, 320, 407);
    self.myImageView.contentMode = UIViewContentModeScaleAspectFit;
    [self.view addSubview:self.myImageView];
}

- (void)presentImage{
    if(regularLogo){
        NSString *key = @"regular-logo";
        NSPurgeableData *data = [cache objectForKey:key];
        if(!data){
            NSString *bundlePath = [[NSBundle mainBundle] bundlePath];
            NSString *imagePath = [NSString stringWithFormat:↵
@"%@/MobileAppMastery-Log.png", bundlePath];
            data = [NSPurgeableData dataWithContentsOfFile:imagePath];
            [cache setObject:data forKey:key];
            NSLog(@"Retrieved resource(%@) and added to cache", key);
        }
        else
            NSLog(@"Just retrieved resource(%@)", key);;
        self.myImageView.image = [UIImage imageWithData:data];
        regularLogo = NO;
    }
    else{
        NSString *key = @"greyscale-logo";
        NSPurgeableData *data = [cache objectForKey:key];
        if(!data){
            NSString *bundlePath = [[NSBundle mainBundle] bundlePath];
            NSString *imagePath = [NSString ↵
stringWithFormat:@"%@/MAM_Logo_Square_No_Words_Grayscale.png", bundlePath];
            data = [NSPurgeableData dataWithContentsOfFile:imagePath];
            [cache setObject:data forKey:key];
            NSLog(@"Retrieved resource(%@) and added to cache", key);
        }
        else
            NSLog(@"Just retrieved resource(%@)", key);
```

```
        self.myImageView.image = [UIImage imageWithData:data];
        regularLogo = YES;
    }
}
}

@end
```

Usage

The application used in this recipe is an iOS single view application. This application type was chosen because the iOS Simulator has the ability to simulate a low memory situation, which makes it possible to see how the NSCache works under this condition. If you need to know how to build your own iOS single view application, see Recipe 1.12.

This example also uses two user controls: a button and an image view. If you want to know more about how to add and use user controls like these, see Recipe 1.13. The images used in the example are mine; if you want to try with your own images, all you need to do is drag your image files into the Supporting Files folder in your Xcode project. Make sure to click "Copy into destination folder" to ensure that the image files are included in the application bundle.

How this application works in general is that the user is presented with a blank screen with a button at the bottom. Each time the user presses the button one of two images is presented. You can see what the application looks like in Figure 4-1.

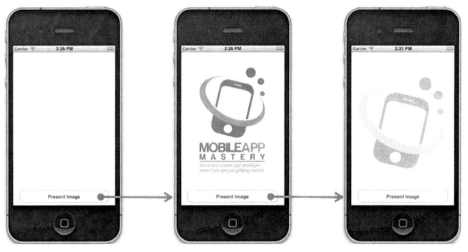

Figure 4-1. *iOS application UI*

Each time the user touches the button, one of the two images is retrieved from the cache. The code knows which image to choose based on the BOOL variable regularLogo.

To test this code once you have everything set up, run the iOS application in the iOS Simulator and then press the Present Image button twice to see both images loaded. If you check in the log, you should see two messages indicating that the images were created for the first time.

```
Retrieved resource(regular-logo) and added to cache
Retrieved resource(greyscale-logo) and added to cache
```

Now press the button twice again. You should see the images presented again in sequence. Check the log again how this worked.

```
Just retrieved resource(regular-logo)
Just retrieved resource(greyscale-logo)
```

This time the images didn't need to be created at all and they were just retrieved from the cache.

Now, let's create a low memory situation in the iOS Simulator to see how the cache helps you. Go to **iOS Simulator ➤ Hardware ➤ Simulate Memory Warning**. Press the button two times again to see the results.

```
Received memory warning.
Retrieved resource(regular-logo) and added to cache
Just retrieved resource(greyscale-logo)
```

As you can see from this output, the regular-logo image had to be re-created because NSCache removed the object when the memory warning was received. The second image didn't get removed (because it was still retained by the image view).

Working With Dates, Times, and Timers

This chapter covers how to work with dates and timers using the Foundation framework with Objective-C.

The recipes in this chapter will show you how to:

- Create today's date using `NSDate`
- Create custom dates using `NSDateComponents`
- Compare dates
- Convert strings to dates
- Format dates for display on user interfaces
- Add and subtract dates
- Use a timer to schedule repeating and non-repeating code

5.1 Creating a Date Object for Today

Problem

You need to represent today's date in your application.

Solution

Use the NSDate class method date to create a date object instance for the current date.

How It Works

NSDate is a class that is generally used with other classes (covered in the upcoming recipes). By itself, NSDate can get today's date, which you can use to present to the console or to the user. To get today's date, use the date function and assign the results of that to an NSDate object variable.

```
NSDate *todaysDate = [NSDate date];
```

See Listing 5-1 for the code.

The Code

Listing 5-1. *main.m*

```
#import <Foundation/Foundation.h>

int main (int argc, const char * argv[])
{

   @autoreleasepool {

        NSDate *todaysDate = [NSDate date];

        NSLog(@"Today's date is %@", todaysDate);

}
    return 0;
}
```

Usage

To use this code, build and run your Mac app from Xcode. View the log to see today's date printed out.

```
Today's date is 2012-06-27 13:14:30 +0000
```

5.2 Creating Custom Dates by Component

Problem

You need to reference dates other than the current date in your application.

Solution

Use `NSDateComponents` to define a specific date and then use `NSCalendar` with your date components to return an `NSDate` object reference that you can use in your application.

How It Works

To create custom dates, you need to use three Foundation classes: `NSDate`, `NSDateComponents`, and `NSCalendar`. `NSDate` acts as the most basic class here to represent dates.

The `NSDateComponents` class represents the details that make up a date and time: day, month, year, and hour. `NSDateComponents` has many date and time details that you can set to completely customize your date.

The `NSCalendar` class is used to represent a real world calendar. This is used to manage the complexities involved with working with calendars. You can specify what calendar to use or simply get the calendar in use by the users' system. Usually, you can assume that you are working with the Gregorian calendar, but you may specify other calendars like the Hebrew or Islamic calendar instead.

To create a custom date, the first thing you do is create a new instance of `NSDateComponents`.

```
NSDateComponents *dateComponents = [[NSDateComponents alloc] init];
```

Then you set all the properties of interest for the custom date. In this recipe, I'm setting the components necessary to represent the original iPhone release date in California, USA.

```
dateComponents.year = 2007;
dateComponents.month = 6;
dateComponents.day = 29;
dateComponents.hour = 12;
dateComponents.minute = 01;
dateComponents.second = 31;
dateComponents.timeZone = [NSTimeZone timeZoneWithAbbreviation:@"PDT"];
```

All you need to do here is use dot notation to set the date properties that you are interested in. The last property requires a special NSTimeZone object. You can specify any time zone that you wish or simply leave this property alone to use the system time zone.

Finally, to actually create your NSDate object, you need a reference to a calendar (usually the current system calendar). You get this reference with the currentCalendar message, [NSCalendar currentCalendar]. Once you have that, you use the dateWithComponents: function to get the date object that matches the specifications that you set out with your date components.

```
NSDate *iPhoneReleaseDate = [[NSCalendar currentCalendar] ↵
dateFromComponents:dateComponents];
```

See Listing 5-2 for the code.

The Code

Listing 5-2. *main.m*

```
#import <Foundation/Foundation.h>

int main (int argc, const char * argv[])
{

    @autoreleasepool {

        NSDateComponents *dateComponents = [[NSDateComponents alloc] init];
        dateComponents.year = 2007;
        dateComponents.month = 6;
        dateComponents.day = 29;
        dateComponents.hour = 12;
        dateComponents.minute = 01;
        dateComponents.second = 31;
        dateComponents.timeZone = [NSTimeZone timeZoneWithAbbreviation:@"PDT"];

        NSDate *iPhoneReleaseDate = [[NSCalendar currentCalendar] ↵
dateFromComponents:dateComponents];

        NSLog(@"The original iPhone went on sale: %@", iPhoneReleaseDate);

    }
    return 0;
}
```

Usage

To use this code, build and run your Mac app from Xcode. You can see the printout of the iPhone release date by inspecting the log.

```
The original iPhone went on sale: 2007-06-29 19:01:31 +0000
```

5.3 Comparing Two Dates

Problem

In your application, you have at least two dates and you need to know how they relate to each other. For instance, did one date come before another? How many days separate these two dates?

Solution

For simple comparisons, use the built-in NSDate comparison functions. To figure out how many days have passed since another date, you need a reference to the system calendar as well as both dates.

How It Works

For this recipe, I'm going to assume that you have the iPhone release date set up still from Recipe 5.2. Let's compare it to today's date. You can get today's date by using the NSDate function date.

The first comparison is whether the iPhone release date was today or not. To find that out, use the isEqualToDate: function and pass it the date that you would like to compare. This function returns a BOOL.

```
NSDate *todaysDate = [NSDate date];

if([todaysDate isEqualToDate:iPhoneReleaseDate])
    NSLog(@"The iPhone was released today!");
else
    NSLog(@"The iPhone was released on some other date");
```

To find out if your date is earlier than another date, use the earlierDate: function with the other date as a parameter. This function returns whatever date is the earlier date.

```
NSDate *earlierDateIs = [todaysDate earlierDate:iPhoneReleaseDate];
```

You can also do the reverse to find out which date is the later date.

```
NSDate *laterDateIs = [todaysDate laterDate:iPhoneReleaseDate];
```

To find out the number of seconds that separate one date from another, use `timeIntervalSinceDate:` passing the second date as a parameter. You get a `double` value equal to the number of seconds between both dates. This is a `typedef` called `NSTimeInterval` (you will see `NSTimeInterval` referenced in other date methods).

You can get richer detail in date comparisons by using the system calendar along with the `NSDateComponents` class. This gives you the time between two dates in the format that you need. So, if you want to know the number of days, hours, minutes, years, months, or some combination of these, you are in luck.

The first step is getting a reference to the user's system calendar.

```
NSCalendar *systemCalendar = [NSCalendar currentCalendar];
```

Next, specify the units you want to use via a bitwise OR of `NSCalendar` constants.

```
unsigned int unitFlags = NSYearCalendarUnit | NSMonthCalendarUnit |
NSDayCalendarUnit;
```

> **NOTE:** Bitwise operations are a way of working with information at a very low level in binary. As you may know, computers represent information in a series of ones and zeros (such as 00000011 for the number three). Bitwise operators compare binary representations of two pieces of information and create a result based on these comparisons. Bitwise OR means that result has a one if either of the pieces of information has a one.

In other words, I want to see the time separating my two dates by year, month, and day. See Table 5-1 for a list of constants that you can use here.

Table 5-1. *NSCalendar Constants*

Constant	Description
NSEraCalendarUnit	Specifies eras
NSYearCalendarUnit	Specifies years

Constant	Description
NSMonthCalendarUnit	Specifies months
NSDayCalendarUnit	Specifies days
NSHourCalendarUnit	Specifies hours
NSMinuteCalendarUnit	Specifies minutes
NSSecondCalendarUnit	Specifies seconds
NSWeekCalendarUnit	Specifies weeks
NSWeekdayCalendarUnit	Specifies weekdays

You can use the NSCalendar function components:fromDate:toDate:options to return an NSDateComponents object filled with data that describes the time difference between the two dates based on what NSCalendar constants you specified.

```
NSDateComponents *dateComparisonComponents = [systemCalendar components:unitFlags
                                                    fromDate:iPhoneReleaseDate
                                                    toDate:todaysDate
                                                    options:NSWrapCalendarComponents];
```

You can access the corresponding properties to get the information you need. For instance, to get the number of years, look at the dateComparisonComponents.year property. See Listing 5-3 for the code.

The Code

Listing 5-3. *Caption*

```
#import <Foundation/Foundation.h>

int main (int argc, const char * argv[])
{

    @autoreleasepool {

        NSDateComponents *dateComponents = [[NSDateComponents alloc] init];
        dateComponents.year = 2007;
        dateComponents.month = 6;
        dateComponents.day = 29;
        dateComponents.hour = 12;
```

```
        dateComponents.minute = 01;
        dateComponents.second = 31;
        dateComponents.timeZone = [NSTimeZone timeZoneWithAbbreviation:@"PDT"];

        NSDate *iPhoneReleaseDate = [[NSCalendar currentCalendar] ↵
dateFromComponents:dateComponents];

        NSLog(@"The original iPhone went on sale: %@", iPhoneReleaseDate);

        NSDate *todaysDate = [NSDate date];

        NSLog(@"Today's date is: %@", todaysDate);

        if([todaysDate isEqualToDate:iPhoneReleaseDate])
            NSLog(@"The iPhone was released today!");
        else
            NSLog(@"The iPhone was released on some other date");

        NSDate *earlierDateIs = [todaysDate earlierDate:iPhoneReleaseDate];

        NSLog(@"The earlier date is: %@", earlierDateIs);

        NSDate *laterDateIs = [todaysDate laterDate:iPhoneReleaseDate];

        NSLog(@"The later date is: %@", laterDateIs);

        NSTimeInterval timeBetweenDates = [todaysDate↵
timeIntervalSinceDate:iPhoneReleaseDate];

        NSLog(@"The iPhone was released %f seconds ago", timeBetweenDates);

        NSCalendar *systemCalendar = [NSCalendar currentCalendar];

        unsigned int unitFlags = NSYearCalendarUnit | NSMonthCalendarUnit|↵
NSDayCalendarUnit;

        NSDateComponents *dateComparisonComponents = ↵
        [systemCalendar components:unitFlags
                        fromDate:iPhoneReleaseDate
                          toDate:todaysDate
                          options:NSWrapCalendarComponents];

        NSLog(@"The iPhone was released %ld years, %ld months and %ld days ago",
            dateComparisonComponents.year,
            dateComparisonComponents.month,
            dateComparisonComponents.day
            );

    }
    return 0;
```

```
}
```

Usage

To use this code, build and run your Mac app from Xcode. View the log messages to see the dates and the results of the comparisons between them.

```
The original iPhone went on sale: 2007-06-29 19:01:31 +0000
Today's date is: 2012-06-27 20:54:56 +0000
The earlier date is: 2007-06-29 19:01:31 +0000
The later date is: 2012-06-27 20:54:56 +0000
The iPhone was released on some other date
The iPhone was released 143776405.074785 seconds ago
The iPhone was released 4 years, 6 months and 20 days ago
```

Note that your output messages will look different than mine because you will be running this code at a different date than me.

5.4 Converting a String to a Date

Problem

You have a string with date information from a strings file and you would like to use this information as a date object.

Solution

Use NSDateFormatter to specify the string format and create the new date object.

How It Works

For this recipe, let's assume that you have date information stored as a string.

```
NSString *dateString = @"02/14/2012";
```

First, you need a date formatter, so use the NSDateFormatter class to create one.

```
NSDateFormatter *df = [[NSDateFormatter alloc] init];
```

Then set the dateFormat property with the format of your string.

```
df.dateFormat = @"MM/dd/yyyy";
```

> **NOTE:** Date formatters use the Unicode date format patterns. See
> http://unicode.org/reports/tr35/tr35-
> 10.html#Date_Format_Patterns for a complete list of the available date
> format patterns.

To create the date object, use the dateFromString: date formatter function.

```
NSDate *valentinesDay = [df dateFromString:dateString];
```

See Listing 5-4 for the code.

The Code

Listing 5-4. *Caption*

```
#import <Foundation/Foundation.h>

int main (int argc, const char * argv[])
{

    @autoreleasepool {

        NSString *dateString = @"02/14/2012";

        NSDateFormatter *df = [[NSDateFormatter alloc] init];

        df.dateFormat = @"MM/dd/yyyy";

        NSDate *valentinesDay = [df dateFromString:dateString];

        NSLog(@"Valentine's Day = %@", valentinesDay);


    }
    return 0;
}
```

Usage

To use this code, build and run your Mac app from Xcode. View the log
message to see the date object that was created from the string.

```
Valentine's Day = 2012-02-14 05:02:00 +0000
```

Your result may appear different than mine as this is based on your local timezone.

5.5 Formatting Dates for Display

Problem

You would like to present your date objects to your user in a format that they recognize and one that looks good in your user interface.

Solution

Use `NSDateFormatter` to create date formats and get data objects formatted as strings that you can present to your users.

How It Works

You specify date formatter dates using the same Unicode data format patterns that you used in Recipe 5.4. So, if you have the date from Recipe 5.4 already in but you want a different format presented to the user, you can set the date format like this:

```
df.dateFormat = @"EEEE, MMMM d";
```

This presents the weekday name of the week, the name of the month, and the numerical day that this date falls on.

To see the results, use the `NSDateFormatter`'s `stringFromDate:` function.

```
NSLog(@"Another Formatted Valentine's Day = %@", [df
stringFromDate:valentinesDay]);
```

This presents the date in a format like this:

```
Tuesday, February 14
```

See Listing 5-5 for the code.

The Code

Listing 5-5. *Caption*

```objc
#import <Foundation/Foundation.h>

int main (int argc, const char * argv[])
{

    @autoreleasepool {

        NSString *dateString = @"02/14/2012";

        NSDateFormatter *df = [[NSDateFormatter alloc] init];

        df.dateFormat = @"MM/dd/yyyy";

        NSDate *valentinesDay = [df dateFromString:dateString];

        NSLog(@"Unformatted Valentine's Day = %@", valentinesDay);

        NSLog(@"Formatted Valentine's Day = %@", [df stringFromDate:valentinesDay]);

        df.dateFormat = @"EEEE, MMMM d";

        NSLog(@"Another Formatted Valentine's Day = %@", ↵
[df stringFromDate:valentinesDay]);

    }
    return 0;
}
```

Usage

To use this code, build and run your Mac app from Xcode. View the log message to see the formatted date objects.

```
Unformatted Valentine's Day = 2012-02-14 05:00:00 +0000
Formatted Valentine's Day = 02/14/2012
Another Formatted Valentine's Day = Tuesday, February 14
```

5.6 Adding and Subtracting Dates

Problem

You want to add or subtract dates in your application.

Solution

Use the `NSDateComponents` and `NSCalendar` classes along with your date object to add or subtract dates. `NSDateComponents` specifies a time length (one day, one week, or another time interval). `NSCalendar` gives you a method to create a new date using the user's calendar along with the specification that you set up in the date components object.

How It Works

Let's keep working with the Valentine's Day date that you created in Recipe 5.4. For this example, you want to get the date for one week before Valentine's Day (perhaps to use as a shopping day).

The first thing you need is a date components object. The `alloc` and `init` constructor is used to create this.

```
NSDateComponents *weekBeforeDateComponents = [[NSDateComponents alloc] init];
```

To work with the interval, you can set any of the properties that you need. For this example, you are only interested in subtracting one week so set the week property of the date components object to -1.

```
weekBeforeDateComponents.week = -1;
```

Now you can get the date for one week in the past by using the user's calendar and the `dateByAddingComponents:toDate:options:` function.

```
NSDate *vDayShoppingDay = [[NSCalendar currentCalendar] ⏎
   dateByAddingComponents:weekBeforeDateComponents
                 toDate:valentinesDay
               options:0];
```

This function returns a new date for the previous week. Also, note that to subtract dates you use this function with negative integers (there is no `dateBySubtractingComponents`). See Listing 5-6 for the code.

The Code

Listing 5-6. *Caption*

```
#import <Foundation/Foundation.h>

int main (int argc, const char * argv[])
{

    @autoreleasepool {

        NSString *dateString = @"02/14/2012";

        NSDateFormatter *df = [[NSDateFormatter alloc] init];

        df.dateFormat = @"MM/dd/yyyy";

        NSDate *valentinesDay = [df dateFromString:dateString];

        NSLog(@"Valentine's Day = %@", valentinesDay);

        NSDateComponents *weekBeforeDateComponents = [[NSDateComponents alloc] init];

        weekBeforeDateComponents.week = -1;

        NSDate *vDayShoppingDay = [[NSCalendar currentCalendar] ↵
        dateByAddingComponents:weekBeforeDateComponents
                    toDate:valentinesDay
                    options:0];

        NSLog(@"Shop for Valentine's Day by %@", vDayShoppingDay);

    }
    return 0;
}
```

Usage

To use this code, build and run your Mac app from Xcode. Check the console to see the result of the date subtraction.

```
Valentine's Day = 2012-02-14 05:00:00 +0000
Shop for Valentine's Day by 2012-02-07 05:00:00 +0000
```

5.7 Using a Timer to Schedule and Repeat Tasks

Problem

Your app needs to schedule code to execute at a particular time. You also want to repeat this task.

Solution

Use `NSTimer` to schedule code to run at a particular time. `NSTimer` needs a date object and a reference to the run loop of an application to work.

> **NOTE:** `NSTimer` requires a run loop, which you will have if you are using your timer from a Mac or iOS app. This recipe requires an app with a run loop. See Recipes 1.11 and 1.12 for procedures on creating Mac and iOS apps, respectively.

How It Works

For this recipe, I will locate the code in the app delegate. Often you will locate timers in custom classes or your app controllers.

Timers work by sending messages to objects starting at a particular date and time. Timers may send messages at intervals if you require repetition in your app. First, you need a date object to represent the date and time the timer will start sending the message to the object.

```
NSDate *scheduledTime = [NSDate dateWithTimeIntervalSinceNow:10.0];
```

This scheduled time is ten seconds after this line of code is reached. You may use any date that you wish here.

Next, create the timer by using the `initWithFireDate:interval:target:selector:userInfo:repeats:` constructor.

```
NSString *customUserObject = @"To demo userInfo";

NSTimer *timer = [[NSTimer alloc] initWithFireDate:scheduledTime
                                    interval:2
```

```
                              target:self
                         selector:@selector(task)
                         userInfo:customUserObject
                          repeats:YES];
```

There are a few things going on here that need some explanation. The first parameter is the date object, which specifies when you want your timer to become active. Next, you have `interval`, which is the number of seconds the timer will wait before sending the message again. And after that is the `target` parameter descriptor. The target is the object where the method is located. The selector parameter requires the name of the method in parentheses preceded by the `@selector` keyword. Since you have the method coded right in the app delegate in the same place as the timer, you can use the `self` keyword here.

The `userInfo` is something you can use for custom specifications for the timer. You can put any object in here and you will have the ability to get a reference to the object in the message that you are executing (the selector parameter above). Here I use a string, but it's common to use a dictionary or other collection for more complex activities.

The `repeats` parameter is where you can specify whether this timer will send the message one time or repeat based on the time interval you provided in the second parameter.

The next thing that you need is a reference to the run loop. You can do that via the `NSRunLoop currentRunLoop` function.

```
NSRunLoop *runLoop = [NSRunLoop currentRunLoop];
```

Now, it's just a matter of adding the timer to the run loop.

```
[runLoop addTimer:timer forMode:NSDefaultRunLoopMode];
```

After ten seconds, the timer will start sending the `task` message to the app every two seconds.

To stop a timer after you have set it up, you can send the timer the invalidate message. This removes the timer from the run loop. It looks like this:

```
[timer invalidate];
```

See Listing 5-7 for the code.

The Code

Listing 5-7. *Caption*

```
#import "AppDelegate.h"
```

```
@implementation AppDelegate

@synthesize window = _window;

- (void)applicationDidFinishLaunching:(NSNotification *)aNotification{

    NSDate *scheduledTime = [NSDate dateWithTimeIntervalSinceNow:10.0];

    NSString *customUserObject = @"To demo userInfo";

    NSTimer *timer = [[NSTimer alloc] initWithFireDate:scheduledTime
                                    interval:2
                                      target:self
                                    selector:@selector(task)
                                    userInfo:customUserObject
                                     repeats:YES];

    NSRunLoop *runLoop = [NSRunLoop currentRunLoop];

    [runLoop addTimer:timer forMode:NSDefaultRunLoopMode];

}

-(void)task:(id)sender{
    NSTimer *localTimer = (NSTimer *)sender;

    NSLog(@"Schedule task has executed with this user info: %@", [localTimer userInfo]);
}

@end
```

Usage

To use this code, build and run your Mac app from Xcode. Pay attention to the console window and notice when the messages start to get written to the log. I've left in the time stamps so you can see how the time interval worked when I did this recipe.

```
2012-01-19 15:23:28.651 Timer[31067:707] Schedule task has executed with this user ↵
info: To demo userInfo
2012-01-19 15:23:30.651 Timer[31067:707] Schedule task has executed with this user ↵
info: To demo userInfo
2012-01-19 15:23:32.651 Timer[31067:707] Schedule task has executed with this user ↵
info: To demo userInfo
```

Chapter 6

Asynchronous Processing

This chapter covers how to add costly tasks to your applications without interrupting the main thread of operations. Objective-C supports many different options to solve this problem and this chapter covers the three most important: NSThread, Grand Central Dispatch, and NSOperationQueue.

The recipes in this chapter will show you how to:

- Create a new thread for a background process
- Send messages to the main thread in order to update the user interface
- Lock threads to keep data structures in sync
- Use Grand Central Dispatch (GCD) to implement asynchronous processing
- Use operation queues to implement asynchronous processing using a more object-oriented approach
- Use serial queues to protect data structures without locking threads to increase multithread performance

> **NOTE:** The topics in this chapter can be complex because multithreading is a difficult problem for software developers. The underlying technology that facilitates multithreading has evolved rapidly over the last few years, which is why you will see a few alternatives here that you can use to solve the problems involved with asynchronous processing.

6.1 Running a Process in a New Thread

Problem

Your application needs to execute a task that will take a long time, but you would like the user interface to remain responsive and otherwise unaffected by the new operation.

Solution

Put the long task into a method and then use NSThread to create a thread separate from the main thread where the new operation is taking place.

How It Works

We refer to executable program like applications as *processes* when they are being executed by the operating system (here either iOS or OSX). Processes are made up of threads in which operations are executed at the same time. These operations could have happened at the same time on different processors or on the same processor using a time-sharing strategy (each thread takes a turn using the computer's processor).

All programs have at least one primary thread referred to as the *main thread*. Applications use the main thread to manage the user interface, but there may be other threads working at the same time doing tasks that are not directly related to the user interface or generally part of the main thread.

> **NOTE:** To follow along with this recipe, you will need to have a Single View
> iPhone application with a button and an activity view. For general information
> on how to use iPhone applications and user controls, see Recipe 1.12 and
> Recipe 1.13. See the complete code listings here for the details on setting up
> the user interface.

To create a new thread in Objective-C, you can use the NSThread class, but first you
need to put all the code that you want to run on the separate thread in a method.

```
-(void) bigTask{
    for(int i=0;i<40000;i++){
        NSString *newString = [NSString stringWithFormat:@"i = %i", i];
        NSLog(@"%@", newString);
    }
    [self.myActivityIndicator stopAnimating];
}
```

This method, bigTask, loops 40,000 times. During each loop a new string is constructed
and then written out to the log. After all this, a message is sent to the activity indicator to
stop spinning, which indicates that the task is complete.

Autorelease

There is one more thing that you should do with bigTask before you move on. It has to
do with memory management, which is covered in more detail in Chapter 8, and is
important when you are dealing with threads. You need to put the code in bigTask into
an autoreleasepool. Autoreleasepool allows Objective-C to use memory resources and
then dispose of the resources as needed. Every thread requires an autoreleasepool or
you will find memory leaks in your app.

To add an autoreleasepool to bigTask, enclose all of bigTask's code in a block starting
with the @autorelease keyword.

```
-(void) bigTask{
    @autoreleasepool {
        for(int i=0;i<40000;i++){
            NSString *newString = [NSString stringWithFormat:@"i = %i", i];
            NSLog(@"%@", newString);
        }
        [self.myActivityIndicator stopAnimating];
    }
}
```

You could simply execute this method directly by assigning bigTask as an action associated with a touch event to a button. However, if you did so, your user interface would be completely unresponsive until the task was complete.

A better way to execute the bigTask is to create a new method for the task of setting up the user interface and then executing the bigTask. You will ultimately assign this method to a button action. Call it bitTaskAction and start the method like this:

```
-(void)bigTaskAction{
    [self.myActivityIndicator startAnimating];
}
```

So far, bigTaskAction just sets up the user interface by sending a message to the activity indicator to start spinning. To execute the big task, use the NSThread class method detachNewThreadSelector:toTarget:withObject:.

```
-(void)bigTaskAction{
    [self.myActivityIndicator startAnimating];

    [NSThread detachNewThreadSelector:@selector(bigTask)
                             toTarget:self
                           withObject:nil];

}
```

This will make a new thread and execute the code in the method that you specify with the @selector keyword. You can also specify the target object, which must be the object where the method from the first parameter is located. If the method accepts a parameter, then you can pass an object using the last parameter in the method. Yours doesn't require a parameter so you simply pass nil.

To make this work with an application, assign the method that spawns the thread as an action to a user control. If you add this to an iPhone app, make sure to add bigTaskAction to the action method.

```
[self.myButton addTarget:self
                  action:@selector(bigTaskAction)
        forControlEvents:UIControlEventTouchUpInside];
```

When a user touches a button on an app like this, the big task will execute in its own thread and not interrupt the user interface at all. See Listings 6-1 through 6-4 for the code.

The Code

Listing 6-1. *AppDelegate.h*

```
#import <UIKit/UIKit.h>
```

```
@class ViewController;

@interface AppDelegate : UIResponder <UIApplicationDelegate>

@property (strong, nonatomic) UIWindow *window;

@property (strong, nonatomic) ViewController *viewController;

@end
```

Listing 6-2. *AppDelegate.m*

```
#import "AppDelegate.h"

#import "ViewController.h"

@implementation AppDelegate

@synthesize window = _window;
@synthesize viewController = _viewController;

- (BOOL)application:(UIApplication *)application didFinishLaunchingWithOptions: ↩
(NSDictionary *)launchOptions{
    self.window = [[UIWindow alloc] initWithFrame:[[UIScreen mainScreen] bounds]];
    // Override point for customization after application launch.
    self.viewController = [[ViewController alloc] initWithNibName:@"ViewController"
                                                    bundle:nil];
    self.window.rootViewController = self.viewController;
    [self.window makeKeyAndVisible];

    return YES;
}

@end
```

Listing 6-3. *ViewController.h*

```objc
#import <UIKit/UIKit.h>

@interface ViewController : UIViewController

@property(strong) UIButton *myButton;
@property(strong) UIActivityIndicatorView *myActivityIndicator;

@end
```

Listing 6-4. *ViewController.m*

```objc
#import "ViewController.h"

@implementation ViewController
@synthesize myButton, myActivityIndicator;

-(void) bigTask{
    @autoreleasepool {
        for(int i=0;i<40000;i++){
            NSString *newString = [NSString stringWithFormat:@"i = %i", i];
            NSLog(@"%@", newString);
        }
        [self.myActivityIndicator stopAnimating];
    }
}
/*
 //do task without using a new thread (watch UI to see how this works)
 -(void)bigTaskAction{
 [self.myActivityIndicator startAnimating];
 [self bigTask];
 }
 */

//do task by detaching a new thread (watch UI to see how this works)
-(void)bigTaskAction{
    [self.myActivityIndicator startAnimating];

    [NSThread detachNewThreadSelector:@selector(bigTask)
                            toTarget:self
                          withObject:nil];

}

- (void)viewDidLoad{
    [super viewDidLoad];

    //Create button
    self.myButton = [UIButton buttonWithType:UIButtonTypeRoundedRect];
```

```objc
    self.myButton.frame = CGRectMake(20, 403, 280, 37);
    [self.myButton addTarget:self
                    action:@selector(bigTaskAction)
            forControlEvents:UIControlEventTouchUpInside];
    [self.myButton setTitle:@"Do Long Task"
                    forState:UIControlStateNormal];

    [self.view addSubview:self.myButton];

    //Create activity indicator
    self.myActivityIndicator = [[UIActivityIndicatorView alloc] init];
    self.myActivityIndicator.frame = CGRectMake(142, 211, 37, 37);
    self.myActivityIndicator.activityIndicatorViewStyle = ↵
UIActivityIndicatorViewStyleWhiteLarge;
    self.myActivityIndicator.hidesWhenStopped = NO;

    [self.view addSubview:self.myActivityIndicator];

}

@end
```

Usage

To use this code, start by setting up a Single View based application in Xcode, like you did in Recipe 1.12. Next, add the code from Listing 6-4 to your own `ViewController` class.

Run the application. In the iOS Simulator you should see an app with one button and a white activity indicator in the middle of the view. Touch the button and examine the log. You should see the `for` loop executing and the activity indicator spinning in the iOS app view. When `bigTask` is complete, the activity indicator will stop spinning.

To compare what would happen without using a new thread, comment out `bigTaskAction` from Listing 6-4 and then comment in the alternate `bigTask` method. See the comments in Listing 6-4 if you are unsure of what method to choose.

Run the application with the alternate `bigTaskAction` and observe how the main thread gets locked up. You will not be able to use the interface, but the `for` loop will continue to execute and you will see the results in the log.

6.2 Communicating Between the Main Thread and a Background Thread

Problem

When you attempt to update the user interface from a background thread, the changes don't occur until the background thread is finished processing, which makes components like progress bars useless. You would like to update your user on the progress of background tasks.

Solution

Use the NSObject method performSelectorOnMainThread:withObject:waitUntilDone: to execute a method on the main thread. You will need to put the code that updates your user interface (or otherwise works with the main thread) in its own method.

How It Works

This recipe continues the work you started in Recipe 6.1. However, you are going to add a UIProgressView object property to your application.

UIProgressView is a UIKit class that you can use to create a user interface element that presents the progress of a task from 0% to 100% and looks like a blue bar that moves across the screen. You are going to use the progress view to show your users how much of the bigTask has been completed.

Here is where you will put the UIProgressView object in your ViewController class. This property belongs in the header file.

```
#import <UIKit/UIKit.h>

@interface ViewController : UIViewController

@property(strong) UIButton *myButton;
@property(strong) UIActivityIndicatorView *myActivityIndicator;
@property(strong) UIProgressView *myProgressView;

@end
```

The property myProgressView must also be added to the @synthesize statement in the ViewController implementation file.

```
#import "ViewController.h"
```

```
@implementation ViewController
@synthesize myButton, myActivityIndicator, myProgressView;

...

@end
```

Note that the entire ViewController implementation is not reproduced here. Take a look at Listing 6-7 to see a complete listing of the code in ViewController in context.

Now, create a method that will update the progress view. This method must be separate from the method where you put the code for the background thread, which is bigTask in this example application.

Name your method updateProgressViewWithPercentage:. The parameter is an NSNumber object indicating how much of the task is complete.

```
-(void)updateProgressViewWithPercentage:(NSNumber *)percentDone{

}
```

Make sure to add this method to your ViewController implementation but before the bigTask method. Alternatively, you can add updateProgressViewWithPercentage: to the ViewController header file as a forward declaration if you'd rather locate the actual method after bigTask.

Next, add the code to update the progress view to the new method. You only need to send one message here to the progress view with the updated information.

```
-(void)updateProgressViewWithPercentage:(NSNumber *)percentDone{
    [self.myProgressView setProgress:[percentDone floatValue]
                            animated:YES];
}
```

As you can see, you are setting the state of the progress view to the percentage that you are getting from the percentDone parameter. setProgress is actually expecting a primitive float type, which means that you must use the NSNumber floatValue method to return the float value version of the NSNumber object. The second parameter allows you to control whether the progress view will update with animation.

This is the method that you will be calling from your background thread. As in Recipe 6.1, you have a method called bigTask where the background thread code is located. There is a slight change in this code: the number to count to is reduced to 10,000 from 40,000 because counting to 40,000 just took too long while testing this code. Here is the updated bigTask:

```
-(void) bigTask{
    @autoreleasepool {
        for(int i=0;i<10000;i++){
```

```
            NSString *newString = [NSString stringWithFormat:@"i = %i", i];
            NSLog(@"%@", newString);
        }
        [self.myActivityIndicator stopAnimating];
    }
}
```

Again, the code for bigTask is located in the ViewController implementation. Before you instruct the user interface to update back on the main thread, you need a few things in place. Since you don't want the interface updating for every single action in the thread, here are some rules to determine when the interface is updated.

You want the interface to update as you reach every 10% of the total task completion time. Since you are counting to 10,000, you can simply update the interface every 1,000 counts. You'll need an integer to help keep track of this, so add it now and assign the initial value to 1000.

```
-(void) bigTask{
    @autoreleasepool {
        int updateUIWhen = 1000;
        for(int i=0;i<10000;i++){
            NSString *newString = [NSString stringWithFormat:@"i = %i", i];
            NSLog(@"%@", newString);
        }
        [self.myActivityIndicator stopAnimating];
    }
}
```

Next, you need to test when your count has reached the value in updateUIWhen. You also need to increment updateUIWhen once you do reach 1,000. Here is one way to do that:

```
-(void) bigTask{
    @autoreleasepool {
        int updateUIWhen = 1000;
        for(int i=0;i<10000;i++){
            NSString *newString = [NSString stringWithFormat:@"i = %i", i];
            NSLog(@"%@", newString);
            if(i == updateUIWhen){
                updateUIWhen = updateUIWhen + 1000;
            }
        }
        [self.myActivityIndicator stopAnimating];
    }
}
```

Now you can figure out the percentage complete by dividing i by 10,000. Put that line of code at the first spot after the opening of the if statement.

```
-(void) bigTask{
    @autoreleasepool {
```

```
            int updateUIWhen = 1000;
            for(int i=0;i<10000;i++){
                NSString *newString = [NSString stringWithFormat:@"i = %i", i];
                NSLog(@"%@", newString);
                if(i == updateUIWhen){
                    float f = (float)i/10000;

                    updateUIWhen = updateUIWhen + 1000;
                }
            }
            [self.myActivityIndicator stopAnimating];
        }
}
```

If you look closely at the new line of code, you will see that i has (float) in front of it. This is called a *type cast*. In this case, you are treating i (which is an integer) as a float type so that you can assign the division result to a float type. You need a float type because your progress view is going to need a value between 0 and 1.

Next, create an NSNumber object because that is what the method that will execute on the main thread will need as a parameter.

```
-(void) bigTask{
    @autoreleasepool {
        int updateUIWhen = 1000;
        for(int i=0;i<10000;i++){
            NSString *newString = [NSString stringWithFormat:@"i = %i", i];
            NSLog(@"%@", newString);
            if(i == updateUIWhen){
                float f = (float)i/10000;
                NSNumber *percentDone = [NSNumber numberWithFloat:f];

                updateUIWhen = updateUIWhen + 1000;
            }
        }
        [self.myActivityIndicator stopAnimating];
    }
}
```

You now have everything you need to send your message to the user interface back on the main thread. To send a message to the main thread, you can use the NSObject method performSelectorOnMainThread:withObject:waitUntilDone:. You need a method to pass with the @selector keyword, an object that will serve as a parameter to the method (the NSNumber you just created) and a BOOL indicating whether you want to block the current thread until the method has completed.

This code will send that message:

```
-(void) bigTask{
    @autoreleasepool {
```

```
        int updateUIWhen = 1000;
        for(int i=0;i<10000;i++){
            NSString *newString = [NSString stringWithFormat:@"i = %i", i];
            NSLog(@"%@", newString);
            if(i == updateUIWhen){
                float f = (float)i/10000;
                NSNumber *percentDone = [NSNumber numberWithFloat:f];
                [self performSelectorOnMainThread: ↵
                        @selector(updateProgressViewWithPercentage:)
                                    withObject:percentDone
                                waitUntilDone:YES];
                updateUIWhen = updateUIWhen + 1000;
            }
        }
        [self.myActivityIndicator stopAnimating];
    }
}
```

Here you are sending a message to the main thread where the user interface is
executing with a parameter that has information about how much of the task is
complete. All the code needed to update the progress view is located in the
updateProgressViewWithPercentage: method.

Next, you need to send yet another message to the main thread after the task is
complete just to make sure the progress view is completely filled up when you are done.
This message looks similar to what you just did.

```
-(void) bigTask{
    @autoreleasepool {
        int updateUIWhen = 1000;
        for(int i=0;i<10000;i++){
            NSString *newString = [NSString stringWithFormat:@"i = %i", i];
            NSLog(@"%@", newString);
            if(i == updateUIWhen){
                float f = (float)i/10000;
                NSNumber *percentDone = [NSNumber numberWithFloat:f];
                [self performSelectorOnMainThread: ↵
                        @selector(updateProgressViewWithPercentage:)
                                    withObject:percentDone
                                waitUntilDone:YES];
                updateUIWhen = updateUIWhen + 1000;
            }
        }
        [self performSelectorOnMainThread:@selector(updateProgressViewWithPercentage:)
                            withObject:[NSNumber numberWithFloat:1.0]
                        waitUntilDone:YES];
        [self.myActivityIndicator stopAnimating];
    }
}
```

See Listings 6-5 through 6-8 for the code.

The Code

Listing 6-5. *AppDelegate.h*

```objc
#import <UIKit/UIKit.h>

@class ViewController;

@interface AppDelegate : UIResponder <UIApplicationDelegate>

@property (strong, nonatomic) UIWindow *window;

@property (strong, nonatomic) ViewController *viewController;

@end
```

Listing 6-6. *AppDelegate.m*

```objc
#import "AppDelegate.h"

#import "ViewController.h"

@implementation AppDelegate

@synthesize window = _window;
@synthesize viewController = _viewController;

- (BOOL)application:(UIApplication *)application didFinishLaunchingWithOptions:↵
(NSDictionary *)launchOptions{
    self.window = [[UIWindow alloc] initWithFrame:[[UIScreen mainScreen] bounds]];
    // Override point for customization after application launch.
    self.viewController = [[ViewController alloc] initWithNibName:@"ViewController"
                                                          bundle:nil];
    self.window.rootViewController = self.viewController;
    [self.window makeKeyAndVisible];
```

```
        return YES;
}

@end
```

Listing 6-7. *ViewController.h*

```objc
#import <UIKit/UIKit.h>

@interface ViewController : UIViewController

@property(strong) UIButton *myButton;
@property(strong) UIActivityIndicatorView *myActivityIndicator;
@property(strong) UIProgressView *myProgressView;

@end
```

Listing 6-8. *ViewController.m*

```objc
#import "ViewController.h"

@implementation ViewController
@synthesize myButton, myActivityIndicator, myProgressView;

-(void)updateProgressViewWithPercentage:(NSNumber *)percentDone{
        [self.myProgressView setProgress:[percentDone floatValue]
                                animated:YES];
}

-(void) bigTask{
    @autoreleasepool {
        int updateUIWhen = 1000;
        for(int i=0;i<10000;i++){
            NSString *newString = [NSString stringWithFormat:@"i = %i", i];
            NSLog(@"%@", newString);
            if(i == updateUIWhen){
                float f = (float)i/10000;
                NSNumber *percentDone = [NSNumber numberWithFloat:f];
                [self performSelectorOnMainThread:  ↵
                        @selector(updateProgressViewWithPercentage:)
                                       withObject:percentDone
                                    waitUntilDone:YES];
                updateUIWhen = updateUIWhen + 1000;
            }
        }
        [self performSelectorOnMainThread:@selector(updateProgressViewWithPercentage:)
                               withObject:[NSNumber numberWithFloat:1.0]
                            waitUntilDone:YES];
        [self.myActivityIndicator stopAnimating];
    }
```

```objectivec
}

//do task by detaching a new thread (watch UI to see how this works)
-(void)bigTaskAction{
    [self.myActivityIndicator startAnimating];

    [NSThread detachNewThreadSelector:@selector(bigTask)
                            toTarget:self
                          withObject:nil];

}

- (void)viewDidLoad{
    [super viewDidLoad];

        //Create button
        self.myButton = [UIButton buttonWithType:UIButtonTypeRoundedRect];
        self.myButton.frame = CGRectMake(20, 403, 280, 37);
        [self.myButton addTarget:self
                          action:@selector(bigTaskAction)
                forControlEvents:UIControlEventTouchUpInside];
        [self.myButton setTitle:@"Do Long Task"
                       forState:UIControlStateNormal];
    [self.view addSubview:self.myButton];

    //Create activity indicator
    self.myActivityIndicator = [[UIActivityIndicatorView alloc] init];
    self.myActivityIndicator.frame = CGRectMake(142, 211, 37, 37);
    self.myActivityIndicator.activityIndicatorViewStyle = ↵
UIActivityIndicatorViewStyleWhiteLarge;
    self.myActivityIndicator.hidesWhenStopped = NO;
    [self.view addSubview:self.myActivityIndicator];

    //Create label
    self.myProgressView = [[UIProgressView alloc] init];
    self.myProgressView.frame = CGRectMake(20, 20, 280, 9);
    [self.view addSubview:self.myProgressView];

}

@end
```

Usage

To use this code, start by setting up a Single View based application in Xcode, like you did in Recipe 1.12. Next, add the code from Listing 6-8tk to your own ViewController class.

Run the application. In the iOS Simulator you should see an app with one button and an empty progress view. You will also see a white activity indicator in the middle of the view. Touch the button to start bigTask in the background thread and examine the log. As bigTask runs, you should see the progress view filling up in 10% increments until the task is complete.

6.3 Locking Threads with NSLock

Problem

Your application uses multiple threads, but at times you need to make sure two threads are not attempting to use the same block of code. Your application could cause conflicts that may result in user confusion or files being accessed too many times.

For example, try to run the application from Recipe 6.2 but touch the button a second time after the progress view starts to fill from the first task. If you look closely, the progress view will start to jump back and forth as each thread changes the progress view's value to the current percentage for that particular thread.

Solution

Use NSLock to make other threads wait until the thread is done processing for key blocks of code.

How It Works

For this example, let's assume that you are starting with the application from Recipe 6.2 and your app behaves as described in the Problem section. What you want to do is make sure that bigTask only executes in one thread at a time. This will make each thread wait its turn.

The first thing you need to do is add an NSLock object to your view controller. The following is an example of setting this up as a property:

```
#import <UIKit/UIKit.h>

@interface ViewController : UIViewController

@property(strong) UIButton *myButton;
@property(strong) UIActivityIndicatorView *myActivityIndicator;
@property(strong) UIProgressView *myProgressView;
@property(strong) NSLock *threadLock;
```

@end

This property must also be included with the @synthesize statement in the view controller's implementation.

```
#import "ViewController.h"

@implementation ViewController
@synthesize myButton, myActivityIndicator, myProgressView, threadLock;

@end
```

> **NOTE:** It is not absolutely necessary to include objects like this as properties. You may also simply add them as a local instance in your view controller implementation. This is a design decision that you must make. I included NSLock like this to stay as consistent as possible with the earlier recipes.

Before you use NSLock, you need to instantiate an object and assign this to the property that you have in place. The best place to do this in a view controller is in the viewDidLoad method.

```
#import "ViewController.h"

@implementation ViewController
@synthesize myButton, myActivityIndicator, myProgressView, threadLock;

- (void)viewDidLoad{
    [super viewDidLoad];

    //Create the NSLock object
    self.threadLock = [[NSLock alloc] init];
}

@end
```

All the code for the view controller is not listed here, but you can see it in Listing 6-11.

Now that you have an NSLock object, all you need to do is lock down your thread. To do this, use the lock message to the NSLock object at the beginning of the thread's code and an unlock message at the end of the thread's code.

This code goes in your bigTask method, which is located in the view controller's implementation.

```
-(void) bigTask{
```

```objc
[self.threadLock lock];
@autoreleasepool {
    int updateUIWhen = 1000;
    for(int i=0;i<10000;i++){
        NSString *newString = [NSString stringWithFormat:@"i = %i", i];
        NSLog(@"%@", newString);
        if(i == updateUIWhen){
            float f = (float)i/10000;
            NSNumber *percentDone = [NSNumber numberWithFloat:f];
            [self performSelectorOnMainThread: ↵
                @selector(updateProgressViewWithPercentage:)
                            withObject:percentDone
                          waitUntilDone:YES];
            updateUIWhen = updateUIWhen + 1000;
        }
    }
    [self performSelectorOnMainThread:@selector(updateProgressViewWithPercentage:)
                        withObject:[NSNumber numberWithFloat:1.0]
                      waitUntilDone:YES];
    [self.myActivityIndicator stopAnimating];
}
[self.threadLock unlock];
}
```

Now you can be sure that this thread will be locked until the thread is done executing. See Listings 6-9 through 6-12 for the code.

The Code

Listing 6-9. *AppDelegate.h*

```objc
#import <UIKit/UIKit.h>

@class ViewController;

@interface AppDelegate : UIResponder <UIApplicationDelegate>

@property (strong, nonatomic) UIWindow *window;

@property (strong, nonatomic) ViewController *viewController;

@end
```

Listing 6-10. *AppDelegate.m*

```objc
#import "AppDelegate.h"

#import "ViewController.h"
```

```objc
@implementation AppDelegate

@synthesize window = _window;
@synthesize viewController = _viewController;

- (BOOL)application:(UIApplication *)application didFinishLaunchingWithOptions: ↵
(NSDictionary *)launchOptions{
    self.window = [[UIWindow alloc] initWithFrame:[[UIScreen mainScreen] bounds]];
    // Override point for customization after application launch.
    self.viewController = [[ViewController alloc] initWithNibName:@"ViewController"
                                                bundle:nil];

    self.window.rootViewController = self.viewController;
    [self.window makeKeyAndVisible];

    return YES;
}

@end
```

Listing 6-11. *ViewController.h*

```objc
#import <UIKit/UIKit.h>

@interface ViewController : UIViewController

@property(strong) UIButton *myButton;
@property(strong) UIActivityIndicatorView *myActivityIndicator;
@property(strong) UIProgressView *myProgressView;
@property(strong) NSLock *threadLock;

@end
```

Listing 6-12. *ViewController.m*

```objc
#import "ViewController.h"

@implementation ViewController
@synthesize myButton, myActivityIndicator, myProgressView, threadLock;

-(void)updateProgressViewWithPercentage:(NSNumber *)percentDone{
    [self.myProgressView setProgress:[percentDone floatValue]
                            animated:YES];
}

-(void) bigTask{
    [self.threadLock lock];
    @autoreleasepool {
        int updateUIWhen = 1000;
        for(int i=0;i<10000;i++){
```

```
                NSString *newString = [NSString stringWithFormat:@"i = %i", i];
                NSLog(@"%@", newString);
                if(i == updateUIWhen){
                    float f = (float)i/10000;
                    NSNumber *percentDone = [NSNumber numberWithFloat:f];
                    [self performSelectorOnMainThread: ↵
                            @selector(updateProgressViewWithPercentage:)
                                        withObject:percentDone
                                     waitUntilDone:YES];
                    updateUIWhen = updateUIWhen + 1000;
                }
            }
        [self performSelectorOnMainThread:@selector(updateProgressViewWithPercentage:)
                            withObject:[NSNumber numberWithFloat:1.0]
                         waitUntilDone:YES];
        [self.myActivityIndicator stopAnimating];
        }
    [self.threadLock unlock];


}


//do task by detaching a new thread (watch UI to see how this works)
-(void)bigTaskAction{
    [self.myActivityIndicator startAnimating];

    [NSThread detachNewThreadSelector:@selector(bigTask)
                            toTarget:self
                          withObject:nil];


}


- (void)viewDidLoad{
    [super viewDidLoad];

    //Create the NSLock object
    self.threadLock = [[NSLock alloc] init];

    //Create button
    self.myButton = [UIButton buttonWithType:UIButtonTypeRoundedRect];
    self.myButton.frame = CGRectMake(20, 403, 280, 37);
    [self.myButton addTarget:self
                    action:@selector(bigTaskAction)
            forControlEvents:UIControlEventTouchUpInside];
     [self.myButton setTitle:@"Do Long Task"
                 forState:UIControlStateNormal];
    [self.view addSubview:self.myButton];

    //Create activity indicator
    self.myActivityIndicator = [[UIActivityIndicatorView alloc] init];
    self.myActivityIndicator.frame = CGRectMake(142, 211, 37, 37);
```

```
    self.myActivityIndicator.activityIndicatorViewStyle = ↵
UIActivityIndicatorViewStyleWhiteLarge;
    self.myActivityIndicator.hidesWhenStopped = NO;
    [self.view addSubview:self.myActivityIndicator];

    //Create label
    self.myProgressView = [[UIProgressView alloc] init];
    self.myProgressView.frame = CGRectMake(20, 20, 280, 9);
    [self.view addSubview:self.myProgressView];

}

@end
```

Usage

To test this code, start by setting up a Single View based application in Xcode, like you did in Recipe 1.12. Next, add the code from Listing 6-12 to your own ViewController class.

Run the application. In the iOS Simulator you should see an app with one button and an empty progress view. You will also see a white activity indicator in the middle of the view. Touch the button two times to start bigTask running in two background threads.

As bigTask runs, you should see the progress view filling up in 10% increments until the task is complete. Observe that the progress view fills up to 100% before going back to 0% and progressing again to 100%. NSLock is doing what it's supposed to do.

6.4 Locking Threads with @synchronized

Problem

Your application uses multiple threads, but at times you need to make sure two threads are not attempting to use the same block of code, and you would like an alternative to NSLock.

> **NOTE:** @synchronized and NSLock solve the same problem with threads, so this recipe will look very similar to Recipe 6.3. These two approaches, while similar, are implemented differently to allow @synchronized the ability to handle

exceptions. This also causes @synchronized to have more of a performance hit than NSLock.

Use the application from Recipe 6.2 as a starting point. The application from Recipe 6.2 will execute the thread as many times as you touch the button, causing the progress view to behave unexpectedly.

Solution

To make sure that only one thread may use a block of code at a time, enclose the entire block of code in curly braces preceded by the @synchronized directive.

How It Works

For this example, let's assume that you are starting with the application from Recipe 6.2 and that your app behaves as described in the Problem section. You want to make sure that bigTask only executes in one thread at a time. This will make each thread wait its turn.

All the code for the view controller is not listed here, but you can see it in Listing 6-15.

Unlike Recipe 6.3, you will not need to add any property code. All you need to do is enclose the code in the bigTask in curly braces with the @synchronized directive.

```
-(void) bigTask{
    @synchronized(self){
        @autoreleasepool {
            int updateUIWhen = 1000;
            for(int i=0;i<10000;i++){
                NSString *newString = [NSString stringWithFormat:@"i = %i", i];
                NSLog(@"%@", newString);
                if(i == updateUIWhen){
                    float f = (float)i/10000;
                    NSNumber *percentDone = [NSNumber numberWithFloat:f];
                    [self performSelectorOnMainThread:  ⏎
                            @selector(updateProgressViewWithPercentage:)
                                        withObject:percentDone
                                     waitUntilDone:YES];
                    updateUIWhen = updateUIWhen + 1000;
                }
            }
            [self performSelectorOnMainThread:  ⏎
                    @selector(updateProgressViewWithPercentage:)
                                withObject:[NSNumber numberWithFloat:1.0]
```

```
                              waitUntilDone:YES];
            [self.myActivityIndicator stopAnimating];
        }
    }
}
```

See Listings 6-13 through 6-16 for the code.

The Code

Listing 6-13. *AppDelegate.h*

```
#import <UIKit/UIKit.h>

@class ViewController;

@interface AppDelegate : UIResponder <UIApplicationDelegate>

@property (strong, nonatomic) UIWindow *window;

@property (strong, nonatomic) ViewController *viewController;

@end
```

Listing 6-14. *AppDelegate.m*

```
#import "AppDelegate.h"

#import "ViewController.h"

@implementation AppDelegate

@synthesize window = _window;
@synthesize viewController = _viewController;

- (BOOL)application:(UIApplication *)application didFinishLaunchingWithOptions: ↩
(NSDictionary *)launchOptions{
    self.window = [[UIWindow alloc] initWithFrame:[[UIScreen mainScreen] bounds]];
    // Override point for customization after application launch.
    self.viewController = [[ViewController alloc] initWithNibName:@"ViewController"
                                                 bundle:nil];
    self.window.rootViewController = self.viewController;
    [self.window makeKeyAndVisible];

    return YES;
}

@end
```

Listing 6-15. *ViewController.h*

```
#import <UIKit/UIKit.h>

@interface ViewController : UIViewController

@property(strong) UIButton *myButton;
@property(strong) UIActivityIndicatorView *myActivityIndicator;
@property(strong) UIProgressView *myProgressView;

@end
```

Listing 6-16. *ViewController.m*

```
#import "ViewController.h"

@implementation ViewController
@synthesize myButton, myActivityIndicator, myProgressView;

-(void)updateProgressViewWithPercentage:(NSNumber *)percentDone{
        [self.myProgressView setProgress:[percentDone floatValue]
                              animated:YES];
}

-(void) bigTask{
    @synchronized(self){
        @autoreleasepool {
            int updateUIWhen = 1000;
            for(int i=0;i<10000;i++){
                NSString *newString = [NSString stringWithFormat:@"i = %i", i];
                NSLog(@"%@", newString);
                if(i == updateUIWhen){
                    float f = (float)i/10000;
                    NSNumber *percentDone = [NSNumber numberWithFloat:f];
                    [self performSelectorOnMainThread:  ↵
                        @selector(updateProgressViewWithPercentage:)
                                        withObject:percentDone
                                        waitUntilDone:YES];
                    updateUIWhen = updateUIWhen + 1000;
                }
            }
            [self performSelectorOnMainThread:  ↵
                @selector(updateProgressViewWithPercentage:)
                                withObject:[NSNumber numberWithFloat:1.0]
                                waitUntilDone:YES];
            [self.myActivityIndicator stopAnimating];
        }
    }
}
```

```objc
//do task by detaching a new thread (watch UI to see how this works)
-(void)bigTaskAction{
    [self.myActivityIndicator startAnimating];

    [NSThread detachNewThreadSelector:@selector(bigTask)
                             toTarget:self
                           withObject:nil];

}

- (void)viewDidLoad{
    [super viewDidLoad];

    //Create button
    self.myButton = [UIButton buttonWithType:UIButtonTypeRoundedRect];
    self.myButton.frame = CGRectMake(20, 403, 280, 37);
    [self.myButton addTarget:self
                      action:@selector(bigTaskAction)
            forControlEvents:UIControlEventTouchUpInside];
    [self.myButton setTitle:@"Do Long Task"
                   forState:UIControlStateNormal];
    [self.view addSubview:self.myButton];

    //Create activity indicator
    self.myActivityIndicator = [[UIActivityIndicatorView alloc] init];
    self.myActivityIndicator.frame = CGRectMake(142, 211, 37, 37);
    self.myActivityIndicator.activityIndicatorViewStyle = ↵
UIActivityIndicatorViewStyleWhiteLarge;
    self.myActivityIndicator.hidesWhenStopped = NO;
    [self.view addSubview:self.myActivityIndicator];

    //Create label
    self.myProgressView = [[UIProgressView alloc] init];
    self.myProgressView.frame = CGRectMake(20, 20, 280, 9);
    [self.view addSubview:self.myProgressView];

}

@end
```

Usage

To test this code, start by setting up a Single View based application in Xcode, like you did in Recipe 1.12. Next, add the code from Listing 6-16 to your own ViewController class.

Run the application. In the iOS Simulator you should see an app with one button and an empty progress view at the top of the view. You will also see a white activity indicator in the middle of the view. Touch the button two times to start bigTask running in two background threads.

As bigTask runs, you should see the progress view filling up in 10% increments until the task is complete. Observe that the progress view fills up to 100% before going back to 0% and progressing again to 100%. @synchronized is doing what it's supposed to do.

6.5 Asynchronous Processing with Grand Central Dispatch (GCD)

Problem

You want to implement asynchronous processing in your application, you plan on supporting your application on newer OSX and iOS systems, and you would rather not use NSThread with the various locking mechanisms required to make your app thread safe.

> **NOTE:** Applications that use multiple threads can become more complicated
> and sometimes slower because developers need to worry about situations
> where regions of code, resources, or data structures may be accessed by
> more than one thread at the same time. Keeping threads locked for short
> periods of time (as in Recipes 6.3 and 6.4) helps to make code thread safe
> (safe for use by multiple threads). However, this can prevent applications from
> making full use of the available resources.

Solution

Consider using Grand Central Dispatch (GCD) as an alternative to NSThread if you know
your users have updated systems (or if you choose to support updated systems only).
GCD solves the same problems as NSThread and follows the same basic idea of
executing code asynchronously. GCD is a newer technology that is more efficient in
computers that have multiple processors. GCD was introduced for OSX in version 10.6
and iOS in version 4.

You don't need to do anything special to add GCD support to your application if you are
developing with a version of OSX that supports GCD. GCD does require the use of a
programming technique called *blocks*, which can take some getting used to.

Blocks are regions of code that are treated like objects. This means that you can put
lines of code between curly brackets and then treat them like an object. Usually, you will
see blocks used as a parameter to a method, and that is how blocks are used in GCD.
You will see how blocks are used with GCD in the following section.

How It Works

For this recipe, you are going to solve the same problem as you did in Recipes 6.1, 6.2,
and 6.3. Essentially, you have an iOS app with a button that sets off a long task and you
want to keep the user interface responsive and let the progress view fill up as the task
executes. This time you will use GCD to fix this problem.

GCD uses blocks instead of methods (with the @selector directive). This means that you
don't need to put all the code that you want to execute into a new method. Instead, you
will pass the code into a GCD function as a parameter right from the action method
bigTaskAction. Use the GCD function dispatch_async to do this.

```
-(void)bigTaskAction{
    [self.myActivityIndicator startAnimating];
```

```
dispatch_async(dispatch_get_global_queue(DISPATCH_QUEUE_PRIORITY_DEFAULT, 0), ^{

    int updateUIWhen = 1000;
    for(int i=0;i<10000;i++){
        NSString *newString = [NSString stringWithFormat:@"i = %i", i];
        NSLog(@"%@", newString);
        if(i == updateUIWhen){
            float f = (float)i/10000;
            NSNumber *percentDone = [NSNumber numberWithFloat:f];

            updateUIWhen = updateUIWhen + 1000;
        }
    }


});
}
```

Let's look at the first line of code with that GCD function.

dispatch_async(dispatch_get_global_queue(DISPATCH_QUEUE_PRIORITY_DEFAULT, 0), ^{

The first part is the name of the function is dispatch_async, which is a GCD function that executes asynchronously. There is also a similar function that executes code synchronously called dispatch_sync. The first parameter that the function requires is a dispatch queue.

dispatch_async(**dispatch_get_global_queue(DISPATCH_QUEUE_PRIORITY_DEFAULT, 0)**, ^{

You are supplying another function that in turn returns the default dispatch queue for this application.

> **NOTE:** GCD has a concept of code queues that are scheduled to run on the next available processor. When you use GCD you need to specify what queue that you want your code to be put into. You are using the default queue here, which you can use for background processing too. You can also use the main queue, which is like the main thread for the user interface.

The next parameter in this function is the code block. You know that you are working with a code block because it starts off with the ^ symbol and has a beginning curly bracket.

dispatch_async(dispatch_get_global_queue(DISPATCH_QUEUE_PRIORITY_DEFAULT, 0), **^{**

All the lines of code that come after are part of the block parameter. This code is scheduled to execute when the next processor is available. The entire GCD function ends with the code);.

So far, all you are doing is scheduling this big task to execute in the background. But, you still want to update the user interface as the task progresses. Instead of performing a selector on the main thread, you can use another GCD function to update the user interface on the main thread. This task should be done synchronously, so use the GCD function along with a main dispatch queue.

```
dispatch_sync(dispatch_get_main_queue(), ^{
    [self.myProgressView setProgress:[percentDone floatValue]
                            animated:YES];

});
```

This takes the place of the method you had to code before. You can just use the variables on hand without worrying about passing parameters, as you can see when you put this GCD call into the context of the entire code block.

```
-(void)bigTaskAction{
    [self.myActivityIndicator startAnimating];

    dispatch_async(dispatch_get_global_queue(DISPATCH_QUEUE_PRIORITY_DEFAULT, 0), ^{

        int updateUIWhen = 1000;
        for(int i=0;i<10000;i++){
            NSString *newString = [NSString stringWithFormat:@"i = %i", i];
            NSLog(@"%@", newString);
            if(i == updateUIWhen){
                float f = (float)i/10000;
                NSNumber *percentDone = [NSNumber numberWithFloat:f];

                dispatch_sync(dispatch_get_main_queue(), ^{
                    [self.myProgressView setProgress:[percentDone floatValue]
                                            animated:YES];

                });

                updateUIWhen = updateUIWhen + 1000;
            }
        }

    });
}
```

> **NOTE:** With GCD dispatch queues you don't know for sure what order code blocks will execute when you use `dispatch_async`. The system picks the most efficient way. So, if order is important (like when you are updating your interface), use `dispatch_sync`.

Finally, just to be complete, you want to finish filling the progress view when the task is complete and stop the activity indicator. Use GCD again to do this by scheduling another task for the main queue at the end of the block of code.

```
-(void)bigTaskAction{
    [self.myActivityIndicator startAnimating];

    dispatch_async(dispatch_get_global_queue(DISPATCH_QUEUE_PRIORITY_DEFAULT, 0), ^{

        int updateUIWhen = 1000;
        for(int i=0;i<10000;i++){
            NSString *newString = [NSString stringWithFormat:@"i = %i", i];
            NSLog(@"%@", newString);
            if(i == updateUIWhen){
                float f = (float)i/10000;
                NSNumber *percentDone = [NSNumber numberWithFloat:f];

                dispatch_sync(dispatch_get_main_queue(), ^{
                    [self.myProgressView setProgress:[percentDone floatValue]
                                            animated:YES];

                });

                updateUIWhen = updateUIWhen + 1000;
            }
        }

        dispatch_sync(dispatch_get_main_queue(), ^{

            [self.myProgressView setProgress:1.0
                                    animated:YES];
            [self.myActivityIndicator stopAnimating];

        });

    });
}
```

See Listings 6-17 through 6-20 for the code.

The Code

Listing 6-17. *AppDelegate.h*

```objc
#import <UIKit/UIKit.h>

@class ViewController;

@interface AppDelegate : UIResponder <UIApplicationDelegate>

@property (strong, nonatomic) UIWindow *window;

@property (strong, nonatomic) ViewController *viewController;

@end
```

Listing 6-18. *AppDelegate.m*

```objc
#import "AppDelegate.h"

#import "ViewController.h"

@implementation AppDelegate

@synthesize window = _window;
@synthesize viewController = _viewController;

- (BOOL)application:(UIApplication *)application didFinishLaunchingWithOptions: ↵
(NSDictionary *)launchOptions{
    self.window = [[UIWindow alloc] initWithFrame:[[UIScreen mainScreen] bounds]];
    // Override point for customization after application launch.
    self.viewController = [[ViewController alloc] initWithNibName:@"ViewController"
                                                          bundle:nil];
    self.window.rootViewController = self.viewController;
    [self.window makeKeyAndVisible];

    return YES;
}

@end
```

Listing 6-19. *ViewController.h*

```objc
#import <UIKit/UIKit.h>

@interface ViewController : UIViewController

@property(strong) UIButton *myButton;
@property(strong) UIActivityIndicatorView *myActivityIndicator;
```

```objc
@property(strong) UIProgressView *myProgressView;

@end
```

Listing 6-20. *ViewController.m*

```objc
#import "ViewController.h"

@implementation ViewController
@synthesize myButton, myActivityIndicator, myProgressView;

-(void)bigTaskAction{
    [self.myActivityIndicator startAnimating];

    dispatch_async(dispatch_get_global_queue(DISPATCH_QUEUE_PRIORITY_DEFAULT, 0), ^{

        int updateUIWhen = 1000;
        for(int i=0;i<10000;i++){
            NSString *newString = [NSString stringWithFormat:@"i = %i", i];
            NSLog(@"%@", newString);
            if(i == updateUIWhen){
                float f = (float)i/10000;
                NSNumber *percentDone = [NSNumber numberWithFloat:f];

                dispatch_sync(dispatch_get_main_queue(), ^{
                    [self.myProgressView setProgress:[percentDone floatValue]
                                            animated:YES];

                });

                updateUIWhen = updateUIWhen + 1000;
            }
        }

        dispatch_sync(dispatch_get_main_queue(), ^{

            [self.myProgressView setProgress:1.0
                                   animated:YES];
            [self.myActivityIndicator stopAnimating];

        });

    });
}

- (void)viewDidLoad{
    [super viewDidLoad];

    //Create button
    self.myButton = [UIButton buttonWithType:UIButtonTypeRoundedRect];
```

```
    self.myButton.frame = CGRectMake(20, 403, 280, 37);
    [self.myButton addTarget:self
                        action:@selector(bigTaskAction)
            forControlEvents:UIControlEventTouchUpInside];
    [self.myButton setTitle:@"Do Long Task"
                    forState:UIControlStateNormal];
    [self.view addSubview:self.myButton];

    //Create activity indicator
    self.myActivityIndicator = [[UIActivityIndicatorView alloc] init];
    self.myActivityIndicator.frame = CGRectMake(142, 211, 37, 37);
    self.myActivityIndicator.activityIndicatorViewStyle = ↵
UIActivityIndicatorViewStyleWhiteLarge;
    self.myActivityIndicator.hidesWhenStopped = NO;
    [self.view addSubview:self.myActivityIndicator];

    //Create label
    self.myProgressView = [[UIProgressView alloc] init];
    self.myProgressView.frame = CGRectMake(20, 20, 280, 9);
    [self.view addSubview:self.myProgressView];

}

@end
```

Usage

To test this code, start by setting up a Single View based application in Xcode, like you did in Recipe 1.12. Next, add the code from Listing 6-20tk to your own ViewController class.

Run the application. In the iOS Simulator you should see an app with one button and an empty progress view. You will also see a white activity indicator in the middle of the view. Touch the button to start the bigTask running. As bigTask runs, you should see the progress view filling up in 10% increments until the task is complete.

Generally speaking, GCD is the preferred way to do background processing. If you are targeting newer systems, GCD should be your first choice when deciding what technology to implement. GCD has been optimized for multi-core applications so you will see a large boast in your application's performance when using GCD on multi-core Macs.

GCD is simpler to use as compared to NSThread since there is no need for an additional object nor is there a need to code an additional method as you would for NSThread. However, you will see plenty of examples of NSThread to do background processing, and that option is available to you.

6.6 Using Serial Queues in GCD

Problem

You use GCD to perform asynchronous processing and you have a situation where you require blocks to execute one at a time in the order in which they are encountered in code. For example, in Recipe 6.5 you run into the same problem as you did earlier in this chapter when users touch the button after the long task is running (the progress view bounces back and forth).

Previously, you solved this problem using NSLock or @synchronized() but these come at a cost, which negates some of the benefits of using GCD in the first place.

Solution

Instead of locking the code, use a GCD serial queue to load up the code blocks to be executed in the order in which the code blocks were placed in the queue. You can use the GCD function dispatch_queue_create(DISPATCH_QUEUE_SERIAL, 0) to create a serial queue. Make sure that the serial queue stays in scope for the lifetime of the object it serves.

How It Works

For the purposes of this recipe, you'll alter Recipe 6.5 to use a serial queue to fix the problem that you run into. The first thing you need is a property for the serial queue.

```
#import <UIKit/UIKit.h>

@interface ViewController : UIViewController

@property(strong) UIButton *myButton;
@property(strong) UIActivityIndicatorView *myActivityIndicator;
@property(strong) UIProgressView *myProgressView;
@property(assign) dispatch_queue_t serialQueue;

@end
```

This could also be a local instance in the view controller, as long as the queue stays in scope as long as needed.

You need to make sure that the serial queue is implemented in the view controller's @synthesize statement as well.

```
#import "ViewController.h"
```

```
@implementation ViewController
@synthesize myButton, myActivityIndicator, myProgressView, serialQueue;

@end
```

The viewDidLoad view controller method is a great place to locate the code required to create the serial queue.

```
#import "ViewController.h"

@implementation ViewController
@synthesize myButton, myActivityIndicator, myProgressView, serialQueue;

...

- (void)viewDidLoad{
    [super viewDidLoad];

    self.serialQueue = dispatch_queue_create(DISPATCH_QUEUE_SERIAL, 0);

}

...

@end
```

This function requires a parameter to specify the type of queue to create. Here you are using DISPATCH_QUEUE_SERIAL because you want a serial queue that ensures that only one block of code executes at a time in the order that each block of code was placed in the queue. Some of the view controller code has been left out; see Listing 6-23 for the entire view controller code.

The next change that you need to make to the Recipe 6.5 code is to replace the default queue used before with the serial queue you just created. This happens in the bigTaskAction method.

```
#import "ViewController.h"

@implementation ViewController
@synthesize myButton, myActivityIndicator, myProgressView, serialQueue;

...

-(void)bigTaskAction{

    dispatch_async(self.serialQueue, ^{

        dispatch_sync(dispatch_get_main_queue(), ^{
            [self.myActivityIndicator startAnimating];
```

```objc
    });

    int updateUIWhen = 1000;
    for(int i=0;i<10000;i++){
        NSString *newString = [NSString stringWithFormat:@"i = %i", i];
        NSLog(@"%@", newString);
        if(i == updateUIWhen){
            float f = (float)i/10000;
            NSNumber *percentDone = [NSNumber numberWithFloat:f];

            dispatch_sync(dispatch_get_main_queue(), ^{
                [self.myProgressView setProgress:[percentDone floatValue]
                                        animated:YES];

            });

            updateUIWhen = updateUIWhen + 1000;
        }
    }

    dispatch_sync(dispatch_get_main_queue(), ^{

        [self.myProgressView setProgress:1.0
                                animated:YES];
        [self.myActivityIndicator stopAnimating];

    });
    });

}

...

@end
```

As you can see, you moved the message to start animating the activity indicator to be inside the main block for this action. You also put it into the main queue because it involved updating the user interface. The reasoning is that you want the activity indicator to start spinning each time a block like this executes in the serial queue. See Listings 6-21 through 6-24 for the code.

The Code

Listing 6-21. *AppDelegate.h*

```objc
#import <UIKit/UIKit.h>

@class ViewController;
```

```
@interface AppDelegate : UIResponder <UIApplicationDelegate>

@property (strong, nonatomic) UIWindow *window;

@property (strong, nonatomic) ViewController *viewController;

@end
```

Listing 6-22. *AppDelegate.m*

```
#import "AppDelegate.h"

#import "ViewController.h"

@implementation AppDelegate

@synthesize window = _window;
@synthesize viewController = _viewController;

- (BOOL)application:(UIApplication *)application didFinishLaunchingWithOptions: ↵
(NSDictionary *)launchOptions{
    self.window = [[UIWindow alloc] initWithFrame:[[UIScreen mainScreen] bounds]];
    // Override point for customization after application launch.
    self.viewController = [[ViewController alloc] initWithNibName:@"ViewController"
                                                    bundle:nil];
    self.window.rootViewController = self.viewController;
    [self.window makeKeyAndVisible];

    return YES;
}

@end
```

Listing 6-23. *ViewController.h*

```
#import <UIKit/UIKit.h>

@interface ViewController : UIViewController

@property(strong) UIButton *myButton;
@property(strong) UIActivityIndicatorView *myActivityIndicator;
@property(strong) UIProgressView *myProgressView;
@property(assign) dispatch_queue_t serialQueue;

@end
```

Listing 6-24. *ViewController.m*

```
#import "ViewController.h"
```

```
@implementation ViewController
@synthesize myButton, myActivityIndicator, myProgressView, serialQueue;

-(void)bigTaskAction{

    dispatch_async(self.serialQueue, ^{

        dispatch_sync(dispatch_get_main_queue(), ^{
            [self.myActivityIndicator startAnimating];
        });

        int updateUIWhen = 1000;
        for(int i=0;i<10000;i++){
            NSString *newString = [NSString stringWithFormat:@"i = %i", i];
            NSLog(@"%@", newString);
            if(i == updateUIWhen){
                float f = (float)i/10000;
                NSNumber *percentDone = [NSNumber numberWithFloat:f];

                dispatch_sync(dispatch_get_main_queue(), ^{
                    [self.myProgressView setProgress:[percentDone floatValue]
                                            animated:YES];

                });

                updateUIWhen = updateUIWhen + 1000;
            }
        }

        dispatch_sync(dispatch_get_main_queue(), ^{

            [self.myProgressView setProgress:1.0
                                    animated:YES];
            [self.myActivityIndicator stopAnimating];

        });
    });

}

- (void)viewDidLoad{
    [super viewDidLoad];

    self.serialQueue = dispatch_queue_create(DISPATCH_QUEUE_SERIAL, 0);

    //Create button
    self.myButton = [UIButton buttonWithType:UIButtonTypeRoundedRect];
    self.myButton.frame = CGRectMake(20, 403, 280, 37);
    [self.myButton addTarget:self
```

```
                    action:@selector(bigTaskAction)
            forControlEvents:UIControlEventTouchUpInside];
    [self.myButton setTitle:@"Do Long Task"
                forState:UIControlStateNormal];
    [self.view addSubview:self.myButton];

    //Create activity indicator
    self.myActivityIndicator = [[UIActivityIndicatorView alloc] init];
    self.myActivityIndicator.frame = CGRectMake(142, 211, 37, 37);
    self.myActivityIndicator.activityIndicatorViewStyle = ↵
UIActivityIndicatorViewStyleWhiteLarge;
    self.myActivityIndicator.hidesWhenStopped = NO;
    [self.view addSubview:self.myActivityIndicator];

    //Create label
    self.myProgressView = [[UIProgressView alloc] init];
    self.myProgressView.frame = CGRectMake(20, 20, 280, 9);
    [self.view addSubview:self.myProgressView];

}

@end
```

Usage

To test out this code, start by setting up an application like the one in
Recipe 6.5.

Run the application. In the iOS Simulator you should see an app with one button and an empty progress view. You will also see a white activity indicator in the middle of the view. Touch the button two times to start bigTask running in two background threads.

As bigTask runs, you should see the progress view filling up in 10% increments until the task is complete. This process will repeat based on the amount of times you touch the button. The progress view should not keep jumping back and forth.

6.7 Implement Asynchronous Processing Using NSOperationQueue

Problem

You would like to add asynchronous processing to your app, but you prefer to use a more object-oriented approach than the GCD approach.

Solution

Use NSOperationQueue if you want to use GCD but would rather not use the GCD library directly.

> **NOTE:** NSOperationQueue is available for iOS 2 and above and OSX 10.5 and above. This makes NSOperationQueue ideal when you want to support applications that run on older systems and you would rather not use NSThread with thread locking. When you use NSOperationQueue, the details of the implementation are hidden from you. Older systems will support NSOperationQueue with threads while newer systems will use GCD.

NSOperationQueue represents a queue of code that will execute. You can use NSOperationQueue to run code in the background or in a main queue for user interface actions.

NSOperationQueue can add code in a few ways. If the OS supports blocks (iOS 4 and above and OSX 10.6 and above), you can just add code directly to a queue using the addOperationWithBlock: method.

If not, you must set up the code that you want to execute as a separate subclass that is a subclass of NSOperation. A subclass of NSOperation will act like a block in that the class will encapsulate data and code that will execute in a queue.

How It Works

For this recipe, you are going to solve the same problem that was presented in Recipe 6.3. But, instead of using threads that you must lock, you will use an operation queue and the main queue to dispatch code asynchronously. Again, start with Recipe 6.2 as a template and change it to use operation queues (see Listings 6-25 through 6-28 for the complete code in context).

First, add local instances for the main queue and a serial queue right in the view controller's implementation.

```
#import "ViewController.h"

@implementation ViewController
@synthesize myButton, myActivityIndicator, myProgressView;
NSOperationQueue *serialQueue;
NSOperationQueue *mainQueue;

@end
```

The main queue is where the user interface gets its instructions. The serial queue executes code blocks one at a time in the order in which they are received, just like the GCD serial queue in Recipe 6.6.

The viewDidLoad method is the ideal place to instantiate these two queue objects.

```objc
#import "ViewController.h"

@implementation ViewController
@synthesize myButton, myActivityIndicator, myProgressView;
NSOperationQueue *serialQueue;
NSOperationQueue *mainQueue;

- (void)viewDidLoad{
    [super viewDidLoad];

    //Create the operation queues
    mainQueue = [NSOperationQueue mainQueue];

    serialQueue = [[NSOperationQueue alloc] init];
    serialQueue.maxConcurrentOperationCount = 1;

}

@end
```

You can just get a reference to the main queue by using the NSOperationQueue mainQueue method. This is a Singleton that always returns an instance of the main queue. You set up the serial queue using the alloc and init constructor. By setting the maxConcurrentOperationCount to one, you are making this a serial queue because it may only do one operation at a time.

Once you have the queues set up, you can use them to schedule your blocks right from the bigTaskAction method.

```objc
-(void)bigTaskAction{

    [serialQueue addOperationWithBlock: ^{

        [mainQueue addOperationWithBlock: ^{

            [self.myActivityIndicator startAnimating];

        }];

        int updateUIWhen = 1000;
        for(int i=0;i<10000;i++){
            NSString *newString = [NSString stringWithFormat:@"i = %i", i];
            NSLog(@"%@", newString);
            if(i == updateUIWhen){
```

```
            float f = (float)i/10000;
            NSNumber *percentDone = [NSNumber numberWithFloat:f];

            [mainQueue addOperationWithBlock: ^{
                [self.myProgressView setProgress:[percentDone floatValue]
                                        animated:YES];

            }];

            updateUIWhen = updateUIWhen + 1000;
        }
    }

    [mainQueue addOperationWithBlock: ^{

        [self.myProgressView setProgress:1.0
                                animated:YES];
        [self.myActivityIndicator stopAnimating];

    }];
  }];
}
```

If you went through Recipe 6.6, you can see that this is essentially following the same pattern as what you did with GCD. See Listings 6-25 through 6-28 for the code.

The Code

Listing 6-25. *AppDelegate.h*

```
#import <UIKit/UIKit.h>

@class ViewController;

@interface AppDelegate : UIResponder <UIApplicationDelegate>

@property (strong, nonatomic) UIWindow *window;

@property (strong, nonatomic) ViewController *viewController;

@end
```

Listing 6-26. *AppDelegate.m*

```
#import "AppDelegate.h"

#import "ViewController.h"

@implementation AppDelegate
```

```
@synthesize window = _window;
@synthesize viewController = _viewController;

- (BOOL)application:(UIApplication *)application didFinishLaunchingWithOptions: ⮐
(NSDictionary *)launchOptions{
    self.window = [[UIWindow alloc] initWithFrame:[[UIScreen mainScreen] bounds]];
    // Override point for customization after application launch.
    self.viewController = [[ViewController alloc] initWithNibName:@"ViewController"
                                                          bundle:nil];
    self.window.rootViewController = self.viewController;
    [self.window makeKeyAndVisible];

    return YES;
}

@end
```

Listing 6-27. *ViewController.h*

```
#import <UIKit/UIKit.h>

@interface ViewController : UIViewController

@property(strong) UIButton *myButton;
@property(strong) UIActivityIndicatorView *myActivityIndicator;
@property(strong) UIProgressView *myProgressView;

@end
```

Listing 6-28. *ViewController.m*

```
#import "ViewController.h"

@implementation ViewController
@synthesize myButton, myActivityIndicator, myProgressView;
NSOperationQueue *serialQueue;
NSOperationQueue *mainQueue;

-(void)bigTaskAction{

    [serialQueue addOperationWithBlock: ^{

        [mainQueue addOperationWithBlock: ^{

            [self.myActivityIndicator startAnimating];

        }];
```

```objc
        int updateUIWhen = 1000;
        for(int i=0;i<10000;i++){
            NSString *newString = [NSString stringWithFormat:@"i = %i", i];
            NSLog(@"%@", newString);
            if(i == updateUIWhen){
                float f = (float)i/10000;
                NSNumber *percentDone = [NSNumber numberWithFloat:f];

                [mainQueue addOperationWithBlock: ^{
                    [self.myProgressView setProgress:[percentDone floatValue]
                                            animated:YES];

                }];

                updateUIWhen = updateUIWhen + 1000;
            }
        }

        [mainQueue addOperationWithBlock: ^{

            [self.myProgressView setProgress:1.0
                                    animated:YES];
            [self.myActivityIndicator stopAnimating];

        }];
    }];
}

- (void)viewDidLoad{
    [super viewDidLoad];

    //Create the operation queues
    mainQueue = [NSOperationQueue mainQueue];

    serialQueue = [[NSOperationQueue alloc] init];
    serialQueue.maxConcurrentOperationCount = 1;

    //Create button
    self.myButton = [UIButton buttonWithType:UIButtonTypeRoundedRect];
    self.myButton.frame = CGRectMake(20, 403, 280, 37);
    [self.myButton addTarget:self
                    action:@selector(bigTaskAction)
            forControlEvents:UIControlEventTouchUpInside];
    [self.myButton setTitle:@"Do Long Task"
                    forState:UIControlStateNormal];
    [self.view addSubview:self.myButton];

    //Create activity indicator
    self.myActivityIndicator = [[UIActivityIndicatorView alloc] init];
    self.myActivityIndicator.frame = CGRectMake(142, 211, 37, 37);
```

```
    self.myActivityIndicator.activityIndicatorViewStyle = ↩
UIActivityIndicatorViewStyleWhiteLarge;
    self.myActivityIndicator.hidesWhenStopped = NO;
    [self.view addSubview:self.myActivityIndicator];

    //Create label
    self.myProgressView = [[UIProgressView alloc] init];
    self.myProgressView.frame = CGRectMake(20, 20, 280, 9);
    [self.view addSubview:self.myProgressView];

}

@end
```

Usage

Run the application. In the iOS Simulator you should see an app with one button and an empty progress view. You will also see a white activity indicator in the middle of the view. Touch the button two times to start bigTask running in two background threads.

As bigTask runs, you should see the progress view filling up in 10% increments until the task is complete. This process will repeat based on the number of times you touched the button. The progress view should not keep jumping back and forth.

Consuming Web Content

This chapter covers how to use web content with Objective-C.

The recipes in this chapter will show you how to:

- Download files with NSURL
- Use web services with XML and JSON
- Parse both XML and JSON data
- Use NSURLConnection to asynchronously consume web content

7.1 Downloading a File

Problem

You want to download a file from the Internet.

Solution

Use NSURL to specify a URL for a file and then use NSData to download the contents of that file into your file system.

> **NOTE:** URL stands for Uniform Resource Locator. A URL is a
> character string that specifies the location of an Internet resource.
> NSURL is a Foundation class that lets you use URLs in Objective-C.

How It Works

For this solution you must have a file available on the Internet that you can
download. I posted a text file to my blog to use in this example. The URL of that
file is:

```
http://howtomakeiphoneapps.com/wp-content/uploads/2012/03/objective-c-recipes-
example-file.txt
```

The first part of this process requires you to create a new NSURL object with the
URL of the resource that you want to download. Using the URL just provided, it
looks like this:

```
NSURL *remoteTextFileURL = [NSURL
URLWithString:@"http://howtomakeiphoneapps.com/wp-
content/uploads/2012/03/objective-c-recipes-example-file.txt"];
```

Next, create a new NSData object with the contents of the NSURL object.

```
NSData *remoteTextFileData = [NSData dataWithContentsOfURL:remoteTextFileURL];
```

You can use the NSData object right in your Objective-C program (see Recipe
4.11 for examples of working with NSData) or save it to the file system like this:

```
[remoteTextFileData writeToFile:@"/Users/Shared/objective-c-recipes-example-file.txt"
                     atomically:YES];
```

See Listing 7-1 for the code.

The Code

Listing 7-1. *main.m*

```
#import <Foundation/Foundation.h>
int main (int argc, const char * argv[]){
    @autoreleasepool {
        NSURL *remoteTextFileURL = [NSURL URLWithString:
@"http://howtomakeiphoneapps.com/wp-content/uploads/2012/03/objective-c-recipes-
example-file.txt"];
        NSData *remoteTextFileData = [NSData dataWithContentsOfURL:remoteTextFileURL];
        [remoteTextFileData writeToFile:@"/Users/Shared/objective-c-recipes-
```

```
example-file.txt"
                              atomically:YES];

    }
    return 0;
}
```

Usage

To try this recipe out, set up a Mac command-line Xcode project and change the code in your `main.m` file to look like the code in Listing 7-1. Build and run the command-line app to download the file into this location on your Mac:

`/Users/Shared/objective-c-recipes-example-file.txt`

Locate and open this file to see if the download was successful.

7.2 Consuming a Web Service Using XML

Problem

You would like to add web services that use XML data to your application.

> **NOTE:** Internet companies publish web services to allow developers to include their services in the developer's applications. Web services work like a web browser. In a web browser, you type in a web address (the request), hit return, and wait for a response from a remote computer on the Internet. When that response comes back, the web browser uses the rules and content in the response to present a web page to you. Web services work the same way except that the application sends the request and gets the response.
>
> Internet companies do their best to formulate web service requests and responses using standard formats that make it easier for the applications to use their services. Web requests are strings of characters (like a web address) while web responses are strings of characters formatted as XML or JSON. XML and JSON will be discussed in full later.

Solution

Formulate a request string based on the documentation that the publisher of the web service provides. Create an NSURL object based on the request string and NSData to download the response from the web service. Use NSXMLParser to go through the XML document that you get back.

How It Works

For this recipe, you are going to learn how to consume a web service that is provided by a company called bitly. This company publishes a web service that you can use to shorten a long URL. All you have to do is send a request to the bitly web service with the long URL along with your bitly credentials in the format that they expect; bitly sends you an XML file with the shortened URL included in the contents.

> **NOTE:** To follow along with this recipe, you need to create a (free) account with bitly and get your own API key and API username. Go to https://bit.ly to get your account.

I'm going to work through this recipe with a command line-based Mac application in Xcode, but you can follow with any project type that you like. Since NSXMLParser uses the Delegation design pattern, you need to locate your code in a class that can adopt a protocol and otherwise support Delegation. Add a new class to your project by going to **File ➤ New File ➤ Objective-C class**. Name the class LinkShortener.

The interface for LinkShortener needs to include a forward declaration for an NSMutableString named recorderString that will record the data you get from the web service. LinkShortener also needs a string for keeping track of the area in the XML file where the XML parser is currently looking. Call that variable currentElement and make both currentElement and recorderString private. Also, you need a forward declaration for the function that you call when you want this object to shorten a URL; call this function getTheShortUrlVersionOfThisLongURL. The interface for LinkShortener should look like this:

```
#import <Foundation/Foundation.h>

@interface LinkShortener : NSObject{
    @private
    NSMutableString *recorderString;
```

```
    NSString *currentElement;
}

-(NSString *)getTheShortURLVersionOfThisLongURL:(NSString *)longURL;

@end
```

How XML Parsing Works

Before we move on, let's discuss what XML is and how `NSXMLParser` reads XML documents. XML stands for EXtensible Markup Language and it's used to store and transport data. XML works by enclosing data with opening and closing tags. Opening tags are characters surrounded by the characters ‹ and ›. Closing tags are characters surrounded by the characters ‹/ and ›. The tags and data together are referred to as an element.

For example, if I had an XML data type for a person, I might use an opening tag like `<Person>`. The closing tag would look like `</Person>`. The characters in the middle are the data. The whole thing together looks like this:

```
<Person>Matthew J. Campbell</Person>
```

XML tags are intended to be descriptive so it's obvious what the tags mean. An entire document will have many tags with data and can be arranged in a hierarchy. So you may have tagged data within other tagged data, like this:

```
<Person>
        <Name>Matthew J. Campbell</Name>
        <Gender>Male</Gender>
</Person>
```

`NSXMLParser` reads through an XML document starting from the beginning, reading element by element until it reaches the end. If `NSXMLParser` was reading the XML above, it would start with the `Person` element, and then move on to the `Name` element, and then the `Gender` element. This method of parsing XML is called Simple API for XML (SAX).

You're going to use delegation to parse the XML data that you get from bitly. As the parser looks at each element in the document, it sends a message to the delegate `LinkShortener` object, giving you a chance to extract the data from each element.

So `LinkShortener` needs to be able to act as a delegate for `NSXMLParser` and this means that you need `LinkShortener` to adopt the `NSXMLParserDelegate` protocol. Do this by including the protocol name right after the `NSObject` superclass.

```
#import <Foundation/Foundation.h>

@interface LinkShortener : NSObject<NSXMLParserDelegate>{
    @private
    NSMutableString *recorderString;
    NSString *currentElement;
}

-(NSString *)getTheShortURLVersionOfThisLongURL:(NSString *)longURL;

@end
```

Now that you have adopted this protocol, you need to implement at least these two delegate methods: parser:didStartElement:namespaceURI:qualifiedName:attributes: and parser:foundCharacters:.

Since your application only needs data from one element in the XML file, you can get away with only these two delegate methods. But, if necessary, you can always implement parser:didEndElement:namespaceURI:qualifiedName: if you want to be notified when the parser encounters a closing tag in the XML data.

Open LinkShortener.m to implement the first delegate method.

```
- (void) parser:(NSXMLParser *)parser
didStartElement:(NSString *)elementName
   namespaceURI:(NSString *)namespaceURI
  qualifiedName:(NSString *)qName
     attributes:(NSDictionary *)attributeDict{

        currentElement = [elementName copy];
        if ([elementName isEqualToString:@"shortUrl"]) {
                recorderString = [[NSMutableString alloc] init];
        }
}
```

Remember that this delegate method executes each time a new XML element is reached (most XML files have lots of elements in them). For this reason, make a copy of the parameter elementName and put it into currentElement. You want to be able to keep track of what element you are in when the other delegate methods execute.

The other significant part of this code is the if statement where you test to see if you are in the element that corresponds to shortUrl. This is the element where bitly puts the shortened URL string. If you do encounter the shortULR element, you will create and initialize a new NSMutableString to be used later to record what is found in the element.

Now you can implement the next delegate method. This delegate method executes each time characters are encountered in an XML element in the file. You can test to see if the XML parser is in the shortUrl element. If the answer is yes, append the characters that are found to the recorderString NSMutableString.

```
- (void)parser:(NSXMLParser *)parser foundCharacters:(NSString *)string{
        if ([currentElement isEqualToString:@"shortUrl"])
                [recorderString appendString:string];

}
```

All of this prepares LinkShortener to receive the XML data. Now you can prepare the request and send that off to the web server to download the response. All of this takes place in the function getTheShortUrlVersionOfThisLongURL:, which you can start coding in the LinkShortener implementation file.

```
-(NSString *)getTheShortUrlVersionOfThisLongURL:(NSString *)longURL{

}
```

The first thing you want to do in this function is to compose the request string. To do this, you compose a string based on the request string that bitly requires along with the longURL parameter and your own API key and API login.

```
#warning Get your API Login from https://bitly.com/a/your_api_key and put it here before ↵
running
NSString *APILogin = @"[YOUR API LOGIN]";
#warning Get your API key from https://bitly.com/a/your_api_key and put it here before ↵
running
NSString *APIKey = @"[YOUR API KEY]";

NSString *requestString = [[NSString alloc] initWithFormat:↵
@"http://api.bit.ly/shorten?version=2.0.1&longUrl=%@&login=%@&apiKey=%@&format=xml",↵
 longURL, APILogin, APIKey];
```

I've included warnings in the example code so that you remember to include your own credentials here. Also, if you look closely at the first part of the request string you'll see that there is a format parameter with the value of xml being returned, (format=xml). This is how you tell bitly that you want the response to come back as XML.

Next, you need an NSURL object, which you can make based on the request string.

```
NSURL *requestURL = [NSURL URLWithString:requestString];
```

To download the data, use NSData as you did in Recipe 7.1.

```
recorderString = nil;
NSData *responseData = [NSData dataWithContentsOfURL:requestURL];
```

Here is a good place to set `recorderString` to nil just in case this function has been used before in this object's lifetime. Now that you've downloaded the data, you may use `NSXMLParser` to go through the XML and pick out the content included in the `shortUrl` element.

To do this, instantiate a new `NSXMLParser` with the downloaded NSData object, set this object's delegate to `self`, and then send the parse message to the `NSXMLParser` object.

```
NSXMLParser *xmlParser = [[NSXMLParser alloc] initWithData:responseData];
xmlParser.delegate = self;
[xmlParser parse];
```

At this point, the XML parser looks through the data and uses the delegate methods previously coded to pick out the meaningful content. Everything that the XML parser finds is recorded in `recorderString`. Once the XML parser is finished, you can return the results back to the caller.

```
if(recorderString)
    return [recorderString copy];
else
    return nil;
```

You can use an `if` statement here to send a copy of `recorderString` if any data was found.

Finally, to use the function from another part of your program, you need to import the `LinkShortener` header file, instantiate a `LinkShortener` object, and then use the function with a long URL. Here is how to do this from `main.m`:

```
#import <Foundation/Foundation.h>
#import "LinkShortener.h"

int main(int argc, const char * argv[]){
    @autoreleasepool {

        NSString *longURL = @"http://howtomakeiphoneapps.com/how-to-↩
asynchronously-add-web-content-to-uitableview-in-ios/1732/";

        LinkShortener *linkShortener = [[LinkShortener alloc] init];

        NSString *shortURL = [linkShortener getTheShortURLVersionOfThisLongURL:longURL];

        NSLog(@"shortURL = %@", shortURL);

    }
    return 0;
```

```
}
```

See Listings 7-2 through 7-4 for the code.

The Code

Listing 7-2. *LinkShortener.h*

```
#import <Foundation/Foundation.h>

@interface LinkShortener : NSObject<NSXMLParserDelegate>{
    @private
    NSMutableString *recorderString;
    NSString *currentElement;
}

-(NSString *)getTheShortURLVersionOfThisLongURL:(NSString *)longURL;

@end
```

Listing 7-3. *LinkShortener.m*

```
#import "LinkShortener.h"

@implementation LinkShortener

-(NSString *)getTheShortURLVersionOfThisLongURL:(NSString *)longURL{

    #warning Get your API Login from https://bitly.com/ and put it here before running
    NSString *APILogin = @"[YOUR API LOGIN]";
    #warning Get your API key from https://bitly.com/ and put it here before running
    NSString *APIKey = @"[YOUR API KEY]";

    NSString *requestString = [[NSString alloc] initWithFormat:↵
@"http://api.bit.ly/shorten?version=2.0.1↵
&longUrl=%@&login=%@&apiKey=%@&format=xml",↵
longURL, APILogin, APIKey];

    NSURL *requestURL = [NSURL URLWithString:requestString];
    recorderString = nil;
    NSData *responseData = [NSData dataWithContentsOfURL:requestURL];
    NSXMLParser *xmlParser = [[NSXMLParser alloc] initWithData:responseData];
    xmlParser.delegate = self;
    [xmlParser parse];

    if(recorderString)
        return [recorderString copy];
    else
        return nil;;
```

```objc
}

- (void) parser:(NSXMLParser *)parser
didStartElement:(NSString *)elementName
   namespaceURI:(NSString *)namespaceURI
  qualifiedName:(NSString *)qName
     attributes:(NSDictionary *)attributeDict{

        currentElement = [elementName copy];
        if ([elementName isEqualToString:@"shortUrl"]) {
                recorderString = [[NSMutableString alloc] init];
        }
}

- (void)parser:(NSXMLParser *)parser foundCharacters:(NSString *)string{
        if ([currentElement isEqualToString:@"shortUrl"])
                [recorderString appendString:string];

}

@end
```

Listing 7-4. *main.m*

```objc
#import <Foundation/Foundation.h>
#import "LinkShortener.h"

int main(int argc, const char * argv[]){
    @autoreleasepool {

        NSString *longURL = @"http://howtomakeiphoneapps.com/↵
how-to-asynchronously-add-web-content-to-uitableview-in-ios/1732/";

        LinkShortener *linkShortener = [[LinkShortener alloc] init];

        NSString *shortURL = [linkShortener getTheShortURLVersionOfThisLongURL:longURL];

        NSLog(@"shortURL = %@", shortURL);

    }
    return 0;
}
```

Usage

To use the URL shortener function, import the header file into the class where
you want to use the functionality. Then instantiate a LinkShortener object from
the LinkShortener class. Finally, to use the function, send the message

getTheShortURLVersionOfThisLongURL: with the long URL as a parameter to the LinkShortener object. The function will return the shortened URL if the web request was successful and nil if the request was not successful. Here is what you should see in your own console log:

shortURL = http://bit.ly/yFmJFh

> **NOTE:** The shortened URL that you receive back from bitly may not look exactly like the one I received when I tested this code.

7.3 Consuming a Web Service Using JSON

Problem

You would like to add web services that use JSON data to your application.

> **NOTE:** JSON is an alternative to XML that many Internet companies use when implementing web services. JSON stands for JavaScript Object Notation and is used for data storage and transportation. Web services that are implemented as REST (REpresentational State Transfer) web services provide both XML and JSON response data. Other types of web services may only provide one or the other.

Solution

As in Recipe 7.2, formulate a request string based on the documentation that the publisher of the web service provides. Create an NSURL object based on the request string and NSData to download the response from the web service. Use NSJSONSerialization to parse the JSON data that you get back.

> **NOTE:** NSJSONSerialization is available starting with Mac OSX 10.7 and iOS 5.0.

How It Works

This recipe uses the same bitly web service and requires the same process to request and download the results as was shown in Recipe 7.2. However, NSJSONSerialization doesn't use delegation, so you don't need to add a new file or class to accommodate JSON parsing with NSJSONSerialization.

Since you don't need a separate class for this, you can locate the code needed to construct the request string wherever in your application you need to use the web service. If you continue to use a command-line Mac app, this code could go right into the main.m file. Here is how to construct the request string:

```
NSString *longURL = @"http://howtomakeiphoneapps.com/↵
how-to-asynchronously-add-web-content-to-uitableview-in-ios/1732/";

#warning Get your API Login from https://bitly.com/ and put it here before running
NSString *APILogin = @"[YOUR API LOGIN]";
#warning Get your API key from https://bitly.com/ and put it here before running
NSString *APIKey = @"[YOUR API KEY]";

NSString *requestString = [[NSString alloc] initWithFormat:↵
@"http://api.bit.ly/shorten?version=2.0.1↵
&longUrl=%@&login=%@&apiKey=%@&format=json", longURL, APILogin, APIKey];
```

Then you can use NSURL and NSData to get the response based on this request string.

```
NSURL *requestURL = [NSURL URLWithString:requestString];

NSData *responseData = [NSData dataWithContentsOfURL:requestURL];
```

JSON Parsing

Next you'll see how to parse JSON. Instead of the tagged data scheme that XML uses, JSON organizes content based on two structures: a collection of name-value pairs and an ordered list of values. A JSON collection of name-value pairs follows the same pattern as an Objective-C NSDictionary while a JSON order list of values corresponds to an Objective-C NSArray.

If you look at a JSON file, you will see these types of structures organized by curly braces instead of the tagged data in an XML file. For example, the JSON version of the Person element described in Recipe 7.2 looks like this:

```
{"Person":"Matthew J. Campbell","Gender":"Male"}
```

Since JSON data is keyed in this way, and the dictionary and array structures map so well to programming languages, JSON is generally much easier to parse. As you'll see in a moment, you have a Foundation function at your disposal that simply turns your JSON response into an NSDictionary with the JSON content ready for you to use.

The first thing you need is an NSError object, which you pass with the JSONObjectWithData:options:error: message that must be sent to NSJSONSerialization.

```
NSError *error = nil;
NSDictionary *bitlyJSON = [NSJSONSerialization JSONObjectWithData:responseData
                                                          options:0
                                                            error:&error];
```

The result of this function is assigned to an NSDictionary that holds the contents of the JSON data. To get to the content that you need, simply access the various objects that are in the dictionary. This often requires you to reference nested dictionaries, arrays, and objects. You need to examine the response data to figure out precisely what you need. Here is what you do to get the bitly short URL from your response data:

```
if(!error){
    NSDictionary *results = [bitlyJSON objectForKey:@"results"];
    NSDictionary *resultsForLongURL = [results objectForKey:longURL];
    NSString *shortURL = [resultsForLongURL objectForKey:@"shortUrl"];
    NSLog(@"shortURL = %@", shortURL);
}
else{
    NSLog(@"There was an error parsing the JSON");
}
```

See Listing 7-5 for the code.

The Code

Listing 7-5. *main.m*

```
#import <Foundation/Foundation.h>

int main(int argc, const char * argv[]){
    @autoreleasepool {

        NSString *longURL = @"http://howtomakeiphoneapps.com/↩
how-to-asynchronously-add-web-content-to-uitableview-in-ios/1732/";

        #warning Get your API Login from https://bitly.com/ and put it here before ↩
running
        NSString *APILogin = @"[YOUR API LOGIN]";
        #warning Get your API key from https://bitly.com/ and put it here before ↩
```

```
running
        NSString *APIKey = @"[YOUR API KEY]";

        NSString *requestString = [[NSString alloc] initWithFormat:
@"http://api.bit.ly/shorten?version=2.0.1↵
&longUrl=%@&login=%@&apiKey=%@&format=json", ↵
longURL, APILogin, APIKey];

        NSURL *requestURL = [NSURL URLWithString:requestString];
        NSData *responseData = [NSData dataWithContentsOfURL:requestURL];

        NSError *error = nil;
        NSDictionary *bitlyJSON = [NSJSONSerialization JSONObjectWithData:responseData
                                                        options:0
                                                          error:&error];
        if(!error){
            NSDictionary *results = [bitlyJSON objectForKey:@"results"];
            NSDictionary *resultsForLongURL = [results objectForKey:longURL];
            NSString *shortURL = [resultsForLongURL objectForKey:@"shortUrl"];
            NSLog(@"shortURL = %@", shortURL);
        }
        else{
            NSLog(@"There was an error parsing the JSON");
        }

    }
    return 0;
}
```

Usage

You can use this code from any area in your application. If you are testing this with a Mac command-line application, you can simply include this code in your main.m file, but you need to obtain an API login and API login from bitly. Examine the console log window to see the results of the web service request. You should see something like this:

```
shortURL = http://bit.ly/yFmJFh
```

> **NOTE:** JSON requires far fewer steps than XML and will probably be your first choice when working with web services (when available). However, be aware that JSON may not always be available from the web service and that you must be using Mac OSX 10.7 or iOS 5 or greater to use JSON.

7.4 Asynchronously Consuming Web Content

Problem

You want to be able to consume web content as a background process so that the network activity doesn't affect your user interface.

Solution

Use `NSURLConnection` and `NSURLRequest` when you want to work with the network asynchronously or if you need more control over the process of using network connections and web requests.

How It Works

The first thing you need is a request string to send to a web server. You could use a request string for a web service (as you did in Recipes 7.2 and 7.3) or you could even put in a web page. For this example, I'll use the RSS feed for my blog since I know it will provide some XML data to download.

> **NOTE:** RSS stands for Really Simple Syndication. RSS is used for publishing content like blog posts and podcasts. RSS files are usually large files that are based on XML but also follow additional specifications that help when publishing content. Adding an RSS feed to your application is an easy way to publish information to your users since most blogging software comes with built-in RSS features.

For this recipe, I'm going to use a Mac Cocoa application. You could also use an iOS application here, but you will have problems if you attempt to use a command-line Mac application. This is because the asynchronous methods used with `NSURLConnection` may take longer to execute than the Mac command-line application's lifecycle, so you may never see the results in the console log.

The code is located in the Mac Cocoa application's `AppDelegate.m` file right in the `applicationDidFinishLaunching:` delegate method. The first thing you need is the request string (which, in this example, is my blog's RSS feed).

```
NSString *requestString = @"http://www.howtomakeiphoneapps.com/feed/";
```

Then you can construct an NSURL object based on the request string.

```
NSURL *requestURL = [NSURL URLWithString:requestString];
```

Use the requestURL object to instantiate a new NSURLRequest.

```
NSURLRequest *request = [[NSURLRequest alloc] initWithURL:requestURL
                                         cachePolicy:NSURLRequestReload↵
IgnoringLocalCacheData
                                         timeoutInterval:10];
```

You also get a chance to specify how you want the request to handle caching and a timeout interval. Next, you need to set up an NSOperationQueue, which will be used with NSURLConnection to execute the web request.

```
NSOperationQueue *backgroundQueue =[[NSOperationQueue alloc] init];
```

Finally, use a class method to execute your web request asynchronously. You need three parameters: the NSURLRequest object, the NSOperationQueue object, and a code block. The code block gives you chance to let NSURLConnection know what code to execute after the data is retrieved.

```
[NSURLConnection sendAsynchronousRequest:request
                      queue:backgroundQueue
              completionHandler:^(NSURLResponse *response, NSData *data, ↵
NSError *error) {

    if(!error){
        NSString *requestResults = [[NSString alloc] initWithData:data
                          encoding:NSStringEncodingConversionAllowLossy];

        NSLog(@"requestResults=%@", requestResults);
    }
    else
        NSLog(@"error=%@", error);

            }];
```

> **NOTE:** This feature is only available starting with Mac OSX 10.7 and iOS 5.0.

Take a close look at the completionHandler block to see how to handle the NSData object that is returned. Usually you test the NSError object to see if everything went well before processing the data. Here all you are doing is writing out the entire RSS feed to the console log, but if you want to process the RSS feed, you can set up an XML parser like the one detailed in Recipe 7.2. See Listings 7-6 through 7-8 for the code.

The Code

Listing 7-6. *main.m*

```
#import <Cocoa/Cocoa.h>

int main(int argc, char *argv[]){
    return NSApplicationMain(argc, (const char **)argv);
}
```

Listing 7-7. *AppDelegate.h*

```
#import <Cocoa/Cocoa.h>

@interface AppDelegate : NSObject <NSApplicationDelegate>

@property (assign) IBOutlet NSWindow *window;

@end
```

Listing 7-8. *AppDelegate.m*

```
#import "AppDelegate.h"

@implementation AppDelegate

@synthesize window = _window;

- (void)applicationDidFinishLaunching:(NSNotification *)aNotification{

    NSString *requestString = @"http://www.howtomakeiphoneapps.com/feed/";

    NSURL *requestURL = [NSURL URLWithString:requestString];

    NSURLRequest *request = [[NSURLRequest alloc] initWithURL:↵
requestURL cachePolicy:NSURLRequestReloadIgnoringLocalCacheData timeoutInterval:10];

    NSOperationQueue *backgroundQueue =[[NSOperationQueue alloc] init];

    [NSURLConnection sendAsynchronousRequest:request
                                 queue:backgroundQueue
                     completionHandler:^(NSURLResponse *response, NSData *data, ↵
NSError *error) {

                if(!error){
                    NSString *requestResults = [[NSString alloc] initWithData:data↵
encoding:NSStringEncodingConversionAllowLossy];
                    NSLog(@"requestResults=%@", requestResults);
                    }
```

```
                            else{
                                NSLog(@"error=%@", error);
                            }

                    }];
        }

@end
```

Usage

To try this recipe out, include the code in the app delegate of a Mac or iOS application. Inspect the log to see the data that was downloaded from the Web. To test the error handling, disconnect your Mac from the network and inspect the log to see what the error object reports. If your web request was successful, you should see something like this appear in your console log:

```
requestResults=<?xml version="1.0" encoding="UTF-8"?>
<rss version="2.0"
        xmlns:content="http://purl.org/rss/1.0/modules/content/"
        xmlns:wfw="http://wellformedweb.org/CommentAPI/"
        xmlns:dc="http://purl.org/dc/elements/1.1/"
        xmlns:atom="http://www.w3.org/2005/Atom"
        xmlns:sy="http://purl.org/rss/1.0/modules/syndication/"
        xmlns:slash="http://purl.org/rss/1.0/modules/slash/"
        >

<channel>
        <title>How to Make iPhone Apps</title>
        <atom:link href="http://howtomakeiphoneapps.com/feed/" rel="self"↵
 type="application/rss+xml" />


. . .
```

This code can be included anywhere in your application where you want to consume web content, but don't interfere with or block other processes like your user interface.

Memory Management

This chapter explores how to manage memory with Objective-C.

The recipes in this chapter will show you how to:

- Understand memory management
- Use reference counting to manage memory
- Use Automatic Reference Counting (ARC) to manage memory
- Use garbage collection (GC) to manage memory on the Mac

8.1 Understanding Memory Management

Problem

You want to understand how to manage memory effectively in your Objective-C applications.

Solution

Memory is one of the finite resources that your Objective-C application requires. Every variable and object that you use in Objective-C takes up some memory. Since memory is a finite resource, it's possible to use up all the memory that you have available.

Programmers who work in C-based programming languages like Objective-C need to think about how to manage memory effectively. This is something new to many programmers who work in Java or with scripting languages. Managing memory is one of the toughest problems we deal with in Objective-C.

The consequences for applications with mismanaged memory are severe: applications can become slow or the system may even shut down an application that is using too much memory. Applications can also leak memory. Memory leaks are caused when objects have memory assigned to them that doesn't get reclaimed by the system even though the object can no longer be reached in the application's code.

Let's go over some of the things to think about when deciding how to deal with memory management.

Object Lifecycle

Just like objects in the real world, Objective-C objects are created, live, and then go away. This is the *object lifecycle*.

In terms of memory management, when an object is born, you set aside memory for the object to use. As the object goes on doing what you have programmed it to do, the object continues to require that memory. Once you no longer need the object, you let the object go away. You can reclaim the memory for that object once it has gone away.

Object Ownership

Object ownership is the concept where one entity is responsible for another. When an entity owns an object, the entity is responsible for cleaning the object up when the entity is done with it. For example, if an object was created and used in the main function, then the main function is responsible for the object. This means that it's the main function's responsibility to clean up the object.

What makes this concept a bit more complicated is that objects can be owned by more than one entity. So, an object may be created and owned in the main function and also be used by another entity that will claim ownership of the object.

A common situation where you will see multiple object ownership is when you use arrays. Arrays are indexed lists of objects, and when you put an object into an array, the array claims ownership of the object. So, if I create an object in the main function and then put that object into an array, both the main function and the array will claim ownership of the object—and both are responsible for cleaning up the object.

Clearly, keeping track of all the possible object relationships that could happen can quickly become daunting without some kind of system to help. Objective-C does provide a system called *reference counting* that can help you keep track of object lifecycles and object ownerships.

Reference Counting

Reference counting is a system for keeping track of how many entities are claiming ownership of an object. Each object has a special number called the *reference count* associated with the object. The reference count represents how many objects claim ownership over the object.

When an object is created, the object gets assigned a reference count of one. This represents the ownership claim of the entity that just created the object. For each entity that claims ownership of the object, the object's reference count gets increased by one.

Once an entity no longer requires ownership of an object, the entity can decrease the reference count of the object. When an object's reference count reaches zero, the system will automatically destroy the object and the system will be able to reclaim the memory.

With reference counting, Objective-C takes care of the actual object destruction. Owner objects are only responsible for releasing their claim of ownership on the object.

Autorelease

There are situations where this reference counting system breaks down because it's unclear who is supposed to claim ownership of an object. For example, some classes provide convenient objects that are meant to be temporary through functions. In such cases, the object creator can't claim ownership because the creator class will never get the chance to release ownership, and you can't assume that the receiver will take responsibility of the created object.

Objective-C helps by providing a way to relinquish ownership of an object in a deferred way. So I can create an object and say that at some point in the relatively near future the object can be destroyed. This is called *autorelease*.

Automatic Reference Counting (ARC)

Automatic Reference Counting, or ARC, is a compiler-level system that automates the process of reference counting. ARC is available starting with iOS

5 and Mac OSX 10.6. with Xcode 4.2 for iOS and Xcode 4.3 for Mac. The recipes in this book have mostly been written using ARC.

ARC essentially automates what you will be doing in this chapter. Before your Objective-C program is compiled, all the code needed for reference counting to work is inserted into your program.

Garbage Collection

Garbage collection is another type of memory management system that is used to automate memory management. This method has the concept of a *garbage collector* that periodically looks for objects that are no longer being used and then takes them away.

Garbage collection is only available for Mac OSX starting with version 10.5. Note that iOS applications can't use garbage collection.

In garbage collection, objects can have either a strong or weak reference to a root object. The root object is usually a top-level application object. For example, a Mac application has an object of type NSApplication that is responsible for the application as a whole. Every other object is contained in the NSApplication object, making the NSApplication object the root object. Objects with a strong reference to the root object can be reached by the root object, while objects with a weak reference can't be reached by the root object.

Periodically, the garbage collection mechanism is activated and any objects with a weak reference are destroyed.

Memory Management Options

With Objective-C, you have three options when you want to implement memory management: manual memory management using reference counting, automatic reference counting (ARC), or garbage collection (excluding iOS applications).

Manual memory management is something that any Objective-C program can use. However, as you'll see in this chapter, manual memory management is a detailed and time-consuming task.

Automatic Reference Counting is available for Mac and iOS but only for more recent versions of the operating systems. Generally, I recommend using ARC if you're developing a new application because it's efficient and it will work on both Mac and iOS. Garbage collection is an option if you are just working on Mac apps.

> **NOTE:** In this chapter, you will see how to do manual memory management as well as garbage collection. ARC isn't specifically covered since it's used in the recipes in the other chapters.

8.2 Setting up an Application without ARC

Problem

You want to set up an application that doesn't use ARC to manage memory.

Solution

When you set up a new Xcode project, you will be presented with a screen that is titled "Choose options for your new project." One of the options is a checkbox that says "Use Automatic Reference Counting." Make sure that this option is left unchecked.

You can set up your project like this for a Mac application, Mac command-line applications, or any iOS application. For the purposes of most of the recipes in this chapter (except for the one on garbage collection), I'll use an iOS application.

How It Works

Xcode sets up your project based on the settings that you provide. When you choose to not use ARC in the options screen, Xcode remembers to compile your project with the compiler setting that indicates to not use ARC. Xcode also allows you to send particular messages required for memory management.

These messages are `retain`, `release`, `autorelease`, and `dealloc`. If you try to use these messages in an ARC project, you will get a compiler error, but with this non-ARC project you'll use these messages to implement the reference counting system.

In fact, if you look at the `AppDelegate.m` file, you will see an example of a `dealloc` method that Xcode automatically coded for you. This `dealloc` method includes some memory management code that I'll cover in the next recipe. See Listings 8-1 through 8-3 for the code.

```
- (void)dealloc{
    [_window release];
    [super dealloc];
}
```

The Code

Listing 8-1. *main.m*

```
#import <UIKit/UIKit.h>

#import "AppDelegate.h"

int main(int argc, char *argv[]){
    @autoreleasepool {
        return UIApplicationMain(argc, argv, nil, NSStringFromClass([AppDelegate ↵
class]));
    }
}
```

Listing 8-2. *AppDelegate.h*

```
#import <UIKit/UIKit.h>

@interface AppDelegate : UIResponder <UIApplicationDelegate>

@property (strong, nonatomic) UIWindow *window;

@end
```

Listing 8-3. *AppDelegate.m*

```
#import "AppDelegate.h"

@implementation AppDelegate

@synthesize window = _window;

- (void)dealloc{
    [_window release];
    [super dealloc];
}

- (BOOL)application:(UIApplication *)application ↵
didFinishLaunchingWithOptions:(NSDictionary *)launchOptions{
    self.window = [[[UIWindow alloc] initWithFrame:[[UIScreen mainScreen] bounds]] ↵
autorelease];
    self.window.backgroundColor = [UIColor whiteColor];
```

```
    [self.window makeKeyAndVisible];
    return YES;
}
```

```
@end
```

Usage

You use this project like any of the others. For now, just take a look at some of the differences in the app delegate that Xcode created for you. The `dealloc` method is included here. If you look closely at the constructor for the `window` property in the `application:applicationDidFinishLaunchingWithOptions:` method, you can see that the `window` object was sent an `autorelease` message. Both of these are examples of what you'll be doing in the next few recipes for memory management.

8.3 Using Reference Counting to Manage Memory

Problem

You want to use an object in your application and need to make sure that the object's memory is being managed effectively.

Solution

When an object is created using the messages `alloc`, `new`, or `copy`, the entity where the constructor code is located claims ownership of the object and the object's reference count is set to one. When the object is no longer needed, the owner is responsible for sending a `release` message to the object.

How It Works

After you create and use an object, send a release message. For example, if I create an `NSObject` with `alloc` and `init`, I use the object. When I finish, I send the `release` message to let Objective-C destroy the object.

```
NSObject *obj = [[NSObject alloc] init];
```

```
NSLog(@"obj's description is %@", [obj description]);

[obj release];
```

In the first line, I use `alloc` to create an NSObject that has a reference count of one. The reference count is still one when I use the object to write out a message to the log. After the third line of code when I sent the release message, the object's reference count becomes zero and Objective-C automatically destroys the object.

That's really all that you need to do. Effective memory management comes down to consistency and absolutely following a series of simple rules. This code reflects the following rule:

> **RULE:** Always match `alloc`, `new`, and `copy` with a release message.

While it's not really needed in this example, it is possible to increment an object's reference count. You can do this by sending the retain message to the object. The retain message means that an entity is claiming ownership of an object. If you sent a retain message to `obj`, you would increase the reference count of `obj` to two.

```
NSObject *obj = [[NSObject alloc] init];

NSLog(@"obj's description is %@", [obj description]);

[obj retain];

[obj release];
```

In effect, you are claiming double ownership of this object. If you just left this code alone, you would have a problem. The object's reference count starts off as one and then goes to two after the retain message. Then the reference count goes back down to one when you release it. But, if you leave the code as-is, Objective-C will never be able to destroy the object because the reference count never reaches zero.

When this happens, you get a memory leak. As mentioned, memory leaks are caused by objects that use memory and never let the system reclaim the memory. If left unchecked, memory leaks can cause your application to slow down or crash.

To fix this problem, you must send another release message to `obj` when you're finished with it.

```
NSObject *obj = [[NSObject alloc] init];

NSLog(@"obj's description is %@", [obj description]);

[obj retain];

[obj release];
```

[obj release];

This leads to another memory management rule.

> **RULE:** Always match each retain with a release.

Basically, you want to make sure your object's reference count is zero when you are finished with the object. See Listing 8-4 for the code.

The Code

Listing 8-4. *main.m*

```
#import <UIKit/UIKit.h>

#import "AppDelegate.h"

int main(int argc, char *argv[]){
    @autoreleasepool {

        NSObject *obj = [[NSObject alloc] init];

        NSLog(@"obj's description is %@", [obj description]);

        [obj retain];

        [obj release];

        [obj release];

        return UIApplicationMain(argc, argv, nil, NSStringFromClass([AppDelegate ↵
class]));
    }
}
```

Usage

You can include the code from Listing 8-4 in your own main function to test it out. By itself, the code doesn't do much other than write to the log, but you need to follow this pattern whenever you use objects while managing memory manually.

8.4 Adding Memory Management to Your Custom Classes

Problem

You have custom classes that could claim ownership of objects and you want to make sure that they will manage memory correctly.

Solution

There are two major situations where memory management becomes an issue in a custom class: property getter and setter code, and the `dealloc` method. Properties need to be configured to claim ownership of objects that are assigned to the instance variables that hold the reference to the object. The `dealloc` method is a special method that Objective-C calls right before an object is destroyed. You need to implement a `dealloc` method for each custom class.

How It Works

The example used in this recipe expands on the `Car` class that you coded back in Recipes 1.4 and 1.6. You are going to add the necessary code to this class to make sure that you are following the memory management rules mentioned in Recipe 8.3.

In case you forgot, here is how to use the `Car` class. Note that I put in a release message this time since you're not using ARC.

```
#import <UIKit/UIKit.h>
#import "AppDelegate.h"
#import "Car.h"

int main(int argc, char *argv[]){
    @autoreleasepool {
```

```
        [Car writeDescriptionToLogWithThisDate:[NSDate date]];

        Car *c = [[Car alloc] init];

        c.name = @"New Car Name";

        [c writeOutThisCarsState];

        [c release];

        return UIApplicationMain(argc, argv, nil, NSStringFromClass([AppDelegate ↲
class]));
    }
}
```

Strong Property References

The first thing that you need to look at here is the property declaration for name.
When you originally coded this, you declared the property like this:

```
@property(strong) NSString *name;
```

The strong keyword means that you are going to take ownership of any object
that is assigned to the name property here.

> **NOTE:** Before ARC was introduced, you would use the retain
> keyword here instead of the strong keyword. You can still use retain
> here if you wish since retain has the same meaning as strong. The
> reason that retain was used before was because this meant that a
> retain message was to be sent to the object after it was assigned.
> You will see both retain and strong.

What you need to do is go back to the getter and setter code and make sure
that you are taking ownership of these objects by sending a retain message.
Right now you have this setter code in the Car implementation:

```
-(void)setName:(NSString *)name{
    name_ = name;
}
```

As you can see, name is not being retained, so you aren't taking ownership of
name. It is possible that you could have a situation where your name property is
assigned to you but then gets released by the other object owners. When you
attempt to use name, you will get a memory warning and your app will crash.

To fix this problem, you must take ownership of name by sending a retain message to name before assigning name to your local instance name_.

```
-(void)setName:(NSString *)name{
    [name retain];
    [name_ release];
    name_ = name;
}
```

As you can see, you also sent a release message to name_ before assigning the new name object to name_. The idea here is that you want to relinquish ownership of any previous name objects you had a claim to and claim ownership of the new name object.

> **NOTE:** You may also use the @synthesize directive here instead of coding your own assessors, and Objective-C will automatically handle the retain and release for you behind the scenes.

The dealloc Method

The dealloc method is called by Objective-C right before an object is destroyed. The purpose of dealloc is to give you a chance to release any objects that you have ownership of before the owner object is destroyed. You need to override the dealloc method for each custom class that you create. You release each of your local instances and then set them to nil.

Here is how you could code a dealloc method for your Car class:

```
-(void)dealloc{
    NSLog(@"%@'s dealloc is executing", self.name);
    [super dealloc];
    [name_ release];
    name_ = nil;
}
```

As you can see, you must send the dealloc method to the superclass first because anything that your parent object is holding on to must be released as well. Here it's very important to release any objects that are marked with a strong reference. You should also set any object to nil here. See Listings 8-5 through 8-7 for the code.

The Code

Listing 8-5. *Car.h*

```objectivec
#import <Foundation/Foundation.h>

@interface Car : NSObject{
@private
    NSString *name_;
}

@property(strong) NSString *name;

+(void)writeDescriptionToLogWithThisDate:(NSDate *)date;

-(void)writeOutThisCarsState;

@end
```

Listing 8-6. *Car.m*

```objectivec
#import "Car.h"

@implementation Car

-(void)setName:(NSString *)name{
    [name retain];
    [name_ release];
    name_ = name;
}

-(NSString *) name{
    return name_;
}

+(void)writeDescriptionToLogWithThisDate:(NSDate *)date{
        NSLog(@"Today's date is %@ and this class represents a car", date);
}

-(void)writeOutThisCarsState{
        NSLog(@"This car is a %@", self.name);
}

-(void)dealloc{
    NSLog(@"%@'s dealloc is executing", self.name);
    [super dealloc];
    [name_ release];
    name_ = nil;
}
```

@end

Listing 8-7. *main.m*

```objc
#import <UIKit/UIKit.h>
#import "AppDelegate.h"
#import "Car.h"

int main(int argc, char *argv[]){
    @autoreleasepool {

        [Car writeDescriptionToLogWithThisDate:[NSDate date]];

        Car *c = [[Car alloc] init];

        c.name = @"New Car Name";

        [c writeOutThisCarsState];

        [c release];

        return UIApplicationMain(argc, argv, nil, NSStringFromClass([AppDelegate ⏎
class]));
    }
}
```

Usage

To use this code, add the Car class from the listings to your Xcode project. You can add the code that creates the Car objects right into your own main.m file to test out this recipe for yourself. Build and run the project to see the results of the program. You can see when the dealloc has executed if you examine the log.

```
This car is a New Car Name
New Car Name's dealloc is executing
```

If you comment out the release message that you sent to c in the main.m file and re-run your Xcode project, you'll see that dealloc was never reached and that the objects in c were never released.

8.5 Using Autorelease

Problem

You want to return an object that was created with an `alloc`, `new`, or `copy` from a function on a custom class. You can't release the object before you return the object to the caller because if the caller attempts to use the object, it will get a memory error and the application will crash. If you don't release the object, you violate the first memory management rule and risk causing a memory leak.

Solution

Before returning an object to a caller, send the `autorelease` message to the object. This is a way to send a deferred `release` message to an object. The idea is that you don't want the object destroyed immediately because the caller needs the object temporarily, but you do want the object to eventually be released and destroyed. Or you may want the caller to claim ownership of the object by sending a `retain` message.

How It Works

`Autorelease` is used in `Foundation` objects that provide functions that return objects but without the usual `alloc` and `init` messages. For instance, `NSDate` has a function `date` that returns an `NSDate` object populated with the current date and time. Although you can see this for yourself, in the `NSDate` `date` function code an `autorelease` message is sent to the object before being returned to you.

```
NSDate *today = [NSDate date];
NSLog(@"Today's date is %@", today);
```

You can use this object and you don't need to worry about releasing the object because you never used the `alloc`, `new`, or `copy` functions to create the `today` object. For your purposes, the reference count is zero and you are not violating the first memory management rule. But you also can't assume that this `today` object will not be destroyed sometime in the future unless you claim ownership.

If you wanted to claim ownership of the `today` object, you could send a `retain` message to the `today` object. This would make the reference count of date equal to one and the object would remain with you even when the deferred `release` message is sent to the object.

For example, if you want to ensure that today would remain for a bit longer, you could do something like this:

```
NSDate *today = [NSDate date];
NSLog(@"Today's date is %@", today);
[today retain];

//do other things...

[today release];
```

Now you know that you can use the today object until you're finished. And you're staying in line with the second memory management rule.

When you create functions like the NSDate date function, you also need to use autorelease. To see how to use autorelease, add a function to the Car class from Recipe 8.4. What you want to do is code a function that will return a Car object to the caller based on a name parameter that the caller provides.

The first thing you need to do is provide a forward declaration in the Car.h file.

```
+(Car *)carWithThisName:(NSString *)carName;
```

You can see that this is a class function because the function starts off with a plus sign. Also, the class Car is specified as the return type, so you know that this function will be returning a Car object. You also have a parameter to allow the caller to specify the name for the Car object that they will get back.

When you move on to the implementation, your first instinct might be to create a new Car object with alloc and init and assign the name property before returning the new object to the caller. Here's what might end up in the implementation (Car.m):

```
+(Car *)carWithThisName:(NSString *)carName{
    Car *car = [[Car alloc] init];
    car.name = carName;

    return car;
}
```

What you're doing is creating a new object and claiming ownership over the object when you use the alloc message. Then you return the object without releasing the object, so you're violating the first rule of memory management. Your caller has no way of knowing that the returned object has a reference count of one, so right now you would end up with a memory leak.

To fix this, all you need to do is send the autorelease message before returning the object to the caller.

```
+(Car *)carWithThisName:(NSString *)carName{
```

```
    Car *car = [[Car alloc] init];
    car.name = carName;
    [car autorelease];

    return car;
}
```

This gives the Car a deferred release message, which makes Car a temporary object.

This example also implies yet another memory management rule.

> **RULE:** Always send an autorelease message to objects in functions before returning them to callers.

There is a complementary rule that goes along with this one.

> **RULE:** Always assume that objects returned from functions are autoreleased and therefore temporary unless retained.

Here is how you could use the Car object:

```
Car *tempCar = [Car carWithThisName:@"Temporary Car"];

[tempCar writeOutThisCarsState];
```

See Listings 8-8 through 8-12 for the code.

The Code

Listing 8-8. *Car.h*

```
#import <Foundation/Foundation.h>

@interface Car : NSObject{
@private
    NSString *name_;
}

@property(strong) NSString *name;

+(void)writeDescriptionToLogWithThisDate:(NSDate *)date;

-(void)writeOutThisCarsState;
```

```
+(Car *)carWithThisName:(NSString *)carName;

@end
```

Listing 8-9. *Car.m*

```
#import "Car.h"

@implementation Car

-(void)setName:(NSString *)name{
    [name retain];
    [name_ release];
    name_ = name;
}

-(NSString *) name{
    return name_;
}

+(void)writeDescriptionToLogWithThisDate:(NSDate *)date{
        NSLog(@"Today's date is %@ and this class represents a car", date);
}

-(void)writeOutThisCarsState{
        NSLog(@"This car is a %@", self.name);
}

-(void)dealloc{
    NSLog(@"%@'s dealloc is executing", self.name);
    [super dealloc];
    [name_ release];
    name_ = nil;
}

+(Car *)carWithThisName:(NSString *)carName{
    Car *car = [[Car alloc] init];
    car.name = carName;
    [car autorelease];

    return car;
}

@end
```

Listing 8-10. *AppDelegate.h*

```
#import <UIKit/UIKit.h>
#import "Car.h"
```

```
@interface AppDelegate : UIResponder <UIApplicationDelegate>

@property (strong, nonatomic) UIWindow *window;

@end
```

Listing 8-11. *AppDelegate.m*

```
#import "AppDelegate.h"

@implementation AppDelegate

@synthesize window = _window;

- (void)dealloc{
    [_window release];
    [super dealloc];
}

- (BOOL)application:(UIApplication *)application ↵
didFinishLaunchingWithOptions:(NSDictionary *)launchOptions{

    Car *tempCar = [Car carWithThisName:@"Temporary Car"];

    [tempCar writeOutThisCarsState];

    self.window = [[[UIWindow alloc] initWithFrame:[[UIScreen mainScreen] bounds]] ↵
autorelease];
    self.window.backgroundColor = [UIColor whiteColor];
    [self.window makeKeyAndVisible];
    return YES;
}

@end
```

Listing 8-12. *main.m*

```
#import <UIKit/UIKit.h>
#import "AppDelegate.h"

int main(int argc, char *argv[])
{
    @autoreleasepool {
        NSDate *today = [NSDate date];
        NSLog(@"Today's date is %@", today);
        [today retain];

        //do other things...

        [today release];
```

```
        return UIApplicationMain(argc, argv, nil, NSStringFromClass([AppDelegate ↵
class]));
    }
}
```

Usage

Add the Car.h and Car.m files to your Xcode project and then include the same code that I did in the app delegation's application:didFinishLaunchingWithOptions: method. Remember that the dealloc method that you coded in Recipe 8.4 writes out a message to the log right before Objective-C destroys a Car object. So you can use this to test if sending the autorelease message really lets the object be destroyed.

When this application runs, you will see the message from the dealloc printed out to the log:

```
Today's date is 2012-06-27 14:29:21 +0000
This car is a Temporary Car
Applications are expected to have a root view controller at the end of application ↵
launch
Temporary Car's dealloc is executing
```

You can see that the Car object's state was written out and that the dealloc executed, even though you never sent a release message.

8.6 Enabling Garbage Collection for Mac Applications

Problem

You want to enable garbage collection on your Mac application as an alternative to manual memory management or ARC.

Solution

Enable garbage collection by changing your Xcode project's Objective-C Garbage Collection Setting build setting to either Supported (-fobjc–gc) or Required (-fobjc-gc-only).

How It Works

To enable garbage collection in your Mac application, select your project and your target (see Figure 8-1 for a reference). Then choose the Build Settings tab and look for the Objective-C Garbage Collection build setting. You can use the search box in the upper right hand corner to find this setting more easily. Choose the option Supported (-fobjc-gc) in both spots.

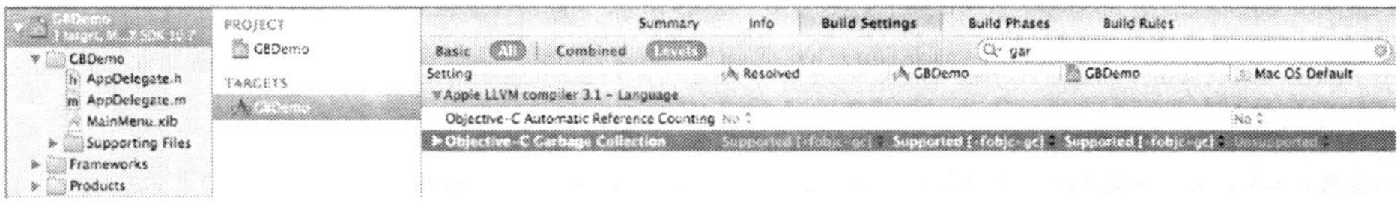

Figure 8-1. *Setting the Objective-C Garbage Collection build setting*

You may also choose the Required (-fobjc-gc-only) option here. The Support option allows you to mix manual memory management with garbage collected memory management while the Required option forces you to use only garbage collection. Once you do this, you can write your code without worrying about manual memory management.

That's all you need to know to get started using garbage collection on the Mac. For the most part, you can treat your Mac applications that are using garbage collection like you would your ARC apps. That is, you can stop worrying about manual memory management.

Chapter

9

Working with Object Graphs

The object graph refers to the objects in an application along with all the object's relationships. In most applications, you will have many objects with many relationships and these can become a bit difficult to manage without some help.

Objective-C comes with some nice features that help you make the most of your object graph. The recipes in this chapter will show you how to:

- Create an object graph
- Use key-value coding (KVC) to dynamically access property values
- Use key paths to access objects in a hierarchy in the object graph
- Use the **Observer** pattern with key-value observing (KVO) to get notifications when property values change
- Use inspection
- Archive and retrieve object graphs

Object-Orientated Vocabulary

Understanding object graphs will be much easier if you recall some object-oriented vocabulary first.

Entity

An *entity* is the abstraction of something that you are working on. Usually, this is something from the real world or a metaphor for an abstract problem. In this chapter, the word "entity" refers to the abstraction itself and not to any particular implementation in code.

Entities are usually described in terms of attributes and behaviors. So, a car entity would have attributes like the color red, four tires, and sport trim. Car behavior would include driving, braking, and turning.

Class

A *class* is the code used to represent an entity inside of your application. This is where you define what an entity is and does inside of your application. The process involves thinking of the entity and using code to represent the entity as an interface and implementation. You code an entity's attributes in a class as properties and an entity's behavior in a class as methods. Many people compare class definitions to blueprints. Coding classes are discussed in detail in Chapter 1 in Recipe 1.3 through Recipe 1.7.

Objects

By itself, a class is just a definition of something and doesn't do much. To use a class, you must instantiate an object from a class. An *object* is a particular instance of a class. You will usually have many objects created from a class definition. Objects are composed of other objects as specified in the object's class definition. You can see a detailed example of creating and using an object from a custom class in Recipe 1.3.

The Object Graph

The *object graph* is an application's network of objects and their relationships. These are the objects that are created and used when a user is actively using an application. The object graph can quickly become very rich and complicated as the user starts to create objects from your class definitions. You can think of your object graph in terms of every object in your application, including system and user interface objects. More likely, you can think of your object graph as the objects that are part of your data model.

> **NOTE:** The data model refers to the Model part of a design pattern called Model-View-Controller (MVC) that splits the responsibilities of an application into three areas: the Model (your representation of the entities you are working with), the View (the user interface), and the Controller (the connection between the Model and the View).

Let's move on to the recipes, beginning with the creation of an object graph.

9.1 Creating an Object Graph

Problem

Your application is working with a rich set of models and you need to set up an object graph that is complex enough to manage your application.

Solution

Use classes to define the properties, methods, and relationships of entities that are necessary to make your application work.

How It Works

For the recipes on KVC, you need a richer object graph to work with. So, let's set up an object graph for an application like a task manager. For such an application, you need a few classes that you can use to set up some objects and relationships.

Working with an Object Graph

In order to make your object graph sufficiently rich, let's set up classes for three entities: Project, Task, and Worker. Project is a class that represents a project that you are working on. A project includes a list of tasks and a worker. Task is a class that represents one thing that you have to do for a project. Worker is a class that represents a person that can do work on a project or task. Let's look at the interfaces for each of these classes so you'll know what you are working with.

Worker

```
#import <Foundation/Foundation.h>

@interface Wrker : NSObject

@property(strong)NSString *name;
@property(strong)NSString *role;

@end
```

Worker holds data for a worker's name and role. In the implementation of Worker, you can override the description function so you can use it later to identify a particular Worker.

```
#import "Worker.h"

@implementation Worker
@synthesize name, role;

-(NSString *)description{
    return [NSString stringWithFormat:@"%@, %@", name, role];
}

@end
```

> **NOTE:** Overriding means that you are replacing a method or function that was defined in the superclass with a new version of that method or function. NSObject already has a function called description that is used when you need a string description of an object. For instance, when you use the %@ format identifier to insert an object into a string, the description function is responsible for providing the string. Overriding description here is an easy way to make sure you can get a sensible description written to the log later.

Task

A task is one activity that needs to be completed for a project. The following is what a header file looks like for the Task class:

```
#import <Foundation/Foundation.h>
#import "Worker.h"

@interface Task : NSObject
```

```
@property(strong)NSString *name;
@property(strong)NSString *details;
@property(strong)NSDate *dueDate;
@property(assign)int priority;
@property(strong)Worker *assignedWorker;

-(void)writeReportToLog;

@end
```

> **NOTE:** Remember that the `strong` keyword is used for objects that you want to claim ownership over, while `assign` is used for primitive types.

As you can see, Task has quite a few properties. The first four are what you might expect to make up a task: the task's name, the task's details, the date the task is due, and the priority. The remaining property, assignedWorker, establishes a *one-to-one relationship* with a Worker object that represents a person assigned to complete this task.

> **NOTE:** Remember that the object graph represents your objects and their relationships. When you add properties to a class that are singular entities, you are establishing a one-to-one relationship. Since you have a Worker object as a property, this means that you can have one worker assigned to each task.

The implementation of Worker includes a report method to write out the status of a task object to the log. Note that I'm leaving some spaces before the content in the log statements so that the output will appear indented when used in conjunction with the Project object's log report output, like so:

```
#import "Task.h"

@implementation Task
@synthesize name, details, dueDate, priority, assignedWorker;

-(void)writeReportToLog{
    NSLog(@"  name = %@", self.name);
    NSLog(@"    description = %@", self.details);
    NSLog(@"    dueDate = %@", self.dueDate);
    NSLog(@"    priority = %i", self.priority);
    NSLog(@"    assignedWorker = %@", self.assignedWorker);
```

```
}

@end
```

Project

`Project` is a higher level entity that has data associated with the project entity itself and relationships with other entities. You can describe a `Project` entity by its name, due date, and description. Like a task, projects have a one-to-one relationship with a worker who is in charge of the project as a whole. Projects also have a *one-to-many relationship* with a list of tasks, since you need to complete a whole series of tasks to get one project finished.

> **NOTE:** You can represent one-to-many relationships in your object graph as well as one-to-one relationships. When you add properties to a class that are collections (like sets, arrays, or dictionaries) you are establishing a one-to-many relationship. Since you have an NSMutableArray object called listOfTasks that follows Project as a property, this means that you can have a collection of tasks associated with a project.

Here is the interface for `Project`:

```
#import <Foundation/Foundation.h>
#import "Task.h"
#import "Worker.h"

@interface Project : NSObject

@property(strong)NSString *name;
@property(strong)NSString *description;
@property(strong)NSDate *dueDate;
@property(strong)NSMutableArray *listOfTasks;
@property(strong)Worker *personInCharge;

-(void)writeReportToLog;

@end
```

Note again how the two relationships here are established: `listOfTasks` is the NSMutableArray that is establishing a one-to-many relationship between `Project` and `Task` and `personInCharge` is establishing a one-to-one relationship between `Project` and `Worker`.

The implementation for `Project` has the code needed to write out a report to the log.

```
#import "Project.h"

@implementation Project
@synthesize name, description, dueDate, listOfTasks, personInCharge;

- (id)init{
    self = [super init];
    if (self) {
        self.listOfTasks = [[NSMutableArray alloc] init];
    }
    return self;
}

-(void)writeReportToLog{
    NSLog(@"PROJECT");
    NSLog(@"   name = %@", self.name);
    NSLog(@"   description = %@", self.description);
    NSLog(@"   dueDate = %@", self.dueDate);
    NSLog(@"   personInCharge = %@", self.personInCharge);
    NSLog(@"TASKS");
    [self.listOfTasks enumerateObjectsUsingBlock:^(id obj, NSUInteger idx, BOOL *stop) {
        [obj writeReportToLog];
    }];
}

@end
```

Also, you need to override the `init` function so you can make sure that the `NSMutableArray` is created and ready to add tasks.

Initializing the Object Graph

To actually use the object graph, you need to create the necessary objects and then assign each to the object relationship to which it belongs. You can do this all in the `main.m` file of a Mac command-line application to model a simple version of an object graph; you will use this in the remaining recipes for this chapter.

The first thing you should do is set up the root object. Every object graph needs to start with at least one root (or first) object. For your example, that is a `Project`.

```
Project *workProject01 =[[Project alloc] init];
workProject01.name = @"Make iOS App";
workProject01.description = @"Make an iOS application for the iPad";
workProject01.dueDate = [NSDate date];
```

This instantiates a `Project` object called `workProject01` and sets the initial properties. Next, you are going to start to establish your first relationship by first creating a `Worker` object for the manager who will be in charge of this project.

```
Worker *personInCharge = [[Worker alloc] init];
personInCharge.name = @"Jane Smith";
personInCharge.role = @"Manager";
```

As you can see, you just create the object and assign some properties to the new Worker object. Now, you can assign this worker to the `wordProject01.personInCharge` property and establish the relationship between this worker and this project.

```
workProject01.personInCharge = personInCharge;
```

Now that this relationship is established, you can use dot notation to either print out the entire `Worker` object or just one of the property values, like role.

```
//Write using description for object
NSLog(@"workProject01.personInCharge = %@", workProject01.personInCharge);
//Just write out role of person in charge
NSLog(@"workProject01.personInCharge.role = %@",
workProject01.personInCharge.role);
```

These two statements print out the following to the log:

```
workProject01.personInCharge = Jane Smith, Manager
workProject01.personInCharge.role = Manager
```

The next part of this exercise takes place in three parts: you create a new task, create a new worker to assign to the task, and then you add the new task to the project's list of tasks. So, you are establishing two relationships this time around.

For the first part, instantiate a new `Task` and set up the property values for it. This part is pretty simple.

```
Task *task01 = [[Task alloc] init];
task01.name = @"Learn Objective-C";
task01.details = @"Learn Objective-C to make Mac apps";
task01.priority = 1;
task01.dueDate = [NSDate date];
```

This just creates the task and sets up some values. Next, you need to do something similar for the new worker.

```
Worker *employee = [[Worker alloc] init];
employee.name = @"David Done";
employee.role = @"Programmer";
```

Finally, you can establish a one-to-one relationship between this task and the new worker. You establish this relationship by assigning `employee` to `task01`, like so:

```
task01.assignedWorker = employee;
```

Now, navigate through to the `employee` object properties using dot notation in a similar way as you did for the `personInCharge` object.

```
//Write using description for object
NSLog(@"task01.assignedWorker = %@", task01.assignedWorker);
//Just write out role of the employee
NSLog(@"task01.assignedWorker.role = %@", task01.assignedWorker.role);
```

These log statements present the following:

```
task01.assignedWorker = David Done, Programmer
task01.assignedWorker.role = Programmer
```

Finally, you are ready to add the task that you just created to the project that you created at the beginning. To do this, you simply add the task to the NSMutableArray `listOfTasks`.

```
[workProject01.listOfTasks addObject:task01];
```

This means that you have one project that has one task associated with the project. You can create as many projects as you like and add them to the list since the relationship between `Project` and `Task` is a one-to-many relationship. See Listing 9-xx for an example of adding a few more tasks to this project.

When you want to reference one of the tasks in this project, you can start by getting a reference to the array. Then select the object either by sending an `objectAtIndex:` message or a `lastObject` message.

```
//Example of using objectAtIndex:
//Task *currentTask = [workProject01.listOfTasks objectAtIndex:0];
Task *currentTask = [workProject01.listOfTasks lastObject];
NSLog(@"currentTask.name = %@", currentTask.name);
```

You should see the following in the log:

```
currentTask.name = Learn Objective-C
```

At this point, you now have a complete object graph to work with. You can send the `writeReportToLog` message to print out the entire contents of the object graph.

```
[workProject01 writeReportToLog];
```

See Listing 9-6 for the details on how that works. Here is the message you would see printed to the log:

```
PROJECT
   name = Make iOS App
   description = Make an iOS application for the iPad
   dueDate = 2012-03-20 15:57:13 +0000
   personInCharge = Jane Smith, Manager
 TASKS
   name = Learn Objective-C
      description = Learn Objective-C to make Mac apps
      dueDate = 2012-03-20 15:57:13 +0000
      priority = 1
      assignedWorker = David Done, Programmer
```

See Listings 9-1 through 9-7.

The Code

Listing 9-1. *Worker.h*

```objc
#import <Foundation/Foundation.h>

@interface Worker : NSObject

@property(strong)NSString *name;
@property(strong)NSString *role;

@end
```

Listing 9-2. *Worker.m*

```objc
#import "Worker.h"

@implementation Worker
@synthesize name, role;

-(NSString *)description{
    return [NSString stringWithFormat:@"%@, %@", name, role];
}

@end
```

Listing 9-3. *Task.h*

```objc
#import <Foundation/Foundation.h>
#import "Worker.h"

@interface Task : NSObject

@property(strong)NSString *name;
```

```objc
@property(strong)NSString *details;
@property(strong)NSDate *dueDate;
@property(assign)int priority;
@property(strong)Worker *assignedWorker;

-(void)writeReportToLog;

@end
```

Listing 9-4. *Task.m*

```objc
#import "Task.h"

@implementation Task
@synthesize name, details, dueDate, priority, assignedWorker;

-(void)writeReportToLog{
    NSLog(@"  name = %@", self.name);
    NSLog(@"    description = %@", self.details);
    NSLog(@"    dueDate = %@", self.dueDate);
    NSLog(@"    priority = %i", self.priority);
    NSLog(@"    assignedWorker = %@", self.assignedWorker);
}

@end
```

Listing 9-5. *Project.h*

```objc
#import <Foundation/Foundation.h>
#import "Task.h"
#import "Worker.h"

@interface Project : NSObject

@property(strong)NSString *name;
@property(strong)NSString *description;
@property(strong)NSDate *dueDate;
@property(strong)NSMutableArray *listOfTasks;
@property(strong)Worker *personInCharge;

-(void)writeReportToLog;

@end
```

Listing 9-6. *Project.m*

```objc
#import "Project.h"

@implementation Project
@synthesize name, description, dueDate, listOfTasks, personInCharge;
```

```objc
- (id)init{
    self = [super init];
    if (self) {
        self.listOfTasks = [[NSMutableArray alloc] init];
    }
    return self;
}

-(void)writeReportToLog{
    NSLog(@"PROJECT");
    NSLog(@"  name = %@", self.name);
    NSLog(@"  description = %@", self.description);
    NSLog(@"  dueDate = %@", self.dueDate);
    NSLog(@"  personInCharge = %@", self.personInCharge);
    NSLog(@"TASKS");
    [self.listOfTasks enumerateObjectsUsingBlock:^(id obj, NSUInteger idx, BOOL *stop) {
        [obj writeReportToLog];
    }];
}

@end
```

Listing 9-7. *main.m*

```objc
#import <Foundation/Foundation.h>
#import "Project.h"
#import "Task.h"

int main(int argc, const char * argv[]){
    @autoreleasepool {
        //Example of object graph
        //Create a new project
        Project *workProject01 =[[Project alloc] init];
        workProject01.name = @"Make iOS App";
        workProject01.description = @"Make an iOS application for the iPad";
        workProject01.dueDate = [NSDate date];

        //Setup a new person to be in charge
        Worker *personInCharge = [[Worker alloc] init];
        personInCharge.name = @"Jane Smith";
        personInCharge.role = @"Manager";

        //Assign person to project
        workProject01.personInCharge = personInCharge;

        //Write using description for object
        NSLog(@"workProject01.personInCharge = %@", workProject01.personInCharge);
        //Just write out role of person in charge
        NSLog(@"workProject01.personInCharge.role = %@", ↵
```

```
workProject01.personInCharge.role);

        //Create new task
        Task *task01 = [[Task alloc] init];
        task01.name = @"Learn Objective-C";
        task01.details = @"Learn Objective-C to make Mac apps";
        task01.priority = 1;
        task01.dueDate = [NSDate date];

        //Set up a new person to assign to the task
        Worker *employee = [[Worker alloc] init];
        employee.name = @"David Done";
        employee.role = @"Programmer";

        //Assign worker to task
        task01.assignedWorker = employee;

        //Write using description for object
        NSLog(@"task01.assignedWorker = %@", task01.assignedWorker);
        //Just write out role of the employee
        NSLog(@"task01.assignedWorker.role = %@", task01.assignedWorker.role);

        //Add task to project
        [workProject01.listOfTasks addObject:task01];

        //To reference a task from the list use the array
        Task *currentTask = [workProject01.listOfTasks lastObject];
        NSLog(@"currentTask.name = %@", currentTask.name);

        //Write out project report:
        [workProject01 writeReportToLog];

        //Note: you will want to do this for each task that the
        //project needs

        //Create new task
        Task *task02 = [[Task alloc] init];
        task02.name = @"Investigate UIKit";
        task02.details = @"Investigate UIKit to see how it works for users.";
        task02.priority = 3;
        task02.dueDate = [NSDate date];

        //Assign worker to task
        task02.assignedWorker = employee;

        //Add task to project
        [workProject01.listOfTasks addObject:task02];

        //Create new task
        Task *task03 = [[Task alloc] init];
```

```
        task03.name = @"Evaluate";
        task03.details = @"Signoff on initial project progress.";
        task03.priority = 1;
        task03.dueDate = [NSDate date];

        //Assign worker to task
        task03.assignedWorker = personInCharge;

        //Add task to project
        [workProject01.listOfTasks addObject:task03];

        //Write out project report
        [workProject01 writeReportToLog];


    }
    return 0;
}
```

Usage

The best way to use this code is to create a Mac command-line application in Xcode and recreate Listings 9-1 through 9-7. Then run the application and inspect the log. You will see something like the following appear, but with different NSDate values:

```
workProject01.personInCharge = Jane Smith, Manager
 workProject01.personInCharge.role = Manager
 task01.assignedWorker = David Done, Programmer
 task01.assignedWorker.role = Programmer
 currentTask.name = Learn Objective-C
 PROJECT
   name = Make iOS App
   description = Make an iOS application for the iPad
   dueDate = 2012-03-20 16:06:55 +0000
   personInCharge = Jane Smith, Manager
 TASKS
   name = Learn Objective-C
     description = Learn Objective-C to make Mac apps
     dueDate = 2012-03-20 16:06:55 +0000
     priority = 1
     assignedWorker = David Done, Programmer
 PROJECT
   name = Make iOS App
   description = Make an iOS application for the iPad
   dueDate = 2012-03-20 16:06:55 +0000
   personInCharge = Jane Smith, Manager
 TASKS
```

```
name = Learn Objective-C
  description = Learn Objective-C to make Mac apps
  dueDate = 2012-03-20 16:06:55 +0000
  priority = 1
  assignedWorker = David Done, Programmer
name = Investigate UIKit
  description = Investigate UIKit to see how it works for users.
  dueDate = 2012-03-20 16:06:55 +0000
  priority = 3
  assignedWorker = David Done, Programmer
name = Evaluate
  description = Signoff on initial project progress.
  dueDate = 2012-03-20 16:06:55 +0000
  priority = 1
  assignedWorker = Jane Smith, Manager
```

This output shows the complete object graph that you will be using as an example throughout this chapter, so this serves as a good reference.

9.2 Using Key-Value Coding

Problem

You would like to get and set property values in your object graph dynamically at runtime without knowing the particular property names beforehand. Since you don't know what properties are to be used, you can't use dot notation to access the property value.

Solution

Use key-value coding (KVC) to get and set properties dynamically. NSObject has built-in methods that let you set or get property values based on a string key that corresponds to the name of a property.

How It Works

Note that you are using the object graph that was created in Recipe 9.1. NSObject has some built-in behavior that indexes each property and each property value in a dictionary data structure. The keys of the dictionary are the declared property names (stored as NSString objects).

Getting Property Values

In order to use this system to get a property value, all you need to do is supply the NSString property name to the NSObject method valueForKey:. Since you don't usually know what kind of object will be returned by valueForKey: you should use the id object type. Name this id object temp and use it throughout this recipe.

```
id temp;
```

To get the name of the project, you need to send the valueForKey: message to the workProject01 and assign the result to temp and use the key @"name".

```
temp = [workProject01 valueForKey:@"name"];
```

To use the value stored in temp, you can treat temp like an NSString object.

```
NSLog(@"temp (from key name) = %@", temp);
```

You should see the following in the log:

```
temp (from key name) = Make iOS App
```

This can be helpful in situations where you just don't know what property value you will need beforehand because you can use strings here. So, instead of including the string directly in the code like I'm doing here, the information could be coming from an external source of input like a text file. This flexibility can provide some dynamic behavior; KVC is also essential to the operation of some systems like data binding and Interface Builder (an Xcode tool used to compose user interfaces without coding).

You can get any type of object with valueForKey:, including custom objects like the Worker object you set up to be in charge of a project.

```
temp = [workProject01 valueForKey:@"personInCharge"];
```

Here is an interesting trick that KVC makes possible. Let's say that you just want to know the name of each task in your project's lists of tasks (a pretty common request). You can use KVC to get an array filled up with just those values. The first thing you want to do is get a reference to the task list.

```
temp = [workProject01 valueForKey:@"listOfTasks"];
```

This works in exactly the same way as the previous examples. Then you want to use valueForKey: again, but this time you send the message to the temp object where you have the task list references and use the @"name" key. This returns an array filled up with each name property value for each Task object inside the task list referenced by the temp object.

```
NSArray *stuffFromTaskList = [temp valueForKey:@"name"];
```

Here, I set the results to an NSArray object because I want to use a particular NSArray enumeration method to demonstrate the results of this operation.

```
[stuffFromTaskList enumerateObjectsUsingBlock:^(id obj, NSUInteger idx, BOOL *stop) {
    NSLog(@"obj: %@", obj);
}];
```

The log should list the following property values:

```
obj: Learn Objective-C
obj: Investigate UIKit
obj: Evaluate
```

Setting Property Values

You can also set property values with KVC. This follows the same pattern as getting property values. You need an NSString key to reference the property and you need to send a message to the object where the property is located.

So, if you want to change the name of the project that you've been working on to "My Pet Project", you could do the following:

```
[workProject01 setValue:@"My Pet Project"
                forKey:@"name"];
```

As before, you can do this with any property. You can also apply a set to each property value in an array. For instance, if you want to reset each task name to "New Task", you would do the following:

```
temp = [workProject01 valueForKey:@"listOfTasks"];
[temp setValue:@"New Task"
        forKey:@"name"];
```

If you were to print out the log report with these changes using the writeReportToLog method, here is what you would now get (updated lines are in bold):

```
PROJECT
   name = My Pet Project
   description = Make an iOS application for the iPad
   dueDate = 2012-03-21 17:01:05 +0000
   personInCharge = Jane Smith, Manager
  TASKS
   name = New Task
      description = Learn Objective-C to make Mac apps
      dueDate = 2012-03-21 17:01:05 +0000
      priority = 1
      assignedWorker = David Done, Programmer
   name = New Task
      description = Investigate UIKit to see how it works for users.
```

```
       dueDate = 2012-03-21 17:01:05 +0000
       priority = 3
       assignedWorker = David Done, Programmer
    name = New Task
       description = Signoff on initial project progress.
       dueDate = 2012-03-21 17:01:05 +0000
       priority = 1
       assignedWorker = Jane Smith, Manager
```

> **NOTE:** The code files that define the `Project`, `Task`, and `Worker` classes
> are the same as in Recipe 9.1.

See Listings 9-8 through 9-14.

The Code

Listing 9-8. *Worker.h*

```
#import <Foundation/Foundation.h>

@interface Worker : NSObject

@property(strong)NSString *name;
@property(strong)NSString *role;

@end
```

Listing 9-9. *Worker.m*

```
#import "Worker.h"

@implementation Worker
@synthesize name, role;

-(NSString *)description{
    return [NSString stringWithFormat:@"%@, %@", name, role];
}

@end
```

Listing 9-10. *Task.h*

```
#import <Foundation/Foundation.h>
#import "Worker.h"

@interface Task : NSObject
```

```
@property(strong)NSString *name;
@property(strong)NSString *details;
@property(strong)NSDate *dueDate;
@property(assign)int priority;
@property(strong)Worker *assignedWorker;

-(void)writeReportToLog;

@end
```

Listing 9-11. *Task.m*

```
#import "Task.h"

@implementation Task
@synthesize name, details, dueDate, priority, assignedWorker;

-(void)writeReportToLog{
    NSLog(@"   name = %@", self.name);
    NSLog(@"    description = %@", self.details);
    NSLog(@"    dueDate = %@", self.dueDate);
    NSLog(@"    priority = %i", self.priority);
    NSLog(@"    assignedWorker = %@", self.assignedWorker);
}

@end
```

Listing 9-12. *Project.h*

```
#import <Foundation/Foundation.h>
#import "Task.h"
#import "Worker.h"

@interface Project : NSObject

@property(strong)NSString *name;
@property(strong)NSString *description;
@property(strong)NSDate *dueDate;
@property(strong)NSMutableArray *listOfTasks;
@property(strong)Worker *personInCharge;

-(void)writeReportToLog;

@end
```

Listing 9-13. *Project.m*

```
#import "Project.h"
```

```
@implementation Project
@synthesize name, description, dueDate, listOfTasks, personInCharge;

- (id)init{
    self = [super init];
    if (self) {
        self.listOfTasks = [[NSMutableArray alloc] init];
    }
    return self;
}

-(void)writeReportToLog{
    NSLog(@"PROJECT");
    NSLog(@"   name = %@", self.name);
    NSLog(@"   description = %@", self.description);
    NSLog(@"   dueDate = %@", self.dueDate);
    NSLog(@"   personInCharge = %@", self.personInCharge);
    NSLog(@"TASKS");
    [self.listOfTasks enumerateObjectsUsingBlock:^(id obj, NSUInteger idx, BOOL *stop) {
        [obj writeReportToLog];
    }];
}

@end
```

Listing 9-14. *main.m*

```
#import <Foundation/Foundation.h>
#import "Project.h"
#import "Task.h"

int main(int argc, const char * argv[]){
    @autoreleasepool {
        //Create a new project
        Project *workProject01 =[[Project alloc] init];
        workProject01.name = @"Make iOS App";
        workProject01.description = @"Make an iOS application for the iPad";
        workProject01.dueDate = [NSDate date];

        //Setup a new person to be in charge
        Worker *personInCharge = [[Worker alloc] init];
        personInCharge.name = @"Jane Smith";
        personInCharge.role = @"Manager";

        //Assign person to project
        workProject01.personInCharge = personInCharge;

        //Create new task
        Task *task01 = [[Task alloc] init];
        task01.name = @"Learn Objective-C";
```

```objc
task01.details = @"Learn Objective-C to make Mac apps";
task01.priority = 1;
task01.dueDate = [NSDate date];

//Setup a new person to assign to the task
Worker *employee = [[Worker alloc] init];
employee.name = @"David Done";
employee.role = @"Programmer";

//Assign worker to task
task01.assignedWorker = employee;

//Add task to project
[workProject01.listOfTasks addObject:task01];

//Create new task
Task *task02 = [[Task alloc] init];
task02.name = @"Investigate UIKit";
task02.details = @"Investigate UIKit to see how it works for users.";
task02.priority = 3;
task02.dueDate = [NSDate date];

//Assign worker to task
task02.assignedWorker = employee;

//Add task to project
[workProject01.listOfTasks addObject:task02];

//Create new task
Task *task03 = [[Task alloc] init];
task03.name = @"Evaluate";
task03.details = @"Signoff on initial project progress.";
task03.priority = 1;
task03.dueDate = [NSDate date];

//Assign worker to task
task03.assignedWorker = personInCharge;

//Add task to project
[workProject01.listOfTasks addObject:task03];

//Use KVC to get property values
//Use id to get a generalized object reference
id temp;

//Get the name of the project:
temp = [workProject01 valueForKey:@"name"];
NSLog(@"temp (from key name) = %@", temp);

//get the person in charge:
```

```
        temp = [workProject01 valueForKey:@"personInCharge"];
        NSLog(@"temp (from key personInCharge) = %@", temp);

        //get the project's task list:
        temp = [workProject01 valueForKey:@"listOfTasks"];
        NSLog(@"temp (from key listOfTasks) = %@", temp);

        NSArray *stuffFromTaskList = [temp valueForKey:@"name"];
        [stuffFromTaskList enumerateObjectsUsingBlock:^(id obj, NSUInteger idx, BOOL ↵
    *stop) {
            NSLog(@"obj: %@", obj);
        }];

        //Use KVC to set property values
        [workProject01 setValue:@"My Pet Project"
                        forKey:@"name"];

        temp = [workProject01 valueForKey:@"listOfTasks"];
        [temp setValue:@"New Task"
            forKey:@"name"];

        //write out the object graph's contents
        [workProject01 writeReportToLog];
    }
    return 0;
}
```

Usage

A Mac command-line is a sufficient base to use to test this code. Recreate all of the code from Listings 9-8 through 9-14, including the code that works with the object graph in the main.m file.

Build and run your application. You should see the output that follows in your console log window. The major change in this recipe was the process of accessing the property values, not the content itself.

```
temp (from key name) = Make iOS App
temp (from key personInCharge) = Jane Smith, Manager
temp (from key listOfTasks) = (
    "<Task: 0x106b16200>",
    "<Task: 0x106b16640>",
    "<Task: 0x106b16730>"
)
 obj: Learn Objective-C
 obj: Investigate UIKit
 obj: Evaluate
```

```
PROJECT
  name = My Pet Project
  description = Make an iOS application for the iPad
  dueDate = 2012-03-21 17:01:05 +0000
  personInCharge = Jane Smith, Manager
TASKS
  name = New Task
    description = Learn Objective-C to make Mac apps
    dueDate = 2012-03-21 17:01:05 +0000
    priority = 1
    assignedWorker = David Done, Programmer
  name = New Task
    description = Investigate UIKit to see how it works for users.
    dueDate = 2012-03-21 17:01:05 +0000
    priority = 3
    assignedWorker = David Done, Programmer
  name = New Task
    description = Signoff on initial project progress.
    dueDate = 2012-03-21 17:01:05 +0000
    priority = 1
    assignedWorker = Jane Smith, Manager
```

This is the results of your navigation and manipulation of the object graph.

9.3 Using Key Paths in Your Object Graph

Problem

You want to access object properties that are deep in your object graph dynamically, but valueForKey: and setValueForKey: only work when you have an object reference at hand.

Solution

Use key paths to get deeply nested object property values from your object graph. NSObject has a function called valueForKeyPath: that will help you get these values.

How It Works

Note that again you are using the object graph that was created in Recipe 9.1. This time, instead of simply providing a key-value as you did in Recipe 9.2, you are going to provide a key path. A *key path* looks like the code that you would write to access an object or property with dot notation except that the key path is a string. For instance, if you want to see the name of the person in charge using standard dot notation, you do the following:

```
id temp;
temp = workProject01.personInCharge.name;
```

Note that you will be reusing `id emp` throughout this recipe. To do the same using a key path, you do this:

```
temp = [workProject01 valueForKeyPath:@"personInCharge.name"];
```

If you want to go one level deeper and get the value of the `NSString` `uppercaseString` function, you can do this:

```
temp = [workProject01 valueForKeyPath:@"personInCharge.name.uppercaseString"];
```

As you might expect, you can also set properties with key paths. For instance, if you want to change the name of the person in charge, you can do this:

```
[workProject01 setValue:@"Mary Steinbeck"
            forKeyPath:@"personInCharge.name"];
```

See Listings 9-15 through 9-21.

> **NOTE:** Key paths work well—with one caveat. There is no way to reference an element of an array. If you want to get the name property value of one of the tasks in the project task list, you're out of luck. The only way to do this is to get a reference to the array first; then you must select the object from the list in the usual ways.

The Code

Listing 9-15. *Worker.h*

```
#import <Foundation/Foundation.h>

@interface Worker : NSObject

@property(strong)NSString *name;
@property(strong)NSString *role;

@end
```

Listing 9-16. *Worker.m*

```
#import "Worker.h"

@implementation Worker
@synthesize name, role;

-(NSString *)description{
    return [NSString stringWithFormat:@"%@, %@", name, role];
}

@end
```

Listing 9-17. *Task.h*

```
#import <Foundation/Foundation.h>
#import "Worker.h"

@interface Task : NSObject

@property(strong)NSString *name;
@property(strong)NSString *details;
@property(strong)NSDate *dueDate;
@property(assign)int priority;
@property(strong)Worker *assignedWorker;

-(void)writeReportToLog;

@end
```

Listing 9-18. *Task.m*

```
#import "Task.h"

@implementation Task
@synthesize name, details, dueDate, priority, assignedWorker;

-(void)writeReportToLog{
    NSLog(@"  name = %@", self.name);
    NSLog(@"    description = %@", self.details);
    NSLog(@"    dueDate = %@", self.dueDate);
    NSLog(@"    priority = %i", self.priority);
    NSLog(@"    assignedWorker = %@", self.assignedWorker);
}

@end
```

Listing 9-19. *Project.h*

```
#import <Foundation/Foundation.h>
#import "Task.h"
#import "Worker.h"

@interface Project : NSObject

@property(strong)NSString *name;
@property(strong)NSString *description;
@property(strong)NSDate *dueDate;
@property(strong)NSMutableArray *listOfTasks;
@property(strong)Worker *personInCharge;

-(void)writeReportToLog;

@end
```

Listing 9-20. *Project.m*

```
#import "Project.h"

@implementation Project
@synthesize name, description, dueDate, listOfTasks, personInCharge;

- (id)init{
    self = [super init];
    if (self) {
        self.listOfTasks = [[NSMutableArray alloc] init];
    }
    return self;
}

-(void)writeReportToLog{
    NSLog(@"PROJECT");
    NSLog(@"  name = %@", self.name);
    NSLog(@"  description = %@", self.description);
    NSLog(@"  dueDate = %@", self.dueDate);
    NSLog(@"  personInCharge = %@", self.personInCharge);
    NSLog(@"TASKS");
    [self.listOfTasks enumerateObjectsUsingBlock:^(id obj, NSUInteger idx, BOOL *stop) {
        [obj writeReportToLog];
    }];
}

@end
```

Listing 9-21. *main.m*

```objc
#import <Foundation/Foundation.h>
#import "Project.h"
#import "Task.h"

int main(int argc, const char * argv[]){
    @autoreleasepool {
        //Create a new project
        Project *workProject01 =[[Project alloc] init];
        workProject01.name = @"Make iOS App";
        workProject01.description = @"Make an iOS application for the iPad";
        workProject01.dueDate = [NSDate date];

        //Setup a new person to be in charge
        Worker *personInCharge = [[Worker alloc] init];
        personInCharge.name = @"Jane Smith";
        personInCharge.role = @"Manager";

        //Assign person to project
        workProject01.personInCharge = personInCharge;

        //Create new task
        Task *task01 = [[Task alloc] init];
        task01.name = @"Learn Objective-C";
        task01.details = @"Learn Objective-C to make Mac apps";
        task01.priority = 1;
        task01.dueDate = [NSDate date];

        //Set up a new person to assign to the task
        Worker *employee = [[Worker alloc] init];
        employee.name = @"David Done";
        employee.role = @"Programmer";

        //Assign worker to task
        task01.assignedWorker = employee;

        //Add task to project
        [workProject01.listOfTasks addObject:task01];

        //Create new task
        Task *task02 = [[Task alloc] init];
        task02.name = @"Investigate UIKit";
        task02.details = @"Investigate UIKit to see how it works for users.";
        task02.priority = 3;
        task02.dueDate = [NSDate date];

        //Assign worker to task
        task02.assignedWorker = employee;
```

```
            //Add task to project
            [workProject01.listOfTasks addObject:task02];

            //Create new task
            Task *task03 = [[Task alloc] init];
            task03.name = @"Evaluate";
            task03.details = @"Signoff on initial project progress.";
            task03.priority = 1;
            task03.dueDate = [NSDate date];

            //Assign worker to task
            task03.assignedWorker = personInCharge;

            //Add task to project
            [workProject01.listOfTasks addObject:task03];

            //Use key paths to get property values
            //Use id to get a generalized object reference
            id temp;

            //Get the name of the person in charge using a dot notation
            temp = workProject01.personInCharge.name;
            NSLog(@"workProject01.personInCharge.name = %@", temp);

            //Get the name of the person in charge using a key path
            temp = [workProject01 valueForKeyPath:@"personInCharge.name"];
            NSLog(@"personInCharge.name = %@", temp);

            //Get the name of the person in charge in uppercase using a key path
            temp = [workProject01 valueForKeyPath:@"personInCharge.name.uppercaseString"];
            NSLog(@"personInCharge.name.uppercaseString = %@", temp);

            //Set the name of the person in charge using a key path
            [workProject01 setValue:@"Mary Steinbeck"
                         forKeyPath:@"personInCharge.name"];

            //write out the object graph's contents
            [workProject01 writeReportToLog];
        }
        return 0;
    }
```

Usage

The easiest way to try this recipe is to set up a command-line Mac application and include the code in Listings 9-15 through 9-21. The class definitions are the same as the ones used in Recipes 9.1 and 9.2.

The key path code is located in the `main.m` file toward the end. When you run this code you will see the results of the key path functions. Look at the name of the person in charge to see the change you made at the end of the code in `main.m`.

```
workProject01.personInCharge.name = Jane Smith
personInCharge.name = Jane Smith
personInCharge.name.uppercaseString = JANE SMITH
PROJECT
   name = Make iOS App
   description = Make an iOS application for the iPad
   dueDate = 2012-03-20 16:06:55 +0000
   personInCharge = Mary Steinbeck, Manager
 TASKS
   name = Learn Objective-C
     description = Learn Objective-C to make Mac apps
     dueDate = 2012-03-20 16:06:55 +0000
     priority = 1
     assignedWorker = David Done, Programmer
   name - Investigate UIKit
     description = Investigate UIKit to see how it works for users.
     dueDate = 2012-03-20 16:06:55 +0000
     priority = 3
     assignedWorker = David Done, Programmer
   name = Evaluate
     description = Signoff on initial project progress.
     dueDate = 2012-03-20 16:06:55 +0000
     priority = 1
     assignedWorker = Mary Steinbeck, Manager
```

In case you don't see the change, Mary Steinbeck is now listed as the person in charge of the project as well as the last task.

9.4 Aggregating Information with Key Paths

Problem

You want to get aggregated information from your object graph. For instance, you may need to know the average priority level of all the tasks in your project's task list.

Solution

Use @count, @sum, @avg, @min, @max, and @distinctUnionOfObjects to get aggregated information from arrays in your object graph.

How It Works

When you use the `valueForKeyPath:` method, you can include the @count, @sum, @avg, @min, @max, and @distinctUnionOfObjects operators in the key path to create the information from the property in the array. The general form of the key path is

`[keypath].[@operator].[property name]`

If you want to get the sum of all the priority values in the task list that you created in Recipe 9.1, you can do this:

```
id sum = [workProject01 valueForKeyPath:@"listOfTasks.@sum.priority"];
```

Remember that `listOfTasks` is an array of `Task` objects. Each `Task` object has an int property named `priority`. These operators work on the value of each priority property for each `Task` object in the array.

Here are some more examples of how to use these operators with the `priority` property:

```
//Get the sum of all the priority values
id sum = [workProject01 valueForKeyPath:@"listOfTasks.@sum.priority"];
NSLog(@"sum of task list priorities = %@", sum);

//Get the average of all the priority values
id average = [workProject01 valueForKeyPath:@"listOfTasks.@avg.priority"];
NSLog(@"average of task list priorities = %@", average);

//Get the minimum of all the priority values
id min = [workProject01 valueForKeyPath:@"listOfTasks.@min.priority"];
NSLog(@"min of task list priorities = %@", min);

//Get the maximum of all the priority values
id max = [workProject01 valueForKeyPath:@"listOfTasks.@max.priority"];
NSLog(@"max of task list priorities = %@", max);
```

You can also get the distinct values from a property. Say that in your task list you have a person assigned to each task. Often the same person is assigned many tasks (like David Done in your object graph). Sometimes you just want a list of each object without the repetition. Maybe you want to send just one e-mail to each person on your project.

To get such a list, use the @distinctUnionOfObjects operator, like so:

```
id listOfWorkers = [workProject01 ↩
valueForKeyPath:@"listOfTasks.@distinctUnionOfObjects.assignedWorker"];
NSLog(@"list of distinct workers from task list = %@", listOfWorkers);
```

This prints out each worker, but only once.

```
list of distinct workers from task list = (
    "David Done, Programmer",
    "Jane Smith, Manager"
)
```

David Done is only listed once, even though he's assigned to two tasks. See Listings 9-22 through 9-28.

The Code

Listing 9-22. *Worker.h*

```
#import <Foundation/Foundation.h>

@interface Worker : NSObject

@property(strong)NSString *name;
@property(strong)NSString *role;

@end
```

Listing 9-23. *Worker.m*

```
#import "Worker.h"

@implementation Worker
@synthesize name, role;

-(NSString *)description{
    return [NSString stringWithFormat:@"%@, %@", name, role];
}

@end
```

Listing 9-24. *Task.h*

```
#import <Foundation/Foundation.h>
#import "Worker.h"

@interface Task : NSObject
```

```
@property(strong)NSString *name;
@property(strong)NSString *details;
@property(strong)NSDate *dueDate;
@property(assign)int priority;
@property(strong)Worker *assignedWorker;

-(void)writeReportToLog;

@end
```

Listing 9-25. *Task.m*

```
#import "Task.h"

@implementation Task
@synthesize name, details, dueDate, priority, assignedWorker;

-(void)writeReportToLog{
    NSLog(@"   name = %@", self.name);
    NSLog(@"    description = %@", self.details);
    NSLog(@"    dueDate = %@", self.dueDate);
    NSLog(@"    priority = %i", self.priority);
    NSLog(@"    assignedWorker = %@", self.assignedWorker);
}

@end
```

Listing 9-26. *Project.h*

```
#import <Foundation/Foundation.h>
#import "Task.h"
#import "Worker.h"

@interface Project : NSObject

@property(strong)NSString *name;
@property(strong)NSString *description;
@property(strong)NSDate *dueDate;
@property(strong)NSMutableArray *listOfTasks;
@property(strong)Worker *personInCharge;

-(void)writeReportToLog;

@end
```

Listing 9-27. *Project.m*

```
#import "Project.h"

@implementation Project
```

```objc
@synthesize name, description, dueDate, listOfTasks, personInCharge;

- (id)init{
    self = [super init];
    if (self) {
        self.listOfTasks = [[NSMutableArray alloc] init];
    }
    return self;
}

-(void)writeReportToLog{
    NSLog(@"PROJECT");
    NSLog(@"  name = %@", self.name);
    NSLog(@"  description = %@", self.description);
    NSLog(@"  dueDate = %@", self.dueDate);
    NSLog(@"  personInCharge = %@", self.personInCharge);
    NSLog(@"TASKS");
    [self.listOfTasks enumerateObjectsUsingBlock:^(id obj, NSUInteger idx, BOOL *stop) {
        [obj writeReportToLog];
    }];
}

@end
```

Listing 9-28. *main.m*

```objc
#import <Foundation/Foundation.h>
#import "Project.h"
#import "Task.h"

int main(int argc, const char * argv[]){
    @autoreleasepool {
        //Create a new project
        Project *workProject01 =[[Project alloc] init];
        workProject01.name = @"Make iOS App";
        workProject01.description = @"Make an iOS application for the iPad";
        workProject01.dueDate = [NSDate date];

        //Set up a new person to be in charge
        Worker *personInCharge = [[Worker alloc] init];
        personInCharge.name = @"Jane Smith";
        personInCharge.role = @"Manager";

        //Assign person to project
        workProject01.personInCharge = personInCharge;

        //Create new task
        Task *task01 = [[Task alloc] init];
        task01.name = @"Learn Objective-C";
        task01.details = @"Learn Objective-C to make Mac apps";
```

```
task01.priority = 1;
task01.dueDate = [NSDate date];

//Set up a new person to assign to the task
Worker *employee = [[Worker alloc] init];
employee.name = @"David Done";
employee.role = @"Programmer";

//Assign worker to task
task01.assignedWorker = employee;

//Add task to project
[workProject01.listOfTasks addObject:task01];

//Create new task
Task *task02 = [[Task alloc] init];
task02.name = @"Investigate UIKit";
task02.details = @"Investigate UIKit to see how it works for users.";
task02.priority = 3;
task02.dueDate = [NSDate date];

//Assign worker to task
task02.assignedWorker = employee;

//Add task to project
[workProject01.listOfTasks addObject:task02];

//Create new task
Task *task03 = [[Task alloc] init];
task03.name = @"Evaluate";
task03.details = @"Signoff on initial project progress.";
task03.priority = 1;
task03.dueDate = [NSDate date];

//Assign worker to task
task03.assignedWorker = personInCharge;

//Add task to project
[workProject01.listOfTasks addObject:task03];

//Use key paths to get aggregated information from arrays
//Get the count
id count = [workProject01 valueForKeyPath:@"listOfTasks.@count.priority"];
NSLog(@"task list count = %@", count);

//Get the sum of all the priority values
id sum = [workProject01 valueForKeyPath:@"listOfTasks.@sum.priority"];
NSLog(@"sum of task list priorities = %@", sum);
```

```
        //Get the average of all the priority values
        id average = [workProject01 valueForKeyPath:@"listOfTasks.@avg.priority"];
        NSLog(@"average of task list priorities = %@", average);

        //Get the minimum of all the priority values
        id min = [workProject01 valueForKeyPath:@"listOfTasks.@min.priority"];
        NSLog(@"min of task list priorities = %@", min);

        //Get the maximum of all the priority values
        id max = [workProject01 valueForKeyPath:@"listOfTasks.@max.priority"];
        NSLog(@"max of task list priorities = %@", max);

        //Get a list of distinct assigned to values
        id listOfWorkers = [workProject01 ↩
valueForKeyPath:@"listOfTasks.@distinctUnionOfObjects.assignedWorker"];
        NSLog(@"list of distinct workers from task list = %@", listOfWorkers);

    }
    return 0;
}
```

Usage

This recipe has the same object graph as the earlier recipes so you can re-use the projects you set up earlier in this chapter if you've been following along. Otherwise, you can set up a Mac command-line app in Xcode and add the files from Listings 9-22 through 9-28. The most important code is located toward the end of the main.m file.

When you build and run your application you will see the results of the aggregated information in your log.

```
task list count = 3
sum of task list priorities = 5
average of task list priorities = 1.6666666666666666666666666666666666666666
min of task list priorities = 1
max of task list priorities = 3
list of distinct workers from task list = (
    "David Done, Programmer",
    "Jane Smith, Manager"
)
```

Note that the order in which your Worker objects appear may not match the order in which my Worker objects appear. This is normal because you can't assume that objects will appear in a given order here.

9.5 Implementing the Observer Pattern

Problem

You want one object to be notified when the property value of another object changes. In particular, you want to notify a controller when a property in the model has changed so that the user interface may be updated.

Solution

Implement an Observer pattern using key-value observing.

How It Works

There are three steps to using key-value observation. First, you need to establish a connection between the object that is being observed and the object that is observing. You do this by sending the `addObserver:forKeyPath:options:context:` message to the object that is to be observed with a reference to the object that is doing the observing.

Next, in the class definition for the object that is doing observing you must override the `NSObject` method called `observeValueForKeyPath:ofObject:change:context:`. This method is invoked whenever a change is made to the observed object. This is where you receive the information that you are interested in, such as the object where the change occurred, the key path, and the changed property value.

Finally, the object that is being observed must remove the observer in the `dealloc` method. This is a method that is called right before the observed object is going to be destroyed, and you have to make sure that observer is removed as well or the observed could be retained and cause a memory leak.

To demonstrate how to do this, you're going to use a subset of the object graph that was created in Recipe 9.1. Your object graph subset only has one `Project` object and one `Worker` object. The `Task` class and task list can both be omitted for now.

What you are about to do is have the person in charge become an observer of the project's name property. Whenever the name property value of the project changes, the person in charge will be notified.

The first step is to go to the part of the code in main.m where you are creating the object graph. Locate the space right after the personInCharge Worker object is instantiated and send the addObserver:forKeyPath:options:context: message to the project with the personInCharge and some other objects. The added code is in bold.

```
//Create a new project
Project *workProject01 =[[Project alloc] init];
workProject01.name = @"Make iOS App";
workProject01.description = @"Make an iOS application for the iPad";
workProject01.dueDate = [NSDate date];

//Setup a new person to be in charge
Worker *personInCharge = [[Worker alloc] init];
personInCharge.name = @"Jane Smith";
personInCharge.role = @"Manager";

//Add personInCharge as an observer:
[workProject01 addObserver:personInCharge
            forKeyPath:@"name"
                options:NSKeyValueObservingOptionNew
                context:nil];
```

This means that the object personInCharge is observing the property value in the key path "name" on the object workProject01. The option NSKeyValueObservingOptionNew means that you will be notified with the updated property value information.

You also have to make sure that you will receive and make use of this information when it arrives to the observer. This happens when you override the observeValueForKeyPath:ofObject:change:context: method in the class definition of your observer. Override this method in the implementation file for the Worker class (Worker.m).

```
#import "Worker.h"

@implementation Worker
@synthesize name, role;

...

-(void)observeValueForKeyPath:(NSString *)keyPath
                    ofObject:(id)object
                       change:(NSDictionary *)change
                      context:(void *)context{
    NSLog(@"'%@' has noticed that the project '%@' has changed", self, object);

    NSLog(@"'%@' was changed to '%@'", keyPath, [change objectForKey:@"new"]);
}
```

@end

When the name property of the workProject01 object changes, this code executes. The parameters will have the information that you are interested in: the key path, a reference to the object that was changed, and a dictionary that has the change that was made. You can use this information to make changes. Here you are simply writing to the log. If you were using key-value observation with a user interface, you could use this information to update the app screen.

Before you test this out, there's one more thing to address. You must take care to remove any observers from an observed object before the object is destroyed. So, go to the Project class declaration and add a dealloc method where you will remove the observer. This code belongs in the Project.m file.

```
#import "Project.h"

@implementation Project
@synthesize name, description, dueDate, personInCharge;

...

-(void)dealloc{
    [self removeObserver:self.personInCharge
                    forKeyPath:@"name"];
}
```

@end

Finally, to test this out, change the name property value of the workProject01 object like this:

```
workProject01.name = @"The Wow Project!";
```

You will see in the log that the personInCharge object was notified and a report was written to the log.

```
'Jane Smith, Manager' has noticed that the project 'Make an iOS application for
the iPad' has changed
'name' was changed to 'The Wow Project!'
```

See Listings 9-29 through 9-33.

The Code

Listing 9-29. *Project.h*

```
#import <Foundation/Foundation.h>
#import "Worker.h"
```

```
@interface Project : NSObject

@property(strong)NSString *name;
@property(strong)NSString *description;
@property(strong)NSDate *dueDate;
@property(strong)Worker *personInCharge;

-(void)writeReportToLog;

@end
```

Listing 9-30. *Project.m*

```
#import "Project.h"

@implementation Project
@synthesize name, description, dueDate, personInCharge;

-(void)writeReportToLog{
    NSLog(@"PROJECT");
    NSLog(@"  name = %@", self.name);
    NSLog(@"  description = %@", self.description);
    NSLog(@"  dueDate = %@", self.dueDate);
    NSLog(@"  personInCharge = %@", self.personInCharge);
}

-(void)dealloc{
    [self removeObserver:self.personInCharge
                    forKeyPath:@"name"];
}

@end
```

Listing 9-31. *Worker.h*

```
#import <Foundation/Foundation.h>

@interface Worker : NSObject

@property(strong)NSString *name;
@property(strong)NSString *role;

@end
```

Listing 9-32. *Worker.m*

```
#import "Worker.h"

@implementation Worker
```

```objc
@synthesize name, role;

-(NSString *)description{
    return [NSString stringWithFormat:@"%@, %@", name, role];
}

-(void)observeValueForKeyPath:(NSString *)keyPath
                     ofObject:(id)object
                       change:(NSDictionary *)change
                      context:(void *)context{
    NSLog(@"'%@' has noticed that the project '%@' has changed", self, object);

    NSLog(@"'%@' was changed to '%@'", keyPath, [change objectForKey:@"new"]);
}

@end
```

Listing 9-33. *main.m*

```objc
#import <Foundation/Foundation.h>
#import "Project.h"

int main(int argc, const char * argv[]){
    @autoreleasepool {
        //Create a new project
        Project *workProject01 =[[Project alloc] init];
        workProject01.name = @"Make iOS App";
        workProject01.description = @"Make an iOS application for the iPad";
        workProject01.dueDate = [NSDate date];

        //Setup a new person to be in charge
        Worker *personInCharge = [[Worker alloc] init];
        personInCharge.name = @"Jane Smith";
        personInCharge.role = @"Manager";

        //Add personInCharge as an observer:
        [workProject01 addObserver:personInCharge
                        forKeyPath:@"name"
                           options:NSKeyValueObservingOptionNew
                           context:nil];


        //Assign person to project
        workProject01.personInCharge = personInCharge;

        //change the name of the project
        workProject01.name = @"The Wow Project!";

    }
    return 0;
```

}

Usage

You can use this code with a simple command-line Mac app. Include the Project class declaration from Listings 9-29 and 9-30. Note that even though these are based on the class definitions from Recipe 9.1 they now include additional code to make them work with key-value observation.

The code in main.m has also been updated from Recipe 9.1 to include code to make key-value observation work. When you build and run your application, you should see something like this appear in your log:

```
'Jane Smith, Manager' has noticed that the project 'Make an iOS application for
the iPad' has changed
'name' was changed to 'The Wow Project!'
```

Key-value observation comes in handy when you want to be able update your user interface. For instance, you may have a view controller in an iOS app set as an observer for a model property so the view controller can update the view as the data model changes.

9.6 Inspecting Classes and Objects

Problem

Your application is dealing with objects that you don't have information about at runtime, but you want to know if you can send messages and otherwise use the objects.

Solution

Use the built-in methods that come with NSObject to inspect classes. You can find out if an object is a type of class, if the object responds to a selector, and if the object is equal to another object.

How It Works

This recipe uses the object graph that you created in Recipe 9.1 but you'll remove the Task class and objects since you don't need the entire hierarchy for this recipe. You need a new class that is a subclass of Worker called Consultant. Here is the interface for and implementation of Consultant:

```
#import "Worker.h"

@interface Consultant : Worker

@end

@implementation Consultant

-(NSString *)description{
    return [NSString stringWithFormat:@"%@, %@", [super description], @"Consultant"];
}

@end
```

Set up the simplified object graph in the main.m file first.

```
//Create a new project
Project *workProject01 =[[Project alloc] init];
workProject01.name = @"Make iOS App";
workProject01.description = @"Make an iOS application for the iPad";
workProject01.dueDate = [NSDate date];

//Set up a new person to be in charge
Worker *personInCharge = [[Worker alloc] init];
personInCharge.name = @"Jane Smith";
personInCharge.role = @"Manager";

//Assign person to project
workProject01.personInCharge = personInCharge;

//Create a consultant
Consultant *consulter = [[Consultant alloc] init];
consulter.name = @"Lone Wolf";
consulter.role = @"Star Programmer";
```

As in Recipe 9.1, this is a project with Jane Smith in charge. This time, though, you omitted the task list and you created a consultant named Lone Wolf.

Now, let's imagine that you are in a situation where you have a reference to an object but you don't know for sure the type of the object. This could happen if you are using key-value coding, or you could have an object reference handed to you in some other situation where you don't know what type of object you are working with. For example,

```
id projectManager = [workProject01 valueForKey:@"personInCharge"];
```

The object variable `projectManager` is just a type of `id`, which doesn't tell you anything (although here you happen to know what's going on because you just created the object graph).

You might guess that `projectManager` is a `Worker` object and you want to send the `writeReportToLog` message to `projectManager`. But since you're not sure, you want to test the object first to see if it responds. One option is to use the `respondsToSelector` message. You can give this message a parameter that references the message that you want to send using the `@selector` keyword. You get back a `BOOL` indicating whether the object will respond.

```
BOOL doesItRespond = [projectManager
respondsToSelector:@selector(writeReportToLog)];
```

You can also find out if an object is a particular class or a subclass of a class. Just send the `isKindOfClass` message to the object with a class object as a parameter. Again, you get a `BOOL` value back telling you if the object is a type of that class or not. In your object graph, both `consulter` and `projectManager` are a kind of `Worker` class and so the following code returns YES for both objects:

```
BOOL isItAKindOfClass = [consulter isKindOfClass:[Worker class]];

isItAKindOfClass = [projectManager isKindOfClass:[Worker class]];
```

You may also want to know if the object is an instance (or object) of a class. This next method returns YES if the object is an instance of the class and NO if anything else (including subclasses of the class). So, if you test both `projectManager` and `consulter` like this

```
BOOL isAnInstanceOfClass = [projectManager isMemberOfClass:[Worker class]];

isAnInstanceOfClass = [consulter isMemberOfClass:[Worker class]];
```

The first function returns YES and the second returns NO. This is because `projectManager` is an instance of `Worker` while `consulter` is merely an instance of a subclass of `Worker`.

Sometimes you have two object references and you need to test to see if they are actually identical objects. To do this, use the `isEqual` message; you get a `BOOL` value of YES back if both objects are the same and a NO back if they are two difference instances.

So for your object graph, you may want to test `projectManager` and consulter to see if they happen to be the same object.

```
BOOL isEqual = [projectManager isEqual:consulter];
```

This is a NO as you probably guessed by looking back at the object creation in the beginning of the code in `main.m`.

However, if you test projectManager and personInCharge, you get a different outcome.

```
isEqual = [projectManager isEqual:personInCharge];
```

This returns YES because while they are different object variable names they are both referencing the same object. See Listings 9-34 through 9-40.

The Code

Listing 9-34. *Project.h*

```
#import <Foundation/Foundation.h>
#import "Worker.h"

@interface Project : NSObject

@property(strong)NSString *name;
@property(strong)NSString *description;
@property(strong)NSDate *dueDate;
@property(strong)Worker *personInCharge;

-(void)writeReportToLog;

@end
```

Listing 9-35. *Project.m*

```
#import "Project.h"

@implementation Project
@synthesize name, description, dueDate, personInCharge;

-(void)writeReportToLog{
    NSLog(@"PROJECT");
    NSLog(@"   name = %@", self.name);
    NSLog(@"   description = %@", self.description);
    NSLog(@"   dueDate = %@", self.dueDate);
    NSLog(@"   personInCharge = %@", self.personInCharge);
}

@end
```

Listing 9-36. *Worker.h*

```
#import <Foundation/Foundation.h>

@interface Worker : NSObject
```

```
@property(strong)NSString *name;
@property(strong)NSString *role;

@end
```

Listing 9-37. *Worker.m*

```
#import "Worker.h"

@implementation Worker
@synthesize name, role;

-(NSString *)description{
    return [NSString stringWithFormat:@"%@, %@", name, role];
}

@end
```

Listing 9-38. *Consultant.h*

```
#import "Worker.h"

@interface Consultant : Worker

@end
```

Listing 9-39. *Consultant.m*

```
#import "Consultant.h"

@implementation Consultant

-(NSString *)description{
    return [NSString stringWithFormat:@"%@, %@", [super description], @"Consultant"];
}

@end
```

Listing 9-40. *main.m*

```
#import <Foundation/Foundation.h>
#import "Project.h"
#import "Consultant.h"

int main(int argc, const char * argv[]){
    @autoreleasepool {
        //Create a new project
        Project *workProject01 =[[Project alloc] init];
        workProject01.name = @"Make iOS App";
        workProject01.description = @"Make an iOS application for the iPad";
```

```objc
        workProject01.dueDate = [NSDate date];

        //Set up a new person to be in charge
        Worker *personInCharge = [[Worker alloc] init];
        personInCharge.name = @"Jane Smith";
        personInCharge.role = @"Manager";

        //Assign person to project
        workProject01.personInCharge = personInCharge;

        //Create a consultant
        Consultant *consulter = [[Consultant alloc] init];
        consulter.name = @"Lone Wolf";
        consulter.role = @"Star Programmer";

        //Get object from key path
        id projectManager = [workProject01 valueForKey:@"personInCharge"];

        //See if the object responds to a selector
        BOOL doesItRespond = [projectManager ⏎
respondsToSelector:@selector(writeReportToLog)];

        if(doesItRespond)
            [projectManager writeReportToLog];
        else
            NSLog(@"'%@' doesn't respond to selector", projectManager);

        //See if consulter is a type of Worker
        BOOL isItAKindOfClass = [consulter isKindOfClass:[Worker class]];

        if(isItAKindOfClass)
            NSLog(@"consulter is a Worker (%@)", consulter);
        else
            NSLog(@"consulter's no Worker");

        //See if projectManager is a type of Worker
        isItAKindOfClass = [projectManager isKindOfClass:[Worker class]];

        if(isItAKindOfClass)
            NSLog(@"projectManager is a Worker (%@)", projectManager);
        else
            NSLog(@"projectManager's no Worker");

        //See if projectManager is an instance of Worker
        BOOL isAnInstanceOfClass = [projectManager isMemberOfClass:[Worker class]];

        if(isAnInstanceOfClass)
            NSLog(@"projectManager is an instance of Worker");
        else
            NSLog(@"projectManager's no Worker");
```

```
        //See if consulter is an instance of Worker
        isAnInstanceOfClass = [consulter isMemberOfClass:[Worker class]];

        if(isAnInstanceOfClass)
            NSLog(@"consulter is an instance of Worker");
        else
            NSLog(@"consulter's no Worker");

        //Compare two objects
        BOOL isEqual = [projectManager isEqual:consulter];

        if(isEqual)
            NSLog(@"'%@' == '%@'", projectManager, consulter);
        else
            NSLog(@"'%@' != '%@'", projectManager, consulter);

        isEqual = [projectManager isEqual:personInCharge];

        if(isEqual)
            NSLog(@"'%@' == '%@'", projectManager, personInCharge);
        else
            NSLog(@"'%@' != '%@'", projectManager, personInCharge);

    }
    return 0;
}
```

Usage

Like the other applications in this chapter, the easiest way to test this for yourself is to use a Mac command-line application with Xcode and add the code from Listings 9-34 through 9-40.

Everything is included in main.m along with if statements that write out the results of each test to the console log. Build and run the application and inspect the console log to see the results. You will see something like the following in your console log:

```
'Jane Smith, Manager' doesn't respond to selector
consulter is a Worker (Lone Wolf, Star Programmer, Consultant)
projectManager is a Worker (Jane Smith, Manager)
projectManager is an instance of Worker
consulter's no Worker
'Jane Smith, Manager' != 'Lone Wolf, Star Programmer, Consultant'
'Jane Smith, Manager' == 'Jane Smith, Manager'
```

9.7 Archiving Your Object Graph

Problem

You want to export you object graph to the file system so you can use your object graph in another application or so you have a backup.

Solution

Adopt and implement the NSCoding protocol in each class that supports archiving. Then use the NSKeyArchiver class to save your root object to the file system.

How It Works

In this recipe, you take the object graph created in Recipe 9.1 and archive the object graph to the file system. Then, with a second application, you read in and decode the saved object graph.

NSCoding

The first step in this process is to adopt the NSCoding protocol in each class where you want to support archiving. To fulfill your NSCoding contract, you must implement two methods: encodeWithCoder: and initWithCoder:. These two methods are what a class will use to encode and decode the class objects.

So adopt and implement the NSCoding protocol for the Worker class. The first step is to adopt the NSCoding protocol in the Worker's interface located in Worker.h.

```
#import <Foundation/Foundation.h>

@interface Worker : NSObject<NSCoding>

@property(strong)NSString *name;
@property(strong)NSString *role;

@end
```

Next, add the implementation for encodeWithCoder: to the Worker's implementation located in Worker.m.

```
#import "Worker.h"

@implementation Worker
@synthesize name, role;

-(NSString *)description{
    return [NSString stringWithFormat:@"%@, %@", name, role];
}

- (void) encodeWithCoder:(NSCoder *)encoder {
    [encoder encodeObject:self.name forKey:@"namekey"];
    [encoder encodeObject:self.role forKey:@"rolekey"];
}

@end
```

This method is used to tell the archive object to store the property values in a file based on the key that is provided. To keep things clear, I used the property name + "key" as the key.

You also need to know how to decode the file and translate that into an object. This is defined in the method initWithCoder:. The init prefix to this method implies that the method makes up part of the constructor and will be used for new object instances.

```
#import "Worker.h"

@implementation Worker
@synthesize name, role;

-(NSString *)description{
    return [NSString stringWithFormat:@"%@, %@", name, role];
}

- (void) encodeWithCoder:(NSCoder *)encoder {
    [encoder encodeObject:self.name forKey:@"namekey"];
    [encoder encodeObject:self.role forKey:@"rolekey"];
}

- (id)initWithCoder:(NSCoder *)decoder {
    self.name = [decoder decodeObjectForKey:@"namekey"];
    self.role = [decoder decodeObjectForKey:@"rolekey"];

    return self;
}

@end
```

The key thing here is that the properties and the keys must match what is defined in the encodeWithCoder: method.

This must be done for each class definition that you want to support archiving. This means that for the object graph from Recipe 9.1, you need to do this for `Project` and `Task` as well (see Listings 9-42 and 9-44 for the code for this).

NSKeyedArchiver

Once all your classes support archiving you can use `NSKeyedArchiver` to save your objects to a file. You need to identify a root, or first, object if your object graph has a hierarchy type of structure. In the 9.1 object graph, `workProject01` is the root object. You also need a file location that you can reference later. This part is very easy.

```
BOOL dataArchived = [NSKeyedArchiver archiveRootObject:workProject01
                                         toFile:@"/Users/Shared/workProject01.dat"];

if(dataArchived)
    NSLog(@"Object graph successfully archived");
else
    NSLog(@"Error attempting to archive object graph");
```

You can simply use a class message to `NSKeyedArchiver` along with a file location to save your object graph to the file. If you ever want to do the opposite and retrieve your object graph, you can do this:

```
Project *storedProject = [NSKeyedUnarchiver ↵
unarchiveObjectWithFile:@"/Users/Shared/workProject01.dat"];

if(storedProject)
    [storedProject writeReportToLog];
else
    NSLog(@"Error attempting to retrieve the object graph");
```

This uses the data from the file to populate your object. This includes the objects in arrays and dictionaries that have relationships with your object (like the task list in Recipe 9.1). You can use this in a completely different application as long as both applications have matching class definitions. See Listings 9-41 through 9-47.

The Code

Listing 9-41. *Project.h*

```
#import <Foundation/Foundation.h>
#import "Task.h"
#import "Worker.h"
```

```objc
@interface Project : NSObject<NSCoding>

@property(strong)NSString *name;
@property(strong)NSString *description;
@property(strong)NSDate *dueDate;
@property(strong)NSMutableArray *listOfTasks;
@property(strong)Worker *personInCharge;


-(void)writeReportToLog;

@end
```

Listing 9-42. *Project.m*

```objc
#import "Project.h"

@implementation Project
@synthesize name, description, dueDate, listOfTasks, personInCharge;

- (id)init{
    self = [super init];
    if (self) {
        self.listOfTasks = [[NSMutableArray alloc] init];
    }
    return self;
}

-(void)writeReportToLog{
    NSLog(@"PROJECT");
    NSLog(@"  name = %@", self.name);
    NSLog(@"  description = %@", self.description);
    NSLog(@"  dueDate = %@", self.dueDate);
    NSLog(@"  personInCharge = %@", self.personInCharge);
    NSLog(@"TASKS");
    [self.listOfTasks enumerateObjectsUsingBlock:^(id obj, NSUInteger idx, BOOL *stop) {
        [obj writeReportToLog];
    }];
}

- (void) encodeWithCoder:(NSCoder *)encoder {
    [encoder encodeObject:self.name forKey:@"namekey"];
    [encoder encodeObject:self.description forKey:@"descriptionkey"];
    [encoder encodeObject:self.dueDate forKey:@"dueDatekey"];
    [encoder encodeObject:self.personInCharge forKey:@"personInChargekey"];
    [encoder encodeObject:self.listOfTasks forKey:@"listOfTaskskey"];
}

- (id)initWithCoder:(NSCoder *)decoder {
    self.name = [decoder decodeObjectForKey:@"namekey"];
    self.description = [decoder decodeObjectForKey:@"descriptionkey"];
```

```
    self.dueDate = [decoder decodeObjectForKey:@"dueDatekey"];
    self.personInCharge = [decoder decodeObjectForKey:@"personInChargekey"];
    self.listOfTasks = [decoder decodeObjectForKey:@"listOfTaskskey"];

    return self;
}

@end
```

Listing 9-43. *Task.h*

```
#import <Foundation/Foundation.h>
#import "Worker.h"

@interface Task : NSObject<NSCoding>

@property(strong)NSString *name;
@property(strong)NSString *details;
@property(strong)NSDate *dueDate;
@property(assign)int priority;
@property(strong)Worker *assignedWorker;

-(void)writeReportToLog;

@end
```

Listing 9-44. *Task.m*

```
#import "Task.h"

@implementation Task
@synthesize name, details, dueDate, priority, assignedWorker;

-(void)writeReportToLog{
    NSLog(@"   name = %@", self.name);
    NSLog(@"    description = %@", self.details);
    NSLog(@"    dueDate = %@", self.dueDate);
    NSLog(@"    priority = %i", self.priority);
    NSLog(@"    assignedWorker = %@", self.assignedWorker);
}

- (void) encodeWithCoder:(NSCoder *)encoder {
    [encoder encodeObject:self.name forKey:@"namekey"];
    [encoder encodeObject:self.details forKey:@"detailskey"];
    [encoder encodeObject:self.dueDate forKey:@"dueDatekey"];
    [encoder encodeObject:[NSNumber numberWithInt:self.priority] forKey:@"prioritykey"];
    [encoder encodeObject:self.assignedWorker forKey:@"assignedWorkerkey"];
}
```

```
- (id)initWithCoder:(NSCoder *)decoder {
    self.name = [decoder decodeObjectForKey:@"namekey"];
    self.details = [decoder decodeObjectForKey:@"detailskey"];
    self.dueDate = [decoder decodeObjectForKey:@"dueDatekey"];
    self.priority = [[decoder decodeObjectForKey:@"prioritykey"] intValue];
    self.assignedWorker = [decoder decodeObjectForKey:@"assignedWorkerkey"];

    return self;
}

@end
```

Listing 9-45. *Worker.h*

```
#import <Foundation/Foundation.h>

@interface Worker : NSObject<NSCoding>

@property(strong)NSString *name;
@property(strong)NSString *role;

@end
```

Listing 9-46. *Worker.m*

```
#import "Worker.h"

@implementation Worker
@synthesize name, role;

-(NSString *)description{
    return [NSString stringWithFormat:@"%@, %@", name, role];
}

- (void) encodeWithCoder:(NSCoder *)encoder {
    [encoder encodeObject:self.name forKey:@"namekey"];
    [encoder encodeObject:self.role forKey:@"rolekey"];
}

- (id)initWithCoder:(NSCoder *)decoder {
    self.name = [decoder decodeObjectForKey:@"namekey"];
    self.role = [decoder decodeObjectForKey:@"rolekey"];

    return self;
}

@end
```

Listing 9-47. *main.m*

```
#import <Foundation/Foundation.h>
#import "Project.h"
#import "Task.h"

int main(int argc, const char * argv[]){
    @autoreleasepool {
        //Example of object graph:
        //Create a new project
        Project *workProject01 =[[Project alloc] init];
        workProject01.name = @"Make iOS App";
        workProject01.description = @"Make an iOS application for the iPad";
        workProject01.dueDate = [NSDate date];

        //Setup a new person to be in charge
        Worker *personInCharge = [[Worker alloc] init];
        personInCharge.name = @"Jane Smith";
        personInCharge.role = @"Manager";

        //Assign person to project
        workProject01.personInCharge = personInCharge;

        //Create new task
        Task *task01 = [[Task alloc] init];
        task01.name = @"Learn Objective-C";
        task01.details = @"Learn Objective-C to make Mac apps";
        task01.priority = 1;
        task01.dueDate = [NSDate date];

        //Setup a new person to assign to the task
        Worker *employee = [[Worker alloc] init];
        employee.name = @"David Done";
        employee.role = @"Programmer";

        //Assign worker to task
        task01.assignedWorker = employee;

        //Add task to project
        [workProject01.listOfTasks addObject:task01];

        //Note: you will want to do this for each task that the
        //project needs

        //Create new task
        Task *task02 = [[Task alloc] init];
        task02.name = @"Investigate UIKit";
        task02.details = @"Investigate UIKit to see how it works for users.";
        task02.priority = 3;
        task02.dueDate = [NSDate date];
```

```
        //Assign worker to task
        task02.assignedWorker = employee;

        //Add task to project
        [workProject01.listOfTasks addObject:task02];

        //Create new task
        Task *task03 = [[Task alloc] init];
        task03.name = @"Evaluate";
        task03.details = @"Signoff on initial project progress.";
        task03.priority = 1;
        task03.dueDate = [NSDate date];

        //Assign worker to task
        task03.assignedWorker = personInCharge;

        //Add task to project
        [workProject01.listOfTasks addObject:task03];

        //Archive object graph:
        BOOL dataArchived = [NSKeyedArchiver archiveRootObject:workProject01
                                          toFile:@"/Users/Shared/workProject01.dat"];

        if(dataArchived)
            NSLog(@"Object graph successfully archived");
        else
            NSLog(@"Error attempting to archive object graph");

        //Retrieve object graph
        Project *storedProject = [NSKeyedUnarchiver ↩
unarchiveObjectWithFile:@"/Users/Shared/workProject01.dat"];
        if(storedProject)
            [storedProject writeReportToLog];
        else
            NSLog(@"Error attempting to retrieve the object graph");

    }
    return 0;
}
```

Usage

To use this code, simply add the files from Listings 9-41 through 9-47 to a Mac command-line application, which you can create easily from Xcode. If you run the application, you will see that the objects are archived and retrieved successfully. To make sure that the archive was created successfully, locate the file on your Mac. You can open this file with a text editor but the contents will not be readable. If you like, you can also try loading the saved object graph into a second application. Copy your Xcode project and paste it into a new location with a different project name. Keep all the code files except for `main.m`. Replace the code in `main.m` with the following code:

```
#import <Foundation/Foundation.h>
#import "Project.h"
#import "Task.h"

int main(int argc, const char * argv[]){
    @autoreleasepool {

        //Retrieve object graph
        Project *storedProject = [NSKeyedUnarchiver ↵
unarchiveObjectWithFile:@"/Users/Shared/workProject01.dat"];

        if(storedProject)
            [storedProject writeReportToLog];
        else
            NSLog(@"Error attempting to retrieve the object graph");

    }
    return 0;
}
```

Build and run this application (making sure you ran the application from the recipe first) and you should see the contents of your object graph print out like this:

```
PROJECT
    name = Make iOS App
    description = Make an iOS application for the iPad
    dueDate = 2012-03-28 21:13:01 +0000
    personInCharge = Jane Smith, Manager
 TASKS
    name = Learn Objective-C
      description = Learn Objective-C to make Mac apps
...
```

Chapter 10

Core Data

Core Data is a technology that is used to solve the problem of data persistence in applications. When users add to the object graph or make changes to the object graph, they generally expect those changes to be reflected in the application the next time that they use it.

For you to provide this, you need to come up with a way for your applications to remember these changes to the object graph. This is what data persistence is all about, and Core Data is the technology that you can use to solve this problem. The recipes in this chapter will show you how to:

- Add Core Data support to your Mac and iOS applications
- Compose an entity description
- Create a managed object
- Execute fetch requests
- Execute fetch requests with NSPredicate
- Execute fetch requests with NSSortDescriptor
- Post changes to your object graph to the data store
- Represent to-many relationships with Core Data

NOTE: Core Data can be pretty complex and requires a few steps to set it up. The first three recipes are required before you can build and test your project.

10.1 Adding Core Data Support to an Application

Problem

You want to add Core Data support to your iOS or Mac application.

Solution

Link to the Core Data framework and add the Core Data stack to the class that you would like to support Core Data.

How It Works

Core Data is used to store object data for an application. While Core Data may use a database or file to hold the object content, you don't need to know these details to use Core Data. You do need to link first to the Core Data framework and set up some Core Data objects in order to use Core Data for your objects.

For this recipe, you're going to re-create the object graph that was used in the Mac app that you created in Recipe 9.1. This time, however, you will use an iOS app and Core Data to compose the object graph. Core Data is something that you can use with either Mac or iOS.

> **NOTE:** Xcode provides a checkbox titled "Use Core Data for Storage" that will do some of this setup work for you automatically. You can use that as an alternative to this recipe, but be aware that the application template won't match exactly what you are doing here.

Link to Core Data Framework

Your iOS application is not necessarily linked to Core Data so you need to do this yourself. To link to a framework, go to your Xcode project's Linked Frameworks pane. See Figure 10-1 to locate this.

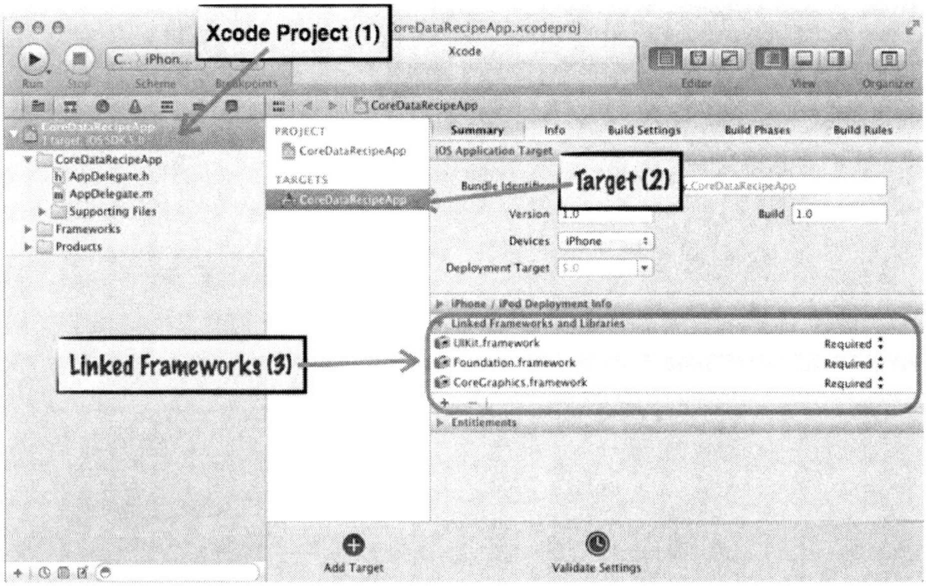

Figure 10-1. *Linking to the Core Data Framework*

Click the plus button in your Linked Frameworks pane (marked (3) in Figure 10-1). You will get a screen with a list of all the available frameworks. There is also a search bar that you can use to filter the list to make it easier to locate the Core Data framework. See Figure 10-2 as a reference.

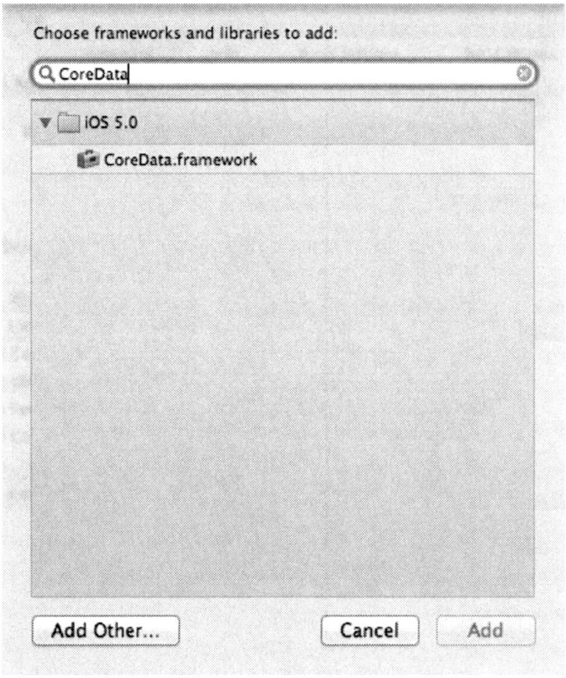

Figure 10-2. *Choosing the Core Data framework*

Select the item named CoreData.framework and click the Add button.

Adding the Core Data Stack

Core Data needs some key objects to work. These objects are referred to as the *Core Data stack*. You need these objects located in the class where you want to implement data persistence. Often you will see the Core Data stack located in the app delegate or a root model class.

In this recipe you are going to add Core Data support to the object graph that you created in Recipe 9.1; you are going to add a new model class that will apply to the entire application. This will serve as your root model and you will locate the Core Data stack here along with an array that will later be used to store a list of projects.

The first step is to create the new root model class that you can simply name AppModel (see Recipe 1.3 for more details on how to add a custom class to your Xcode project). The first thing that you need to add to the AppModel class is a function that returns the URL that you are going to use for your data store.

> **NOTE:** The data store is the file that stores the data on the user's device in the application's Documents directory. This can be a SQLite database or another file. While you need to supply Core Data with this URL, you don't need to worry about the specifics of the database, nor do you need to create the database yourself. If the file or database is not present, Core Data will create it for you.

Here is the function that returns the URL of the data store:

```objc
#import "AppModel.h"

@implementation AppModel

- (NSURL *)dataStoreURL {

    NSString *docDir =
[NSSearchPathForDirectoriesInDomains(NSDocumentDirectory, ↵
NSUserDomainMask, YES) lastObject];

    return [NSURL fileURLWithPath:[docDir ↵
stringByAppendingPathComponent:@"DataStore.sql"]];
}

@end
```

Next, add the managed object model to `AppModel`. The managed object model maintains a collection of data schemas. *Data schemas* are specifications of collections of the entities that make up your object graph. These specifications are used by Core Data to figure out how to make object data persistent. In a later recipe, you will compose the documents that Core Data uses for these data schemas.

You are going to add the managed object model to `AppModel` by adding a property of type `NSManagedObjectModel`. This property is marked as `readonly` in the `AppModel` interface. Since `NSManagedObjectModel` is a Core Data class, you need to import Core Data into `AppModel` here as well.

```objc
#import <Foundation/Foundation.h>
#import <CoreData/CoreData.h>

@interface AppModel : NSObject

-(NSURL *)dataStoreURL;

@property (nonatomic, strong, readonly) NSManagedObjectModel *managedObjectModel;
```

@end

Moving over to the AppModel implementation file, you must code your own assessor for this readonly property.

```
#import "AppModel.h"

@implementation AppModel
NSManagedObjectModel *_managedObjectModel;

...

- (NSManagedObjectModel *)managedObjectModel {
    if (_managedObjectModel) {
        return _managedObjectModel;
    }
    _managedObjectModel = [NSManagedObjectModel mergedModelFromBundles:nil];
    return _managedObjectModel;
}
```

@end

This readonly property assessor is lazily creating the managed object model only if the object hasn't already been created. The managed object model will be created with each schema that you have included in your project.

Next you need the persistent store coordinator. This part of the Core Data stack is responsible for connecting the data store to the managed object model. The persistent store coordinator is also used by the managed object content (you add this next) to persist changes to the object graph.

You add this Core Data stack object to the AppModel class following the same pattern used for the managed object model.

```
- (NSPersistentStoreCoordinator *)persistentStoreCoordinator {
    if (_persistentStoreCoordinator) {
        return _persistentStoreCoordinator;
    }

    NSError *error = nil;
    _persistentStoreCoordinator = [[NSPersistentStoreCoordinator alloc] ↵
initWithManagedObjectModel:[self managedObjectModel]];
    if (![_persistentStoreCoordinator addPersistentStoreWithType:NSSQLiteStoreType
                                               configuration:nil
                                                         URL:[self dataStoreURL]
                                                     options:nil
                                                       error:&error]) {
        NSLog(@"Unresolved Core Data error with persistentStoreCoordinator: %@, %@", ↵
error, [error userInfo]);
```

```
    }

    return _persistentStoreCoordinator;
}
```

This one is a little more involved because you need to create the store coordinator with a reference to the managed object model and you need to add the data store reference so Core Data knows where to manage the object data.

> **NOTE:** You are not explicitly listing the interface for the persistent store coordinator or the managed object context here since they follow the same pattern as the managed object model. Listing 10-2 shows the entire interface.

Of course, the persistent store coordinator and the next Core Data stack object you add both need a property declaration like the managed object model did. These all follow the same pattern so I won't repeat that code here, but you can look at Listing 10-2 for the remaining property declarations.

Next, you need the managed object context. This core data stack object is responsible for managing a collection of managed objects. *Managed objects* are the objects for which Core Data is responsible. These are the objects that need data persistence.

The managed object context acts like a scratch pad for all the changes to the object graph. At key points in an application's lifecycle, you will use the managed object context to retrieve objects and post the changes to the object graph back to the data store. Here is how to add the managed object context:

```
- (NSManagedObjectContext *)managedObjectContext {
    if (_managedObjectContext) {
        return _managedObjectContext;
    }

    if ([self persistentStoreCoordinator]) {
        _managedObjectContext = [[NSManagedObjectContext alloc] init];
        [_managedObjectContext setPersistentStoreCoordinator:[self ↵
persistentStoreCoordinator]];
    }

    return _managedObjectContext;
}
```

As you can see from the function, the managed object context simply needs a reference to the persistent store coordinator to function. That's the Core Data stack for iOS. This gives you Core Data support, but there are other steps you need to take before you can show how Core Data works in a real application.

See Listings 10-1 through 10-4.

The Code

Listing 10-1. *AppModel.h*

```
#import <Foundation/Foundation.h>
#import <CoreData/CoreData.h>

@interface AppModel : NSObject

-(NSURL *)dataStoreURL;

@property (nonatomic, strong, readonly) NSManagedObjectModel *managedObjectModel;
@property (nonatomic, strong, readonly) NSPersistentStoreCoordinator ↵
*persistentStoreCoordinator;
@property (nonatomic, strong, readonly) NSManagedObjectContext *managedObjectContext;

@end
```

Listing 10-2. *AppModel.m*

```
#import "AppModel.h"

@implementation AppModel
NSManagedObjectModel *_managedObjectModel;
NSPersistentStoreCoordinator *_persistentStoreCoordinator;
NSManagedObjectContext *_managedObjectContext;

- (NSURL *)dataStoreURL {

    NSString *docDir = [NSSearchPathForDirectoriesInDomains(NSDocumentDirectory, ↵
NSUserDomainMask, YES) lastObject];

    return [NSURL fileURLWithPath:[docDir
stringByAppendingPathComponent:@"DataStore.sql"]];
}

- (NSManagedObjectModel *)managedObjectModel {
    if (_managedObjectModel) {
        return _managedObjectModel;
    }
    _managedObjectModel = [NSManagedObjectModel mergedModelFromBundles:nil];
    return _managedObjectModel;
}
```

```objc
- (NSPersistentStoreCoordinator *)persistentStoreCoordinator {
    if (_persistentStoreCoordinator) {
        return _persistentStoreCoordinator;
    }

    NSError *error = nil;
    _persistentStoreCoordinator = [[NSPersistentStoreCoordinator alloc] ↵
initWithManagedObjectModel:[self managedObjectModel]];
    if (![_persistentStoreCoordinator addPersistentStoreWithType:NSSQLiteStoreType
                                            configuration:nil
                                                    URL:[self dataStoreURL]
                                                options:nil
                                                    error:&error]) {
        NSLog(@"Unresolved Core Data error with persistentStoreCoordinator: %@, %@", ↵
error, [error userInfo]);
    }

    return _persistentStoreCoordinator;
}

- (NSManagedObjectContext *)managedObjectContext {
    if (_managedObjectContext) {
        return _managedObjectContext;
    }

    if ([self persistentStoreCoordinator]) {
        _managedObjectContext = [[NSManagedObjectContext alloc] init];
        [_managedObjectContext setPersistentStoreCoordinator:[self ↵
persistentStoreCoordinator]];
    }

    return _managedObjectContext;
}

@end
```

Listing 10-3. *AppDelegate.h*

```
#import <UIKit/UIKit.h>

@interface AppDelegate : UIResponder <UIApplicationDelegate>

@property (strong, nonatomic) UIWindow *window;

@end
```

Listing 10-4. *AppDelegate.m*

```
#import "AppDelegate.h"

@implementation AppDelegate
@synthesize window = _window;

- (BOOL)application:(UIApplication *)application didFinishLaunchingWithOptions: ⏎
(NSDictionary *)launchOptions{
    self.window = [[UIWindow alloc] initWithFrame:[[UIScreen mainScreen] bounds]];
    self.window.backgroundColor = [UIColor whiteColor];
    [self.window makeKeyAndVisible];
    return YES;
}

@end
```

Usage

Core Data requires you to set up a few things before you can actually test code. For now, you can simply link to the Core Data framework and add the AppModel class to an iOS app. Build your application and make sure that you don't see any errors. The upcoming recipes will assume that you have the Core Data stack in place.

10.2 Adding an Entity Description

Problem

You need to describe the entity that will be managed by Core Data.

Solution

Add a data model file to your application and then use the data model editor to describe your entity.

How It Works

You can use Xcode to lay out entities and attributes. Store these entity descriptions in a special file called a data model. For this recipe, you will create an entity description for the entity project. This is the same project that you set up in Recipe 9.1.

The first thing you need to do is add the data model to your application. From Xcode, go to File ➤ New ➤ File. Then choose iOS ➤ Core Data ➤ Data Model. You can name the file whatever you want, but I'll leave the default name of Model. You should see a new file named Model.xcdatamodeld appear in the Project Navigator. If you select this file, you will see something like Figure 10-3 appear in the editor screen.

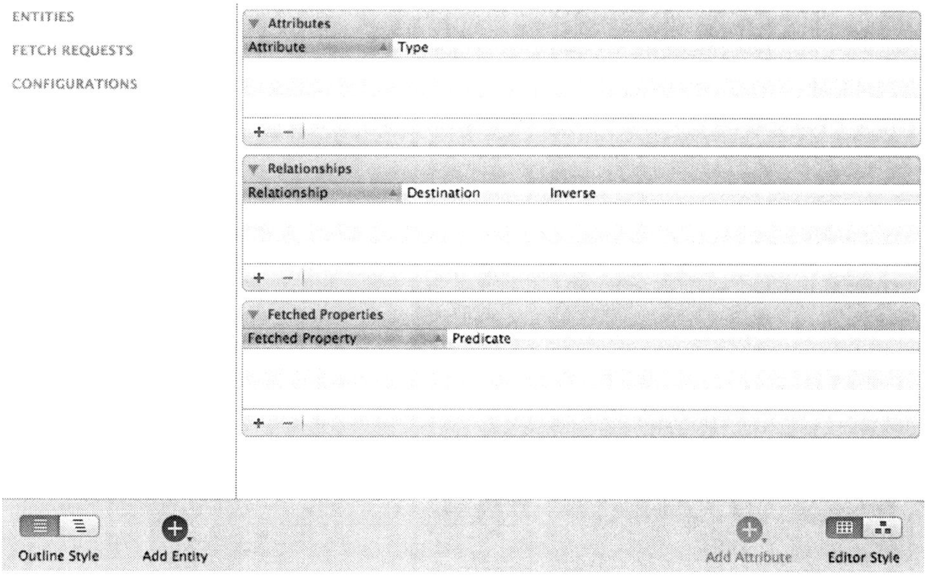

Figure 10-3. *Data model editor*

The data model editor is where you will describe the Project entity. Click the Add Entity button in the bottom left area in the screen. A new entry will appear at the top left area in the data model editor under the title entity. Name your entity `Project`.

Once you have an entity started, you can describe the entity by adding attributes to it. These attributes will be turned into code properties later. Based on Recipe 9-1, you already know that `Project` has these attributes: name, description, and a due date.

> **NOTE:** The `Project` class from Recipe 9.1 also had `Worker` and `listOfTasks` properties. These are a little bit more involved, so you'll revisit these two properties in the upcoming recipe on establishing relationships in Core Data.

To add an attribute to the `Project` entity, make sure that the `Project` entity is selected in the data model editor and click the Add Attribute button in the bottom right area of the data model editor. The attribute will appear in the center top area of the data model editor and you can type in the name of the attribute (name, in this case).

To the right of the attribute `name` you can also choose a data type. Click the drop-box toward the right and select the data type String for the `name` attribute. Repeat this process for the `description` attribute, but change the name to `descrip`.

> **NOTE:** The word "description" is already used by a Core Data class so you can't use it for the `Project` entity because there will be a conflict.

Name the due date attribute `dueDate` and set Date as the data type.

When you are finished your data model should look like Figure 10-4.

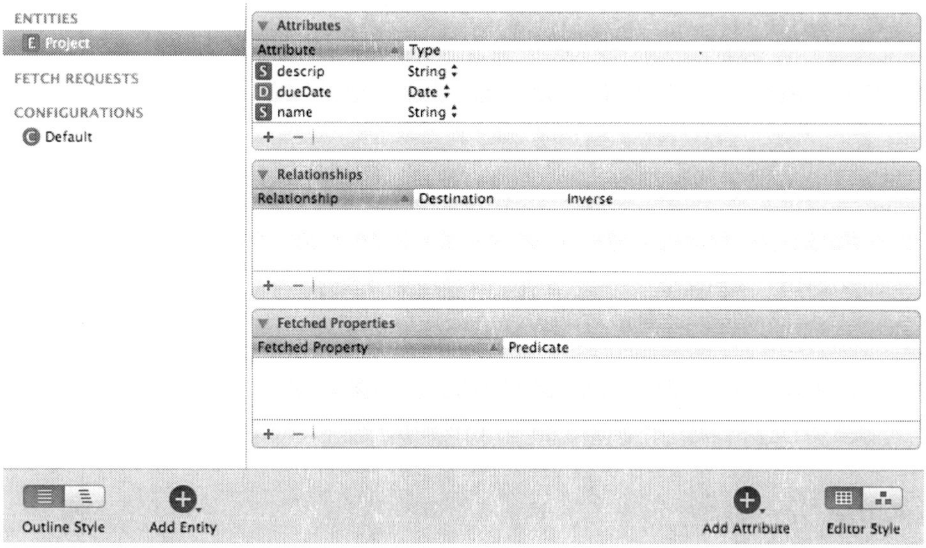

Figure 10-4. *Completed project data model*

That's all there is to using the data model editor to describe an entity.

The Code

> **NOTE:** The code that appears in Listings 10-5 and 10-6 is the default code that Xcode automatically generates when you create a new iOS application. I've made no modifications to it.

Listing 10-5. *AppDelegate.h*

```
#import <UIKit/UIKit.h>

@interface AppDelegate : UIResponder <UIApplicationDelegate>

@property (strong, nonatomic) UIWindow *window;

@end
```

Listing 10-6. *AppDelegate.m*

```
#import "AppDelegate.h"

@implementation AppDelegate
@synthesize window = _window;

- (BOOL)application:(UIApplication *)application didFinishLaunchingWithOptions: ↵
(NSDictionary *)launchOptions{
    self.window = [[UIWindow alloc] initWithFrame:[[UIScreen mainScreen] bounds]];
    self.window.backgroundColor = [UIColor whiteColor];
    [self.window makeKeyAndVisible];
    return YES;
}

@end
```

Usage

Now you're ready to move on to Recipe 10.3 and continue setting up Core Data.

10.3 Adding a Managed Object to an Application

Problem

The entity that you composed in Recipe 10.2 needs an Objective-C class so that you can use it in code.

Solution

Use Xcode to automatically generate a code file based on the entity description that you set up in Recipe 10.2.

How It Works

Core Data uses entity descriptions to set up a database schema and to code a class that you can use in your application. All you need to do is add a new Core Data file to your Xcode project. For this recipe, I'm going to assume that you have already set up the Core Data stack from Recipe 10.1 and the project entity description from Recipe 10.2.

Select the data model file that you created in Recipe 10.2. Also, make sure to select the `Project` entity. Then choose File ➤ New ➤ File. Then choose iOS ➤ Core Data ➤ NSManaged Object subclass. In the dialog that pops up, click Create.

You will see that two files have been generated for you: `Project.h` and `Project.m`. If you click on `Project.h`, you will see this interface:

```
#import <Foundation/Foundation.h>
#import <CoreData/CoreData.h>

@interface Project : NSManagedObject

@property (nonatomic, retain) NSString * descrip;
@property (nonatomic, retain) NSDate * dueDate;
@property (nonatomic, retain) NSString * name;

@end
```

This looks like a typical Objective-C class except that `Project` is a subclass of `NSManagedObject` and you're importing the Core Data framework. Being a subclass of `NSManagedObject` is required for Core Data to be able to take responsibility for `Project`.

Here is what the implementation for `Project` looks like:

```
#import "Project.h"

@implementation Project

@dynamic descrip;
@dynamic dueDate;
@dynamic name;

@end
```

What's notable about this is that these property declarations all come from the entity description that you coded in Recipe 10.2. Also, note the @dynamic keyword here. @dynamic is used like @synthesize to deal with the property assessor code.

> **NOTE:** @dynamic means that the class will deal with the property assessor code at runtime. Normally, if you were to use the @dynamic code on your own, you would need some way to have your class respond to requests for property value getting and setting. NSManagedObject does this for you in the background using key-value coding.

That's all you need to do to create the Project managed object. See Listings 10-7 through 10-12.

The Code

Listing 10-7. *AppDelegate.h*

```
#import <UIKit/UIKit.h>

@interface AppDelegate : UIResponder <UIApplicationDelegate>

@property (strong, nonatomic) UIWindow *window;

@end
```

Listing 10-8. *AppDelegate.m*

```
#import "AppDelegate.h"

@implementation AppDelegate
@synthesize window = _window;

- (BOOL)application:(UIApplication *)application didFinishLaunchingWithOptions:
(NSDictionary *)launchOptions{
    self.window = [[UIWindow alloc] initWithFrame:[[UIScreen mainScreen] bounds]];
    self.window.backgroundColor = [UIColor whiteColor];
    [self.window makeKeyAndVisible];
    return YES;
}

@end
```

Listing 10-9. *AppModel.h*

```
#import <Foundation/Foundation.h>
#import <CoreData/CoreData.h>

@interface AppModel : NSObject

-(NSURL *)dataStoreURL;

@property (nonatomic, strong, readonly) NSManagedObjectModel *managedObjectModel;
@property (nonatomic, strong, readonly) NSPersistentStoreCoordinator ↵
*persistentStoreCoordinator;
@property (nonatomic, strong, readonly) NSManagedObjectContext *managedObjectContext;

@end
```

Listing 10-10. *AppModel.m*

```
#import "AppModel.h"

@implementation AppModel
NSManagedObjectModel *_managedObjectModel;
NSPersistentStoreCoordinator *_persistentStoreCoordinator;
NSManagedObjectContext *_managedObjectContext;

- (NSURL *)dataStoreURL {

    NSString *docDir = [NSSearchPathForDirectoriesInDomains(NSDocumentDirectory, ↵
NSUserDomainMask, YES) lastObject];

    return [NSURL fileURLWithPath:[docDir ↵
stringByAppendingPathComponent:@"DataStore.sql"]];
}

- (NSManagedObjectModel *)managedObjectModel {
    if (_managedObjectModel) {
        return _managedObjectModel;
    }
    _managedObjectModel = [NSManagedObjectModel mergedModelFromBundles:nil];
    return _managedObjectModel;
}

- (NSPersistentStoreCoordinator *)persistentStoreCoordinator {
    if (_persistentStoreCoordinator) {
        return _persistentStoreCoordinator;
    }

    NSError *error = nil;
    _persistentStoreCoordinator = [[NSPersistentStoreCoordinator alloc] ↵
initWithManagedObjectModel:[self managedObjectModel]];
```

```
    if (![_persistentStoreCoordinator addPersistentStoreWithType:NSSQLiteStoreType
                                            configuration:nil
                                                      URL:[self dataStoreURL]
                                                  options:nil
                                                    error:&error]) {
        NSLog(@"Unresolved Core Data error with persistentStoreCoordinator: %@, %@", ↵
error, [error userInfo]);
    }

    return _persistentStoreCoordinator;
}

- (NSManagedObjectContext *)managedObjectContext {
    if (_managedObjectContext) {
        return _managedObjectContext;
    }

    if ([self persistentStoreCoordinator]) {
        _managedObjectContext = [[NSManagedObjectContext alloc] init];
        [_managedObjectContext setPersistentStoreCoordinator:[self ↵
persistentStoreCoordinator]];
    }

    return _managedObjectContext;
}

@end
```

Listing 10-11. *Project.h*

```
#import <Foundation/Foundation.h>
#import <CoreData/CoreData.h>

@interface Project : NSManagedObject

@property (nonatomic, retain) NSString * descrip;
@property (nonatomic, retain) NSDate * dueDate;
@property (nonatomic, retain) NSString * name;

@end
```

Listing 10-12. *Project.m*

```
#import "Project.h"

@implementation Project

@dynamic descrip;
@dynamic dueDate;
@dynamic name;
```

```
@end
```

Usage

You are getting closer to testing Core Data out, but as of yet there is still nothing to test with this code. In the next recipe, you'll start to see how this all starts to come together.

10.4 Adding a Managed Object to Core Data

Problem

You want to use objects that are managed by Core Data.

Solution

Use the managed object context to create a new managed object and save the managed object to the data store.

How It Works

For this recipe, you will work on the Xcode project from Recipe 10.3 that has the Core Data stack and `Project` managed object class already set up. To create a new managed object, use the managed object context with the `NSEntityDescription` class function `insertNewObjectForEntityForName:inManagedObjectContext:`. This function needs the name of the managed object class `Project` and it returns a reference to the managed object that was just created.

```
Project *managedProject = (Project *)[NSEntityDescription ↵
insertNewObjectForEntityForName:@"Project"↵
inManagedObjectContext:[self managedObjectContext]];
```

This gives you a `Project` object named `managedProject`. The first thing you should do is set some of this project's properties.

```
managedProject.name = @"New Project";
managedProject.descrip = @"This is a new project";
managedProject.dueDate = [NSDate date];
```

This `managedProject` object only exists in the managed object context at first. The managed object context functions like a scratch pad where you can place objects before they are ready to be stored in the data store.

Posting Back to the Data Store

Now that you have created content, you need to use the managed object context to post this change back to the data store. To do this, send the `save` message to the managed object context.

```
[[self managedObjectContext] save:nil];
```

Note that this line of code is how you send the `save` message from the `AppModel` class. If you want to send the save message from another class, like the app delegate, you can send the save message to the local `AppModel` reference; you can see this in Listing 10-14.

After you do this, you've posted all the changes to the managed object context that were made since the last `save` message was sent. You can use an `NSError` object here as a parameter if you wish; for this example I simply used `nil`. You can retrieve this object from the data store at a later date.

Note that you include this code in the `init` function, so take a look at Listings 10-13 through 10-18 to see how this all fits into `AppModel` in context. The code to create a new project managed object is put into a function that returns a `Project` object so it's easier to test from other classes like the app delegate.

The Code

Listing 10-13. *AppDelegate.h*

```objc
#import <UIKit/UIKit.h>
#import "AppModel.h"

@interface AppDelegate : UIResponder <UIApplicationDelegate>

@property (strong, nonatomic) UIWindow *window;

@end
```

Listing 10-14. *AppDelegate.m*

```objc
#import "AppDelegate.h"

@implementation AppDelegate
@synthesize window = _window;
```

```
- (BOOL)application:(UIApplication *)application didFinishLaunchingWithOptions: ↵
(NSDictionary *)launchOptions{

    //Create a new AppModel instance
    AppModel *dataModel = [[AppModel alloc] init];

    //Get a new project from dateModel and use it
    Project *newProject = [dataModel makeNewProject];
    newProject.name = @"App Delegate's Project";
    NSLog(@"project.name = %@", newProject.name);
    NSLog(@"project.descrip = %@", newProject.descrip);
    NSLog(@"project.dueDate = %@\n", newProject.dueDate);

    //Post changes back to date store
    [[dataModel managedObjectContext] save:nil];

    self.window = [[UIWindow alloc] initWithFrame:[[UIScreen mainScreen] bounds]];
    self.window.backgroundColor = [UIColor whiteColor];
    [self.window makeKeyAndVisible];
    return YES;
}

@end
```

Listing 10-15. *AppModel.h*

```
#import <Foundation/Foundation.h>
#import <CoreData/CoreData.h>
#import "Project.h"

@interface AppModel : NSObject

-(NSURL *)dataStoreURL;
-(Project *)makeNewProject;

@property (nonatomic, strong, readonly) NSManagedObjectModel *managedObjectModel;
@property (nonatomic, strong, readonly) NSPersistentStoreCoordinator ↵
*persistentStoreCoordinator;
@property (nonatomic, strong, readonly) NSManagedObjectContext *managedObjectContext;

@end
```

Listing 10-16. *AppModel.m*

```
#import "AppModel.h"

@implementation AppModel
NSManagedObjectModel *_managedObjectModel;
NSPersistentStoreCoordinator *_persistentStoreCoordinator;
```

```objc
NSManagedObjectContext *_managedObjectContext;

-(Project *)makeNewProject{

    Project *managedProject = (Project *)[NSEntityDescription ↵
insertNewObjectForEntityForName:@"Project"↵
inManagedObjectContext:[self managedObjectContext]];

    managedProject.name = @"New Project";
    managedProject.descrip = @"This is a new project";
    managedProject.dueDate = [NSDate date];

    return managedProject;

}

- (NSURL *)dataStoreURL {

    NSString *docDir = [NSSearchPathForDirectoriesInDomains(NSDocumentDirectory, ↵
NSUserDomainMask, YES) lastObject];

    return [NSURL fileURLWithPath:[docDir ↵
stringByAppendingPathComponent:@"DataStore.sql"]];
}

- (NSManagedObjectModel *)managedObjectModel {
    if (_managedObjectModel) {
        return _managedObjectModel;
    }
    _managedObjectModel = [NSManagedObjectModel mergedModelFromBundles:nil];
    return _managedObjectModel;
}

- (NSPersistentStoreCoordinator *)persistentStoreCoordinator {
    if (_persistentStoreCoordinator) {
        return _persistentStoreCoordinator;
    }

    NSError *error = nil;
    _persistentStoreCoordinator = [[NSPersistentStoreCoordinator alloc] ↵
initWithManagedObjectModel:[self managedObjectModel]];
    if (![_persistentStoreCoordinator addPersistentStoreWithType:NSSQLiteStoreType
                                            configuration:nil
                                                      URL:[self dataStoreURL]
                                                  options:nil
                                                    error:&error]) {
        NSLog(@"Unresolved Core Data error with persistentStoreCoordinator: %@, %@", ↵
error, [error userInfo]);
    }
```

```
    return _persistentStoreCoordinator;
}

- (NSManagedObjectContext *)managedObjectContext {
    if (_managedObjectContext) {
        return _managedObjectContext;
    }

    if ([self persistentStoreCoordinator]) {
        _managedObjectContext = [[NSManagedObjectContext alloc] init];
        [_managedObjectContext setPersistentStoreCoordinator:[self ↵
persistentStoreCoordinator]];
    }

    return _managedObjectContext;
}

@end
```

Listing 10-17. *Project.h*

```
#import <Foundation/Foundation.h>
#import <CoreData/CoreData.h>

@interface Project : NSManagedObject

@property (nonatomic, retain) NSString * descrip;
@property (nonatomic, retain) NSDate * dueDate;
@property (nonatomic, retain) NSString * name;

@end
```

Listing 10-18. *Project.m*

```
#import "Project.h"

@implementation Project

@dynamic descrip;
@dynamic dueDate;
@dynamic name;

@end
```

Usage

At long last, you can now test out this Core Data code for yourself. Add the
code from Listings 10-13 through 10-18 and then build and run your Xcode

project. When you run your application you will see the following in your console log window:

```
project.name = App Delegate's Project
project.descrip = This is a new project
project.dueDate = 2012-04-10 14:07:00 +0000
```

Take a look at AppDelegate.m to see how this output was created. A Project managed object instance was created from the AppModel class and returned to the app delegate. As you can see, this process isn't much different than using other Objective-C classes and objects.

10.5 Retrieving Objects from the Data Store

Problem

You want users to retrieve objects from the data store that they have worked on earlier.

Solution

Use a fetch request to retrieve objects that are already in the data store.

How It Works

A *fetch request* is the action of getting objects out of a data store. Use the NSFetchRequest class to create the request and NSEntityDescription to specify the type of entity that you want to retrieve from the data store.

You can create an NSFetchRequest object using the alloc and init constructors.

```
NSFetchRequest *request = [[NSFetchRequest alloc] init];
```

You also need an entity description so Core Data knows what it's supposed to fetch.

```
NSEntityDescription *entity = [NSEntityDescription entityForName:@"Project"
                                  inManagedObjectContext:[self ↵
managedObjectContext]];

NSEntityDescription *entity = [NSEntityDescription entityForName:@"Project"
```

```
                                    inManagedObjectContext:[self managedObjectContext]];
```

You then must assign the entity object to the fetch request's entity property.

```
request.entity = entity;
```

Finally, you can execute the fetch request. The results will be returned back to you as an array.

```
NSArray *listOfProjects = [[self managedObjectContext] executeFetchRequest:request ⏎
error:nil];
```

You can use this array to reference the managed objects that you have available from the data store. If there are no objects yet, the array will still be created but it will have a count of 0.

Here is an example of how you might use this array of project objects:

```
//List out contents of each project
if([listOfProjects count] == 0)
    NSLog(@"There are no projects in the data store yet");
else {
    NSLog(@"HERE ARE THE PROJECTS IN THE DATA STORE");
    [listOfProjects enumerateObjectsUsingBlock:^(id obj, NSUInteger idx, BOOL *stop) {
        NSLog(@"-----");
        NSLog(@"project.name = %@", [obj name]);
        NSLog(@"project.descrip = %@", [obj descrip]);
        NSLog(@"project.dueDate = %@\n", [obj dueDate]);
    }];
}
```

See Listings 10-19 through 10-24.

The Code

Listing 10-19. *AppDelegate.h*

```
#import <UIKit/UIKit.h>
#import "AppModel.h"

@interface AppDelegate : UIResponder <UIApplicationDelegate>

@property (strong, nonatomic) UIWindow *window;

@end
```

Listing 10-20. *AppDelegate.m*

```objc
#import "AppDelegate.h"

@implementation AppDelegate
@synthesize window = _window;

- (BOOL)application:(UIApplication *)application ⮐
didFinishLaunchingWithOptions:(NSDictionary *)launchOptions{

    //Create a new AppModel instance
    AppModel *dataModel = [[AppModel alloc] init];

    //Get a new project from dateModel and use it
    Project *newProject = [dataModel makeNewProject];
    newProject.name = @"App Delegate's Project";
    NSLog(@"project.name = %@", newProject.name);
    NSLog(@"project.descrip = %@", newProject.descrip);
    NSLog(@"project.dueDate = %@\n", newProject.dueDate);

    //Post changes back to date store
    [[dataModel managedObjectContext] save:nil];

    //Get all the projects in the data store
    NSFetchRequest *request = [[NSFetchRequest alloc] init];
    NSEntityDescription *entity = [NSEntityDescription entityForName:@"Project"
                                        inManagedObjectContext:[dataModel ⮐
managedObjectContext]];
    request.entity = entity;
    NSArray *listOfProjects = [[dataModel managedObjectContext] ⮐
executeFetchRequest:request error:nil];

    //List out contents of each project
    if([listOfProjects count] == 0)
        NSLog(@"There are no projects in the data store yet");
    else {
        NSLog(@"HERE ARE THE PROJECTS IN THE DATA STORE");
      [listOfProjects enumerateObjectsUsingBlock:^(id obj, NSUInteger idx, BOOL *stop) {
            NSLog(@"-----");
            NSLog(@"project.name = %@", [obj name]);
            NSLog(@"project.descrip = %@", [obj descrip]);
            NSLog(@"project.dueDate = %@\n", [obj dueDate]);
      }];
    }


    self.window = [[UIWindow alloc] initWithFrame:[[UIScreen mainScreen] bounds]];
    self.window.backgroundColor = [UIColor whiteColor];
    [self.window makeKeyAndVisible];
    return YES;
```

```
}

@end
```

Listing 10-21. *AppModel.h*

```
#import <Foundation/Foundation.h>
#import <CoreData/CoreData.h>
 #import "Project.h"

@interface AppModel : NSObject

-(NSURL *)dataStoreURL;
-(Project *)makeNewProject;

@property (nonatomic, strong, readonly) NSManagedObjectModel *managedObjectModel;
@property (nonatomic, strong, readonly) NSPersistentStoreCoordinator ↵
*persistentStoreCoordinator;
@property (nonatomic, strong, readonly) NSManagedObjectContext *managedObjectContext;

@end
```

Listing 10-22. *AppModel.m*

```
#import "AppModel.h"

@implementation AppModel
NSManagedObjectModel *_managedObjectModel;
NSPersistentStoreCoordinator *_persistentStoreCoordinator;
NSManagedObjectContext *_managedObjectContext;

-(Project *)makeNewProject{

    Project *managedProject = (Project *)[NSEntityDescription ↵
insertNewObjectForEntityForName:@"Project"↵
inManagedObjectContext:[self managedObjectContext]];

    managedProject.name = @"New Project";
    managedProject.descrip = @"This is a new project";
    managedProject.dueDate = [NSDate date];

    return managedProject;

}

- (NSURL *)dataStoreURL {

    NSString *docDir = [NSSearchPathForDirectoriesInDomains(NSDocumentDirectory, ↵
NSUserDomainMask, YES) lastObject];
```

```
        return [NSURL fileURLWithPath:[docDir ↩
stringByAppendingPathComponent:@"DataStore.sql"]];
}

- (NSManagedObjectModel *)managedObjectModel {
    if (_managedObjectModel) {
        return _managedObjectModel;
    }
    _managedObjectModel = [NSManagedObjectModel mergedModelFromBundles:nil];
    return _managedObjectModel;
}

- (NSPersistentStoreCoordinator *)persistentStoreCoordinator {
    if (_persistentStoreCoordinator) {
        return _persistentStoreCoordinator;
    }

    NSError *error = nil;
    _persistentStoreCoordinator = [[NSPersistentStoreCoordinator alloc] ↩
initWithManagedObjectModel:[self managedObjectModel]];
    if (![_persistentStoreCoordinator addPersistentStoreWithType:NSSQLiteStoreType
                                            configuration:nil
                                                      URL:[self dataStoreURL]
                                                  options:nil
                                                    error:&error]) {
        NSLog(@"Unresolved Core Data error with persistentStoreCoordinator: %@, %@", ↩
error, [error userInfo]);
    }

    return _persistentStoreCoordinator;
}

- (NSManagedObjectContext *)managedObjectContext {
    if (_managedObjectContext) {
        return _managedObjectContext;
    }

    if ([self persistentStoreCoordinator]) {
        _managedObjectContext = [[NSManagedObjectContext alloc] init];
        [_managedObjectContext setPersistentStoreCoordinator:[self ↩
persistentStoreCoordinator]];
    }

    return _managedObjectContext;
}

@end
```

Listing 10-23. *Project.h*

```
#import <Foundation/Foundation.h>
#import <CoreData/CoreData.h>

@interface Project : NSManagedObject

@property (nonatomic, retain) NSString * descrip;
@property (nonatomic, retain) NSDate * dueDate;
@property (nonatomic, retain) NSString * name;

@end
```

Listing 10-24. *Project.m*

```
#import "Project.h"

@implementation Project

@dynamic descrip;
@dynamic dueDate;
@dynamic name;

@end
```

Usage

Test this code by adding Listings 10-19 through 10-24 to your own Xcode project. If you build and run this a few times, you will notice that the list from the data store grows by one project for each run. This happens because the new project that was created in the beginning in the app delegate is being added to all the projects that were already present in the data store. If you were to run this app for the first time, your output would look something like this:

```
project.name = App Delegate's Project
project.descrip = This is a new project
project.dueDate = 2012-04-12 15:08:13 +0000
HERE ARE THE PROJECTS IN THE DATA STORE
-----
project.name = App Delegate's Project
project.descrip = This is a new project
project.dueDate = 2012-04-12 15:08:13 +0000
```

> **NOTE:** The managed object context retrieves all the objects in the data store as well as the objects that are in the managed object context but not yet posted to the data store.

10.6 Posting Changes to the Data Store

Problem

As your users work with your application they makes changes to the content that you want to save to the data store.

Solution

Test the managed object context to see if any changes have been made to the user's object graph. If there have been changes, you can either roll back and get rid of the changes or save the changes back to the data store.

How It Works

Managed objects are used like other Objective-C objects. You can use dot notation to change the content in a managed object. Once you do this, the managed object context becomes aware that changes have been made to the object graph.

For example, if you change the content in the project from Recipe 10.5, you would just do something like this:

```
newProject.name = @"Project Has New Name";
newProject.descrip = @"Here is a new revision of the project";
```

What is different from what you've done in previous chapters is that the managed object context has become aware of the changes you've made. You can ask the managed object context if any changes have been made to the object graph by sending the hasChanges message to the context, like so:

```
if([[dataModel managedObjectContext] hasChanges])
    NSLog(@"The object graph has changed");
```

Sometimes you might want to ask the managed object context if anything has changed at key points in an application's lifecycle. If there are changes, you can either save them to the data store or discard them. Here is how you might save changes:

```
if([[dataModel managedObjectContext] hasChanges])
    [[dataModel managedObjectContext] save:nil];
```

Of course, you already saw this operation when you created the first project. You could have also discarded the changes by sending a `rollback` message to the managed object context.

```
if([[dataModel managedObjectContext] hasChanges])
    [[dataModel managedObjectContext] rollback];
```

When you want to delete a managed object you must use the managed object context deleteObject method.

```
[[dataModel managedObjectContext] deleteObject:newProject];
```

You still can roll back or save this change permanently like you did when you changed the property values by sending either the `rollback` or `save` message to the managed object context. See Listings 10-25 through 10-30.

The Code

Listing 10-25. *AppDelegate.h*

```
#import <UIKit/UIKit.h>
#import "AppModel.h"

@interface AppDelegate : UIResponder <UIApplicationDelegate>

@property (strong, nonatomic) UIWindow *window;

@end
```

Listing 10-26. *AppDelegate.m*

```
#import "AppDelegate.h"

@implementation AppDelegate
@synthesize window = _window;

- (BOOL)application:(UIApplication *)application ↵
didFinishLaunchingWithOptions:(NSDictionary *)launchOptions{

    //Create a new AppModel instance
    AppModel *dataModel = [[AppModel alloc] init];

    //Make some projects
```

```
    Project *p1 = [dataModel makeNewProject];
    p1.name = @"Proj1";

    Project *p2 = [dataModel makeNewProject];
    p2.name = @"Proj2";

    Project *p3 = [dataModel makeNewProject];
    p3.name = @"Proj3";

    Project *p4 = [dataModel makeNewProject];
    p4.name = @"Proj4";

    [[dataModel managedObjectContext] save:nil];

    //Get all the projects in the data store
    NSFetchRequest *request = [[NSFetchRequest alloc] init];
    NSEntityDescription *entity = [NSEntityDescription entityForName:@"Project"
                                        inManagedObjectContext:[dataModel ↩
managedObjectContext]];
    request.entity = entity;
    NSArray *listOfProjects = [[dataModel managedObjectContext] ↩
executeFetchRequest:request error:nil];

    //Print out contents of all the projects
    NSLog(@"-----");
    NSLog(@"NEW PROJECTS IN CONTEXT");
    [listOfProjects enumerateObjectsUsingBlock:^(id obj, NSUInteger idx, BOOL *stop) {
        NSLog(@"project.name = %@", [obj name]);
    }];

    //Rollback example
    Project *rollbackProject = [listOfProjects objectAtIndex:0];
    rollbackProject.name = @"Rollback Project";

    //Look at changed object
    NSLog(@"-----");
    NSLog(@"CHANGED PROJECTS IN CONTEXT");
    [listOfProjects enumerateObjectsUsingBlock:^(id obj, NSUInteger idx, BOOL *stop) {
        NSLog(@"project.name = %@", [obj name]);
    }];

    //Discard changes
    if([[dataModel managedObjectContext] hasChanges])
        [[dataModel managedObjectContext] rollback];

    //Look at object after rollback
    NSLog(@"-----");
    NSLog(@"PROJECTS IN CONTEXT AFTER ROLLBACK");
    [listOfProjects enumerateObjectsUsingBlock:^(id obj, NSUInteger idx, BOOL *stop) {
        NSLog(@"project.name = %@", [obj name]);
```

```
    }];

    //Delete second and third projects
    [[dataModel managedObjectContext] deleteObject:p2];
    [[dataModel managedObjectContext] deleteObject:p3];

    //save back to data store
    [[dataModel managedObjectContext] save:nil];

    //Get all the projects in the data store
    request = [[NSFetchRequest alloc] init];
    entity = [NSEntityDescription entityForName:@"Project"
                        inManagedObjectContext:[dataModel managedObjectContext]];
    request.entity = entity;
    listOfProjects = [[dataModel managedObjectContext] executeFetchRequest:request ↵
error:nil];

    //Look at objects after deletion
    NSLog(@"-----");
    NSLog(@"PROJECTS IN CONTEXT AFTER DELETION");
    [listOfProjects enumerateObjectsUsingBlock:^(id obj, NSUInteger idx, BOOL *stop) {
        NSLog(@"project.name = %@", [obj name]);
    }];

    self.window = [[UIWindow alloc] initWithFrame:[[UIScreen mainScreen] bounds]];
    self.window.backgroundColor = [UIColor whiteColor];
    [self.window makeKeyAndVisible];
    return YES;
}

@end
```

Listing 10-27. *AppModel.h*

```
#import <Foundation/Foundation.h>
#import <CoreData/CoreData.h>
 #import "Project.h"

@interface AppModel : NSObject

-(NSURL *)dataStoreURL;
-(Project *)makeNewProject;

@property (nonatomic, strong, readonly) NSManagedObjectModel *managedObjectModel;
@property (nonatomic, strong, readonly) NSPersistentStoreCoordinator ↵
*persistentStoreCoordinator;
@property (nonatomic, strong, readonly) NSManagedObjectContext *managedObjectContext;

@end
```

Listing 10-28. *AppModel.m*

```objc
#import "AppModel.h"

@implementation AppModel
NSManagedObjectModel *_managedObjectModel;
NSPersistentStoreCoordinator *_persistentStoreCoordinator;
NSManagedObjectContext *_managedObjectContext;

-(Project *)makeNewProject{

    Project *managedProject = (Project *)[NSEntityDescription ↵
insertNewObjectForEntityForName:@"Project"↵
inManagedObjectContext:[self managedObjectContext]];

    managedProject.name = @"New Project";
    managedProject.descrip = @"This is a new project";
    managedProject.dueDate = [NSDate date];

    return managedProject;

}

- (NSURL *)dataStoreURL {

    NSString *docDir = [NSSearchPathForDirectoriesInDomains(NSDocumentDirectory, ↵
NSUserDomainMask, YES) lastObject];

    return [NSURL fileURLWithPath:[docDir
stringByAppendingPathComponent:@"DataStore.sql"]];
}

- (NSManagedObjectModel *)managedObjectModel {
    if (_managedObjectModel) {
        return _managedObjectModel;
    }
    _managedObjectModel = [NSManagedObjectModel mergedModelFromBundles:nil];
    return _managedObjectModel;
}

- (NSPersistentStoreCoordinator *)persistentStoreCoordinator {
    if (_persistentStoreCoordinator) {
        return _persistentStoreCoordinator;
    }

    NSError *error = nil;
    _persistentStoreCoordinator = [[NSPersistentStoreCoordinator alloc] ↵
initWithManagedObjectModel:[self managedObjectModel]];
    if (![_persistentStoreCoordinator addPersistentStoreWithType:NSSQLiteStoreType
```

```
                                        configuration:nil
                                             URL:[self dataStoreURL]
                                         options:nil
                                           error:&error]) {
        NSLog(@"Unresolved Core Data error with persistentStoreCoordinator: %@, %@", ↵
error, [error userInfo]);
    }

    return _persistentStoreCoordinator;
}

- (NSManagedObjectContext *)managedObjectContext {
    if (_managedObjectContext) {
        return _managedObjectContext;
    }

    if ([self persistentStoreCoordinator]) {
        _managedObjectContext = [[NSManagedObjectContext alloc] init];
        [_managedObjectContext setPersistentStoreCoordinator:[self ↵
persistentStoreCoordinator]];
    }

    return _managedObjectContext;
}

@end
```

Listing 10-29. *Project.h*

```
#import <Foundation/Foundation.h>
#import <CoreData/CoreData.h>

@interface Project : NSManagedObject

@property (nonatomic, retain) NSString * descrip;
@property (nonatomic, retain) NSDate * dueDate;
@property (nonatomic, retain) NSString * name;

@end
```

Listing 10-30. *Project.m*

```
#import "Project.h"

@implementation Project

@dynamic descrip;
@dynamic dueDate;
@dynamic name;
```

```
@end
```

Usage

Add the code from Listings 10-25 through 10-30 to your Xcode project to test it for yourself. The recipe is a little bit more involved than the main recipe text. The main difference is that it contains four separate projects so that you can clearly see the effects of saving, rolling back, and deleting managed objects from the data store.

The first time that you run your application you should observe something like this in the console log window:

```
-----
NEW PROJECTS IN CONTEXT
project.name = Proj3
project.name = Proj4
project.name = Proj1
project.name = Proj2
-----
CHANGED PROJECTS IN CONTEXT
project.name = Rollback Project
project.name = Proj4
project.name = Proj1
project.name = Proj2
-----
PROJECTS IN CONTEXT AFTER ROLLBACK
project.name = Proj3
project.name = Proj4
project.name = Proj1
project.name = Proj2
-----
PROJECTS IN CONTEXT AFTER DELETION
project.name = Proj4
project.name = Proj1
```

> **NOTE:** The order in which the projects appear may be different for you.

10.7 Using One-To-One Relationships with Core Data

Problem

Your object graph requires you to represent a one-to-one relationship and you want this content managed by Core Data.

Solution

Create at least two entities in the data model and then add a relationship between these entities in the data model editor.

How It Works

You are getting closer to implementing the object graph from Recipe 9.1 in Core Data. What you want to do is add a Worker entity to your data model. Remember that the Worker class from Recipe 9.1 had a name property and a role property. Worker objects could be assigned to projects and tasks. You are going to just recreate the Project to Worker relationship here.

> **NOTE:** You are about to make a big change to your data model. Since the data model is cached after the first time it runs, you can't change the data model without breaking the application. So you need to make sure to delete the application from the iOS Simulator before testing the changes that you are about to make to the data model. Go to the iOS Simulator and click iOS Simulator ➤ Reset Content and Settings. Click the Reset button that pops up.

First, add a new Worker entity to your data model. Follow the same procedure as Recipe 10.2 to add the Worker entity. Your updated model should look like Figure 10-5 when you are finished.

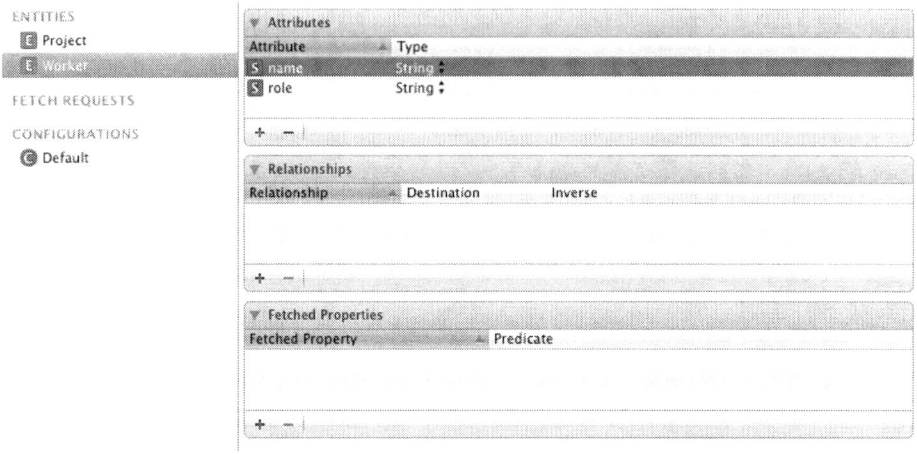

Figure 10-5. *Worker entity*

Next, you need to establish a relationship between `Project` and `Worker`. To establish the relationship, select `Project` in the data model editor and then click the plus button in the Relationships pane of the data model editor. Name the relationship `personInCharge` and set the Destination to `Worker`.

Now you need to define the inverse (or opposite) relationship. This gives you a way to reference the project that a worker is working on.

Select the `Worker` entity and then click the plus button in the Relationships pane of the data model editor. Name the relationship `Project` and set the Destination to `Project`. Select `personInCharge` for the Inverse.

To see everything that you just did at one time, select each entity in the data model editor while holding down the Command key. Both entities will be highlighted and you will see all the attributes and relationships listed at once. Your data model editor should look like Figure 10-6.

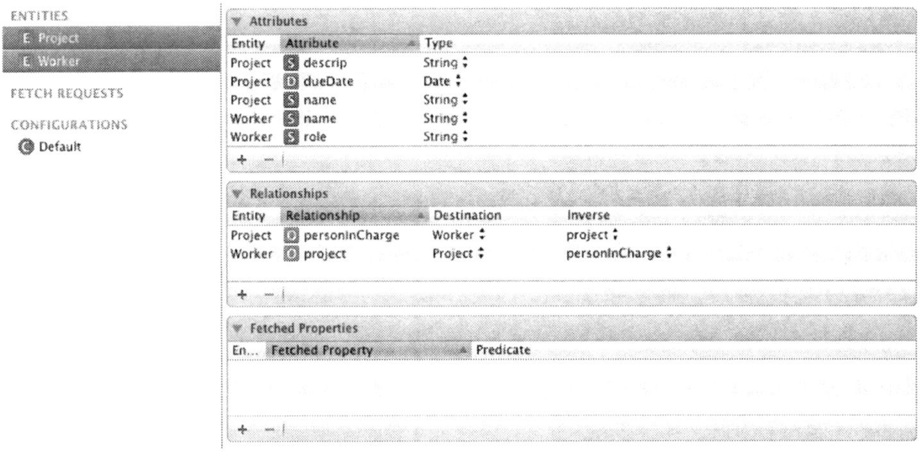

Figure 10-6. *Project-to-Worker and Worker-to-Project relationship*

Keeping both the Project and Worker entities highlighted, go to File ➤ New ➤ File. Then choose iOS ➤ Core Data ➤ NSManagedObject subclass. Click Next and then Create. You will get a warning dialog because you are going to write over the previous Project class file. That is ok since you do need to update it, so click Replace.

In your Xcode project you should have files for the Project and Worker managed object classes. Let's take a look at the Project class interface.

```
#import <Foundation/Foundation.h>
#import <CoreData/CoreData.h>

@class Worker;

@interface Project : NSManagedObject

@property (nonatomic, retain) NSString * descrip;
@property (nonatomic, retain) NSDate * dueDate;
@property (nonatomic, retain) NSString * name;
@property (nonatomic, retain) Worker *personInCharge;

@end
```

The relationship for the person in charge is represented by that last property, personInCharge. You can use this property to get a reference to the Worker object with which you have the one-to-one relationship.

Now look at the Worker class interface to see how the opposite relationship is represented.

```
#import <Foundation/Foundation.h>
#import <CoreData/CoreData.h>

@class Project;

@interface Worker : NSManagedObject

@property (nonatomic, retain) NSString * name;
@property (nonatomic, retain) NSString * role;
@property (nonatomic, retain) Project *project;

@end
```

This gives you the opportunity to get a reference to the project when you only have a reference to the worker on hand.

All of this gives you the infrastructure to set up your relationships and entities. But you now need to add the code to create the objects and establish the relationships. In the Core Data recipes you've done so far you've been using the makeNewProject function in AppModel to do this for you. Logically enough, you need to use a makeNewWorker function to create a Worker instance for you in AppModel.

Change the interface for AppModel to accommodate the function that you need to create a new Worker instance.

```
#import <Foundation/Foundation.h>
#import <CoreData/CoreData.h>
#import "Project.h"
#import "Worker.h"

@interface AppModel : NSObject

-(NSURL *)dataStoreURL;

@property (nonatomic, strong, readonly) NSManagedObjectModel *managedObjectModel;
@property (nonatomic, strong, readonly) NSPersistentStoreCoordinator ↵
*persistentStoreCoordinator;
@property (nonatomic, strong, readonly) NSManagedObjectContext *managedObjectContext;

-(Project *)makeNewProject;
-(Worker *)makeNewWorker;

@end
```

The makeNewWorker function can be coded like this:

```
#import "AppModel.h"

@implementation AppModel
```

...

```objc
-(Worker *)makeNewWorker{
    Worker *managedWorker = (Worker *)[NSEntityDescription ↵
insertNewObjectForEntityForName:@"Worker" ↵
inManagedObjectContext:[self managedObjectContext]];

    managedWorker.name = @"New Worker";
    managedWorker.Role = @"Works on projects";

    return managedWorker;
}
```

...

```objc
@end
```

You establish the relationship itself in the makeNewProject function.

```objc
#import "AppModel.h"

@implementation AppModel
```

...

```objc
-(Project *)makeNewProject{

    Project *managedProject = (Project *)[NSEntityDescription ↵
insertNewObjectForEntityForName:@"Project" ↵
inManagedObjectContext:[self managedObjectContext]];

    managedProject.name = @"New Project";
    managedProject.descrip = @"This is a new project";
    managedProject.dueDate = [NSDate date];

    managedProject.personInCharge = [self makeNewWorker];

    return managedProject;

}
```

...

```objc
@end
```

Now, if you use AppModel to create a new project, you automatically have a Worker assigned and the relationship is established. For instance, you could do something like this:

```
//Create a new AppModel instance
AppModel *dataModel = [[AppModel alloc] init];

//Make some projects
Project *p1 = [dataModel makeNewProject];
p1.name = @"Proj1";

NSLog(@"p1.name = %@, p1.personInCharge = %@", p1.name, p1.personInCharge.name);
```

This will print out the following content to the console log:

```
p1.name = Proj1, p1.personInCharge = New Worker
w.project.name = Proj1
```

See Listings 10-31 through 10-38.

The Code

Listing 10-31. *AppModel.h*

```
#import <Foundation/Foundation.h>
#import <CoreData/CoreData.h>
#import "Project.h"
#import "Worker.h"

@interface AppModel : NSObject

-(NSURL *)dataStoreURL;

@property (nonatomic, strong, readonly) NSManagedObjectModel *managedObjectModel;
@property (nonatomic, strong, readonly) NSPersistentStoreCoordinator
*persistentStoreCoordinator;
@property (nonatomic, strong, readonly) NSManagedObjectContext *managedObjectContext;

-(Project *)makeNewProject;
-(Worker *)makeNewWorker;

@end
```

Listing 10-32. *AppModel.m*

```
#import "AppModel.h"

@implementation AppModel
NSManagedObjectModel *_managedObjectModel;
NSPersistentStoreCoordinator *_persistentStoreCoordinator;
NSManagedObjectContext *_managedObjectContext;

-(Project *)makeNewProject{
```

```objc
    Project *managedProject = (Project *)[NSEntityDescription ↵
insertNewObjectForEntityForName:@"Project" ↵
inManagedObjectContext:[self managedObjectContext]];

    managedProject.name = @"New Project";
    managedProject.descrip = @"This is a new project";
    managedProject.dueDate = [NSDate date];

    managedProject.personInCharge = [self makeNewWorker];

    return managedProject;

}

-(Worker *)makeNewWorker{
    Worker *managedWorker = (Worker *)[NSEntityDescription ↵
insertNewObjectForEntityForName:@"Worker" ↵
inManagedObjectContext:[self managedObjectContext]];

    managedWorker.name = @"New Worker";
    managedWorker.Role = @"Works on projects";

    return managedWorker;
}

- (NSURL *)dataStoreURL {

    NSString *docDir = [NSSearchPathForDirectoriesInDomains(NSDocumentDirectory, ↵
NSUserDomainMask, YES) lastObject];

    return [NSURL fileURLWithPath:[docDir ↵
stringByAppendingPathComponent:@"DataStore.sql"]];
}

- (NSManagedObjectModel *)managedObjectModel {
    if (_managedObjectModel) {
        return _managedObjectModel;
    }
    _managedObjectModel = [NSManagedObjectModel mergedModelFromBundles:nil];
    return _managedObjectModel;
}

- (NSPersistentStoreCoordinator *)persistentStoreCoordinator {
    if (_persistentStoreCoordinator) {
        return _persistentStoreCoordinator;
    }

    NSError *error = nil;
    _persistentStoreCoordinator = [[NSPersistentStoreCoordinator alloc] ↵
```

```
initWithManagedObjectModel:[self managedObjectModel]];
    if (![_persistentStoreCoordinator addPersistentStoreWithType:NSSQLiteStoreType
                                            configuration:nil
                                                    URL:[self dataStoreURL]
                                                options:nil
                                                  error:&error]) {
        NSLog(@"Unresolved Core Data error with persistentStoreCoordinator: %@, %@", ↵
error, [error userInfo]);
    }

    return _persistentStoreCoordinator;
}

- (NSManagedObjectContext *)managedObjectContext {
    if (_managedObjectContext) {
        return _managedObjectContext;
    }

    if ([self persistentStoreCoordinator]) {
        _managedObjectContext = [[NSManagedObjectContext alloc] init];
        [_managedObjectContext setPersistentStoreCoordinator:[self ↵
persistentStoreCoordinator]];
    }

    return _managedObjectContext;
}

@end
```

Listing 10-33. *Worker.h*

```
#import <Foundation/Foundation.h>
#import <CoreData/CoreData.h>

@class Project;

@interface Worker : NSManagedObject

@property (nonatomic, retain) NSString * name;
@property (nonatomic, retain) NSString * role;
@property (nonatomic, retain) Project *project;

@end
```

Listing 10-34. *Worker.m*

```
#import "Worker.h"
#import "Project.h"
```

```
@implementation Worker

@dynamic name;
@dynamic role;
@dynamic project;

@end
```

Listing 10-35. *Project.h*

```
#import <Foundation/Foundation.h>
#import <CoreData/CoreData.h>

@class Worker;

@interface Project : NSManagedObject

@property (nonatomic, retain) NSString * descrip;
@property (nonatomic, retain) NSDate * dueDate;
@property (nonatomic, retain) NSString * name;
@property (nonatomic, retain) Worker *personInCharge;

@end
```

Listing 10-36. *Project.m*

```
#import "Project.h"
#import "Worker.h"

@implementation Project

@dynamic descrip;
@dynamic dueDate;
@dynamic name;
@dynamic personInCharge;

@end
```

Listing 10-37. *AppDelegate.h*

```
#import <UIKit/UIKit.h>
#import "AppModel.h"

@interface AppDelegate : UIResponder <UIApplicationDelegate>

@property (strong, nonatomic) UIWindow *window;

@end
```

Listing 10-38. *AppDelegate.m*

```objc
#import "AppDelegate.h"

@implementation AppDelegate
@synthesize window = _window;

- (BOOL)application:(UIApplication *)application ↵
didFinishLaunchingWithOptions:(NSDictionary *)launchOptions{

    //Create a new AppModel instance
    AppModel *dataModel = [[AppModel alloc] init];

    //Make some projects
    Project *p1 = [dataModel makeNewProject];
    p1.name = @"Proj1";

    NSLog(@"p1.name = %@, p1.personInCharge = %@", p1.name, p1.personInCharge.name);

    Worker *worker = p1.personInCharge;
    NSLog(@"w.project.name = %@", worker.project.name);

    self.window = [[UIWindow alloc] initWithFrame:[[UIScreen mainScreen] bounds]];
    self.window.backgroundColor = [UIColor whiteColor];
    [self.window makeKeyAndVisible];
    return YES;
}

@end
```

Usage

Add the code from Listings 10-31 through 10-38 to your app. If you have been following along with the previous recipes and want to reuse your Xcode project, make sure to delete the application from the iOS Simulator before attempting to test this code.

Build and run your application to see the following output in the console log:

```
p1.name = Proj1, p1.personInCharge = New Worker
w.project.name = Proj1
```

10.8 Using One-To-Many Relationships with Core Data

Problem

Your object graph requires you to represent a one-to-many relationship and you want this content managed by Core Data.

Solution

Create at least two entities in the data model and then add a one-to-many relationship between these entities in the data model editor.

How It Works

You're getting closer to implementing the object graph from Recipe 9.1 in Core Data. What you want to do is add a task entity to your data model. Remember that the Task class from Recipe 9.1 has name, details, dueDate, and priority properties. Task also has a Worker property which you will leave for the next recipe. Tasks are contained in projects so the relationship is going to go from Project to Task. There will be many tasks for each project. You are going to just recreate the Project to Task relationship here.

> **NOTE:** You are about to make another big change to your data model. Since the data model is cached after the first time it runs, you can't change the data model without breaking the application. So you need to make sure to delete the application from the iOS Simulator before testing the changes that you are about to make to the data model. Go to the iOS Simulator and click iOS Simulator ➤ Reset Content and Settings. Click the Reset button that pops up.

Just like in Recipe 10.7, you are going to add another entity to the data model. This entity is called Task and the attributes will match the Task properties from Recipe 9.2. The Task entity description will look like Figure 10-7.

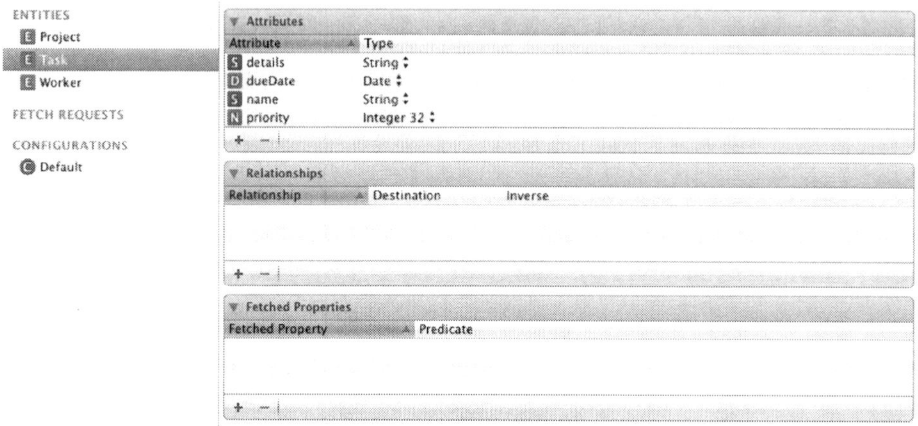

Figure 10-7. *Task entity*

Now you are going to start to establish the relationship between `Project` and `Task`. Select the `Project` entity and click the plus sign in the Relationships pane in the data model editor. Name the relationship `listOfTasks` and set the Destination to `Task`.

To set up the inverse relationship, select the `Task` entity and click the plus sign in the Relationships pane in the data model editor. Name the relationship `project` and set the Destination to `Project`. Choose `listOfTasks` as the Inverse.

Select all three entities in the data model to see everything at once. Alternatively, you can also hold down the Shift key and then click the first and last entity to select all the entities. You should have something that looks like Figure 10-8.

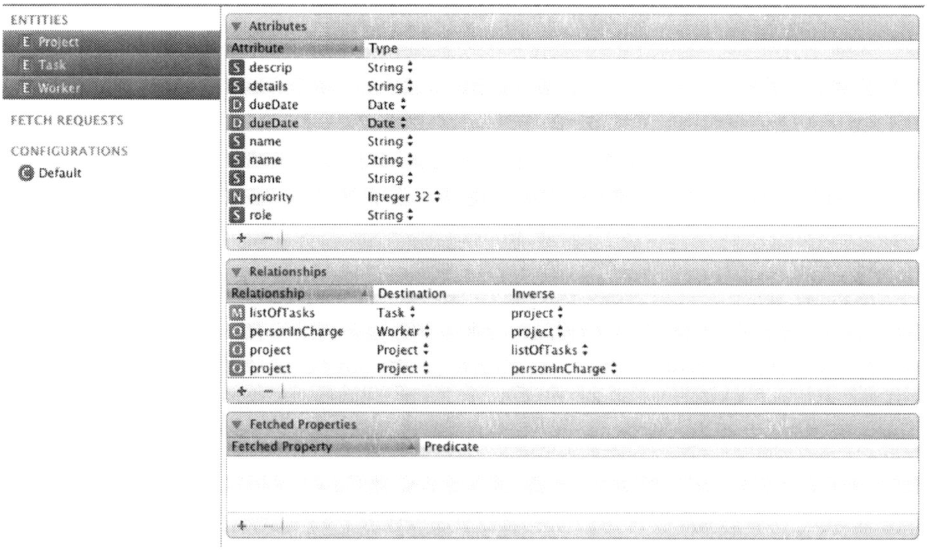

Figure 10-8. *Project, Task, and Worker with relationships*

To see the data model in a more visual way, you can change the editor style by clicking the segmented button in the bottom right hand area of the data model editor (the "Editor Styles: Table, Graph" button). This provides a graphical display that highlights the entities and their relationships. See Figure 10-9 for an example of what it looks like. You may need to move the entities around a little to get them to appear as they do in Figure 10-9.

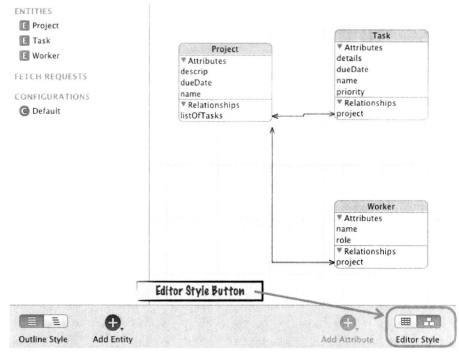

Figure 10-9. *Visual editor style*

You still need to make the Project to Task relationship a one-to-many relationship. To do so, select the listOfTasks relationship and use the data model inspector to change listOfTasks from a one-to-one relationship to a one-to-many relationship.

Select listOfTasks and then open the data model inspector, which is on the right hand side of the data model editor. Make sure that the right pane in Xcode is visible and that you have the data model inspector open (see Figure 10-10).

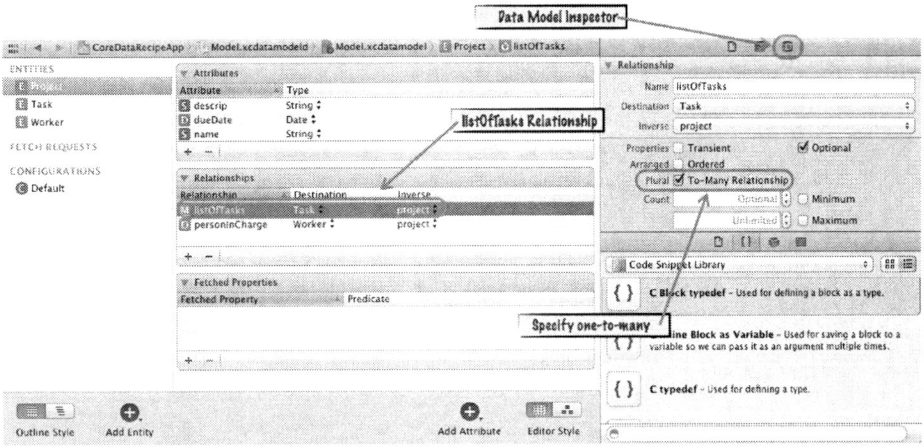

Figure 10-10. *Specifying one-to-many relationships*

In the data inspector, click the checkbox named Plural that reads To-Many Relationship.

Now you are ready to create your managed objects. Make sure each entity is selected in the data model editor and then choose File ➤ New ➤ File. Then choose iOS ➤ Core Data ➤ NSManaged Object subclas**s**. In the dialog that pops up, click Create. You need to allow Xcode to replace the file here.

Look at the `Project` interface to see how the one-to-many relationship is represented in code.

```
#import <Foundation/Foundation.h>
#import <CoreData/CoreData.h>

@class Worker;

@interface Project : NSManagedObject

@property (nonatomic, retain) NSString * descrip;
@property (nonatomic, retain) NSDate * dueDate;
@property (nonatomic, retain) NSString * name;
@property (nonatomic, retain) Worker *personInCharge;
@property (nonatomic, retain) NSSet *listOfTasks;
@end

@interface Project (CoreDataGeneratedAccessors)

- (void)addListOfTasksObject:(NSManagedObject *)value;
- (void)removeListOfTasksObject:(NSManagedObject *)value;
- (void)addListOfTasks:(NSSet *)values;
```

```
- (void)removeListOfTasks:(NSSet *)values;
```

@end

The property that holds the references to all your tasks is an NSSet named
listOfTasks. The additional interface code is given to make it easier to add and
remove items into the NSSet property. All you need to do to add Task objects
into the project is to use these accessors. For example,

```
//Make a task
Task *t1 = (Task *)[NSEntityDescription insertNewObjectForEntityForName:@"Task" ↵
inManagedObjectContext:[dataModel managedObjectContext]];

t1.name = @"Task 1";
t1.details = @"Task details";
t1.dueDate = [NSDate date];
t1.priority = [NSNumber numberWithInt:1];

//Add the task to the project
[p1 addListOfTasksObject:t1];

//Make a task
Task *t2 = (Task *)[NSEntityDescription insertNewObjectForEntityForName:@"Task" ↵
inManagedObjectContext:[dataModel managedObjectContext]];

t2.name = @"Task 2";
t2.details = @"Task details";
t2.dueDate = [NSDate date];
t2.priority = [NSNumber numberWithInt:1];

//Add the task to the project
[p1 addListOfTasksObject:t2];
```

Now you can use the tasks that are associated with the project. To print these
tasks out to the log, you could do something like this:

```
//Get all the projects in the data store
NSFetchRequest *request = [[NSFetchRequest alloc] init];
NSEntityDescription *entity = [NSEntityDescription entityForName:@"Project"
                                  inManagedObjectContext:[dataModel ↵
managedObjectContext]];

request.entity = entity;
NSArray *listOfProjects = [[dataModel managedObjectContext] ↵
executeFetchRequest:request error:nil];

//Print out contents of all the projects (including the tasks)
NSLog(@"-----");
NSLog(@"NEW PROJECTS IN CONTEXT");
[listOfProjects enumerateObjectsUsingBlock:^(id obj, NSUInteger idx, BOOL *stop) {
```

```
        NSLog(@"project.name = %@", [obj name]);
        [[obj listOfTasks] enumerateObjectsUsingBlock:^(id obj, BOOL *stop) {
            NSLog(@" task.name = %@", [obj name]);
        }];
}];
```

See Listings 10-39 through 10-48.

The Code

Listing 10-39. *AppDelegate.h*

```
#import <UIKit/UIKit.h>
#import "AppModel.h"

@interface AppDelegate : UIResponder <UIApplicationDelegate>

@property (strong, nonatomic) UIWindow *window;

@end
```

Listing 10-40. *AppDelegate.m*

```
#import "AppDelegate.h"

@implementation AppDelegate
@synthesize window = _window;

- (BOOL)application:(UIApplication *)application ↵
didFinishLaunchingWithOptions:(NSDictionary *)launchOptions{

    //Create a new AppModel instance
    AppModel *dataModel = [[AppModel alloc] init];

    //Make a project
    Project *p1 = [dataModel makeNewProject];
    p1.name = @"Proj1";

    //Make a task
    Task *t1 = (Task *)[NSEntityDescription insertNewObjectForEntityForName:@"Task" ↵
inManagedObjectContext:[dataModel managedObjectContext]];

    t1.name = @"Task 1";
    t1.details = @"Task details";
    t1.dueDate = [NSDate date];
    t1.priority = [NSNumber numberWithInt:1];
```

```objc
    //Add the task to the project
    [p1 addListOfTasksObject:t1];

    //Make a task
    Task *t2 = (Task *)[NSEntityDescription insertNewObjectForEntityForName:@"Task"
                                            inManagedObjectContext:  ↩
[dataModel managedObjectContext]];

    t2.name = @"Task 2";
    t2.details = @"Task details";
    t2.dueDate = [NSDate date];
    t2.priority = [NSNumber numberWithInt:1];

    //Add the task to the project
    [p1 addListOfTasksObject:t2];

    //Get all the projects in the data store
    NSFetchRequest *request = [[NSFetchRequest alloc] init];
    NSEntityDescription *entity = [NSEntityDescription entityForName:@"Project"
                                       inManagedObjectContext:[dataModel ↩
managedObjectContext]];

    request.entity = entity;
    NSArray *listOfProjects = [[dataModel managedObjectContext] ↩
executeFetchRequest:request error:nil];

    //print out contents of all the projects (including the tasks):
    NSLog(@"-----");
    NSLog(@"NEW PROJECTS IN CONTEXT");
    [listOfProjects enumerateObjectsUsingBlock:^(id obj, NSUInteger idx, BOOL *stop) {
        NSLog(@"project.name = %@", [obj name]);
        [[obj listOfTasks] enumerateObjectsUsingBlock:^(id obj, BOOL *stop) {
            NSLog(@" task.name = %@", [obj name]);
        }];
    }];

    self.window = [[UIWindow alloc] initWithFrame:[[UIScreen mainScreen] bounds]];
    self.window.backgroundColor = [UIColor whiteColor];
    [self.window makeKeyAndVisible];
    return YES;
}

@end
```

Listing 10-41. *AppModel.h*

```objc
#import <Foundation/Foundation.h>
#import <CoreData/CoreData.h>
#import "Project.h"
#import "Worker.h"
```

```
#import "Task.h"

@interface AppModel : NSObject

-(NSURL *)dataStoreURL;

@property (nonatomic, strong, readonly) NSManagedObjectModel *managedObjectModel;
@property (nonatomic, strong, readonly) NSPersistentStoreCoordinator ↵
*persistentStoreCoordinator;
@property (nonatomic, strong, readonly) NSManagedObjectContext *managedObjectContext;

-(Project *)makeNewProject;
-(Worker *)makeNewWorker;
-(Task *)makeNewTask;

@end
```

Listing 10-42. *AppModel.m*

```
#1import "AppModel.h"

@implementation AppModel
NSManagedObjectModel *_managedObjectModel;
NSPersistentStoreCoordinator *_persistentStoreCoordinator;
NSManagedObjectContext *_managedObjectContext;

-(Project *)makeNewProject{

    Project *managedProject = (Project *)[NSEntityDescription ↵
insertNewObjectForEntityForName:@"Project" ↵
inManagedObjectContext:[self managedObjectContext]];

    managedProject.name = @"New Project";
    managedProject.descrip = @"This is a new project";
    managedProject.dueDate = [NSDate date];

    managedProject.personInCharge = [self makeNewWorker];

    return managedProject;

}

-(Worker *)makeNewWorker{
    Worker *managedWorker = (Worker *)[NSEntityDescription ↵
insertNewObjectForEntityForName:@"Worker" ↵
inManagedObjectContext:[self managedObjectContext]];

    managedWorker.name = @"New Worker";
    managedWorker.Role = @"Works on projects";
```

```
        return managedWorker;
}

-(Task *)makeNewTask{
    Task *managedTask = (Task *)[NSEntityDescription ↩
insertNewObjectForEntityForName:@"Task" ↩
inManagedObjectContext:[self managedObjectContext]];

    managedTask.name = @"New Task";
    managedTask.details = @"Task details";
    managedTask.dueDate = [NSDate date];
    managedTask.priority = [NSNumber numberWithInt:1];

    return managedTask;
}

- (NSURL *)dataStoreURL {

    NSString *docDir = [NSSearchPathForDirectoriesInDomains(NSDocumentDirectory, ↩
NSUserDomainMask, YES) lastObject];

    return [NSURL fileURLWithPath:[docDir ↩
stringByAppendingPathComponent:@"DataStore.sql"]];
}

- (NSManagedObjectModel *)managedObjectModel {
    if (_managedObjectModel) {
        return _managedObjectModel;
    }
    _managedObjectModel = [NSManagedObjectModel mergedModelFromBundles:nil];
    return _managedObjectModel;
}

- (NSPersistentStoreCoordinator *)persistentStoreCoordinator {
    if (_persistentStoreCoordinator) {
        return _persistentStoreCoordinator;
    }

    NSError *error = nil;
    _persistentStoreCoordinator = [[NSPersistentStoreCoordinator alloc] ↩
initWithManagedObjectModel:[self managedObjectModel]];
    if (![_persistentStoreCoordinator addPersistentStoreWithType:NSSQLiteStoreType
                                                    configuration:nil
                                                              URL:[self dataStoreURL]
                                                          options:nil
                                                            error:&error]) {
        NSLog(@"Unresolved Core Data error with persistentStoreCoordinator: %@, %@", ↩
error, [error userInfo]);
    }
```

```objc
    return _persistentStoreCoordinator;
}

- (NSManagedObjectContext *)managedObjectContext {
    if (_managedObjectContext) {
        return _managedObjectContext;
    }

    if ([self persistentStoreCoordinator]) {
        _managedObjectContext = [[NSManagedObjectContext alloc] init];
        [_managedObjectContext setPersistentStoreCoordinator:[self ↵
persistentStoreCoordinator]];
    }

    return _managedObjectContext;
}

@end
```

Listing 10-43. *Project.h*

```objc
#import <Foundation/Foundation.h>
#import <CoreData/CoreData.h>

@class Worker;

@interface Project : NSManagedObject

@property (nonatomic, retain) NSString * descrip;
@property (nonatomic, retain) NSDate * dueDate;
@property (nonatomic, retain) NSString * name;
@property (nonatomic, retain) Worker *personInCharge;
@property (nonatomic, retain) NSSet *listOfTasks;
@end

@interface Project (CoreDataGeneratedAccessors)

- (void)addListOfTasksObject:(NSManagedObject *)value;
- (void)removeListOfTasksObject:(NSManagedObject *)value;
- (void)addListOfTasks:(NSSet *)values;
- (void)removeListOfTasks:(NSSet *)values;

@end
```

Listing 10-44. *Project.m*

```objc
#import "Project.h"
#import "Worker.h"
```

```
@implementation Project

@dynamic descrip;
@dynamic dueDate;
@dynamic name;
@dynamic personInCharge;
@dynamic listOfTasks;

@end
```

Listing 10-45. *Worker.h*

```
#import <Foundation/Foundation.h>
#import <CoreData/CoreData.h>

@class Project;

@interface Worker : NSManagedObject

@property (nonatomic, retain) NSString * name;
@property (nonatomic, retain) NSString * role;
@property (nonatomic, retain) Project *project;

@end
```

Listing 10-46. *Worker.m*

```
#import "Worker.h"
#import "Project.h"

@implementation Worker

@dynamic name;
@dynamic role;
@dynamic project;

@end
```

Listing 10-47. *Task.h*

```
#import <Foundation/Foundation.h>
#import <CoreData/CoreData.h>

@class Project;

@interface Task : NSManagedObject

@property (nonatomic, retain) NSString * name;
@property (nonatomic, retain) NSString * details;
@property (nonatomic, retain) NSString * dueDate;
```

```
@property (nonatomic, retain) NSNumber * priority;
@property (nonatomic, retain) Project *project;

@end
```

Listing 10-48. *Task.m*

```
#import "Task.h"
#import "Project.h"

@implementation Task

@dynamic name;
@dynamic details;
@dynamic dueDate;
@dynamic priority;
@dynamic project;

@end
```

Usage

To use this code, add the entities as described in the "How It Works" section.
Include the code from Listings 10-39 through 10-48 for the `AppDelegate` and the
`AppModel` classes. Build and run your project and you should see output that
looks like this:

```
-----
NEW PROJECTS IN CONTEXT
project.name = Proj1
 task.name = Task 1
 task.name = Task 2
```

10.9 Managing Data Store Versioning

Problem

You have an application that is already deployed to your customers and you
want to make a change to the data model. You know if you just make the
change to the existing data model you will break your user's application.

Solution

Add a new version of your data model to your application based on your original
data model. Set the new version of your data model to be the current model
used by the application. Finally, add some options to your persistent store
coordinator to make sure that the updated data model is used.

How It Works

As you probably realize by now, if you are developing an application and then
decide to make a change to the data model, your application will crash when
you try to test your code. This is because the application is trying to use the
managed object model that was created during the first run with an updated
managed object model that you just created.

Normally you can just delete your application from the iOS Simulator (or Mac
desktop) and start over without any problems. However, if you have people
already using your application, you need to make sure that you can use the new
data model version without breaking their application or losing their content.

To demonstrate this recipe, go back to the application created in Recipe 10.8
and add a new relationship to the task entity. In the original object graph from
Recipe 9.1, the Task class had a one-to-one relationship with the Worker class.
Add this relationship now with a new version of the data model.

First, add some options to the persistent store coordinator. Set two flags to YES
to allow automatic versioning. These flags are
NSMigratePersistentStoresAutomaticallyOption and
NSInferMappingModelAutomaticallyOption; to use them you must put them both
in an NSDictionary object with their values set to YES. You add this update to
the persistent store coordinator in the AppModel.m file where you have the
persistent store coordinator coded.

```
#import "AppModel.h"

@implementation AppModel

...

- (NSPersistentStoreCoordinator *)persistentStoreCoordinator {
    if (_persistentStoreCoordinator) {
        return _persistentStoreCoordinator;
    }

    NSError *error = nil;
```

```
    NSDictionary *options = [NSDictionary dictionaryWithObjectsAndKeys: ⮐
[NSNumber numberWithBool:YES], NSMigratePersistentStoresAutomaticallyOption, ⮐
[NSNumber numberWithBool:YES], NSInferMappingModelAutomaticallyOption, nil];

    _persistentStoreCoordinator = [[NSPersistentStoreCoordinator alloc] ⮐
initWithManagedObjectModel:[self managedObjectModel]];

    if (![_persistentStoreCoordinator addPersistentStoreWithType:NSSQLiteStoreType
                                        configuration:nil
                                                  URL:[self dataStoreURL]
                                              options:options
                                                error:&error]) {
        NSLog(@"Unresolved Core Data error with persistentStoreCoordinator: %@, %@", ⮐
error, [error userInfo]);
    }

    return _persistentStoreCoordinator;
}

...

@end
```

To make the change a bit clearer, I've highlighted the additional code in bold.

Now you can go ahead and create a new version of the data model based on the original. Select your data model, which is the file named Model.xcdatamodeld. Then go to Editor ➤ Add Model Version. Name your version Model 2 and select Model in the "Based on Model" drop-down box.

When you look at your data model file, you will see that there are two data model files, Model.xcdatamodeld and Model 2.xcdatamodeld. Right now, they are identical and you can see each data model by clicking on the respective file.

Now set the current data model to Model 2. This is how you let Core Data know that you are using the new version. You do this by selecting the top level in the data model. Make sure that the right pane is showing the File Inspector. Locate the drop-down box labeled Current. Select Model 2 from the Current drop-down box (see Figure 10-11).

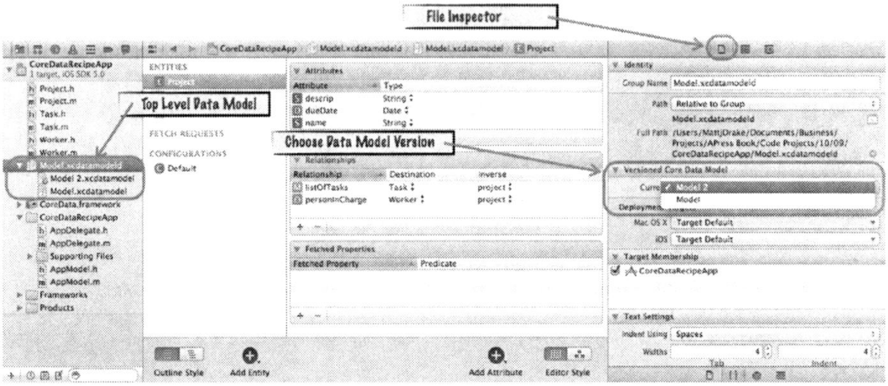

Figure 10-11. *Setting the current data model versions*

Now add the Task to Worker one-to-one relationship. First, select Model 2 so you know that you're working on the new version. To establish the relationship, select Task in the data model editor and then click the plus button in the Relationships pane of the data model editor. Name the relationship assignedTo and set the Destination to Worker.

Now you need to define the inverse (or opposite) relationship. This gives you a way to reference the task that a worker is working on. Select the Worker entity and click the plus button in the Relationships pane of the data model editor. Name the relationship task and set the Destination to Task. Select assignedTo for the Inverse.

To see everything that you just did at one time, select each entity in the data model editor while holding down the Command key. Both entities will be highlighted and you will see all the attributes and relationships listed at once. Your data model editor should look like Figure 10-12.

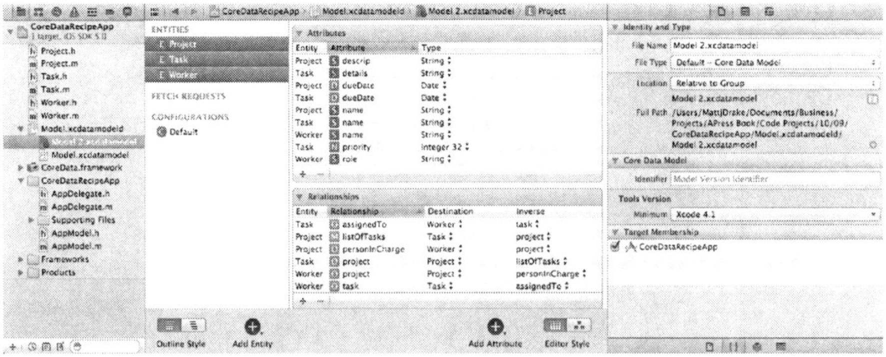

Figure 10-12. *Task to Worker and Worker to Task relationship*

Keeping all the entities highlighted, go to File ➤ New ➤ File. Then choose iOS ➤
Core Data ➤ NSManagedObject subclass. Click Next and then Create. You will
get a warning dialog because you are going to write over the previous Project
class file. That's ok since you do need to update it, so click Replace.

Now you can use your Core Data without breaking your application.

```
//Create a new AppModel instance
AppModel *dataModel = [[AppModel alloc] init];

//Make a project
Project *p1 = [dataModel makeNewProject];
p1.name = @"Proj1";

//Make a task
Task *t1 = (Task *)[NSEntityDescription insertNewObjectForEntityForName:@"Task"

inManagedObjectContext:[dataModel managedObjectContext]];
t1.name = @"Task 1";
t1.details = @"Task details";
t1.dueDate = [NSDate date];
t1.priority = [NSNumber numberWithInt:1];

//Assign a worker to this task:
Worker *managedWorker = (Worker *)[NSEntityDescription
insertNewObjectForEntityForName:@"Worker"

inManagedObjectContext:[dataModel managedObjectContext]];
managedWorker.name = @"John";
managedWorker.Role = @"Programmer";
```

t1.assignedTo = managedWorker;

Core Data will take care of managing the two versions for each user's
application without any more intervention from you. See Listings 10-49 through
10-58.

The Code

Listing 10-49. *AppDelegate.h*

```
#import <UIKit/UIKit.h>
#import "AppModel.h"

@interface AppDelegate : UIResponder <UIApplicationDelegate>

@property (strong, nonatomic) UIWindow *window;
```

@end

Listing 10-50. *AppDelegate.m*

```
#import "AppDelegate.h"

@implementation AppDelegate
@synthesize window = _window;

- (BOOL)application:(UIApplication *)application ↩
didFinishLaunchingWithOptions:(NSDictionary *)launchOptions{

    //Create a new AppModel instance
    AppModel *dataModel = [[AppModel alloc] init];

    //Make a project
    Project *p1 = [dataModel makeNewProject];
    p1.name = @"Proj1";

    //Make a task
    Task *t1 = (Task *)[NSEntityDescription insertNewObjectForEntityForName:@"Task" ↩
inManagedObjectContext:[dataModel managedObjectContext]];

    t1.name = @"Task 1";
    t1.details = @"Task details";
    t1.dueDate = [NSDate date];
    t1.priority = [NSNumber numberWithInt:1];


    //Assign a worker to this task:
    Worker *managedWorker = (Worker *)[NSEntityDescription ↩
insertNewObjectForEntityForName:@"Worker" ↩
inManagedObjectContext:[dataModel managedObjectContext]];

    managedWorker.name = @"John";
    managedWorker.Role = @"Programmer";

    t1.assignedTo = managedWorker;

    //Add the task to the project
    [p1 addListOfTasksObject:t1];

    //Make a task
    Task *t2 = (Task *)[NSEntityDescription insertNewObjectForEntityForName:@"Task"
                                            inManagedObjectContext: ↩
[dataModel managedObjectContext]];

    t2.name = @"Task 2";
    t2.details = @"Task details";
    t2.dueDate = [NSDate date];
```

```
    t2.priority = [NSNumber numberWithInt:1];

    //Add the task to the project
    [p1 addListOfTasksObject:t2];

    //Get all the projects in the data store
    NSFetchRequest *request = [[NSFetchRequest alloc] init];
    NSEntityDescription *entity = [NSEntityDescription entityForName:@"Project"
                                         inManagedObjectContext:[dataModel ↩
managedObjectContext]];

    request.entity = entity;
    NSArray *listOfProjects = [[dataModel managedObjectContext] ↩
executeFetchRequest:request error:nil];

    //print out contents of all the projects (including the tasks):
    NSLog(@"-----");
    NSLog(@"NEW PROJECTS IN CONTEXT");
    [listOfProjects enumerateObjectsUsingBlock:^(id obj, NSUInteger idx, BOOL *stop) {
        NSLog(@"project.name = %@", [obj name]);
        [[obj listOfTasks] enumerateObjectsUsingBlock:^(id obj, BOOL *stop) {
            NSLog(@" task.name = %@", [obj name]);
            NSLog(@" task.assignedTo = %@", [[obj assignedTo] name]);
        }];
    }];

    self.window = [[UIWindow alloc] initWithFrame:[[UIScreen mainScreen] bounds]];
    self.window.backgroundColor = [UIColor whiteColor];
    [self.window makeKeyAndVisible];
    return YES;
}

@end
```

Listing 10-51. *AppModel.h*

```
#import <Foundation/Foundation.h>
#import <CoreData/CoreData.h>
#import "Project.h"
#import "Worker.h"
#import "Task.h"

@interface AppModel : NSObject

-(NSURL *)dataStoreURL;

@property (nonatomic, strong, readonly) NSManagedObjectModel *managedObjectModel;
@property (nonatomic, strong, readonly) NSPersistentStoreCoordinator ↩
*persistentStoreCoordinator;
@property (nonatomic, strong, readonly) NSManagedObjectContext *managedObjectContext;
```

```
-(Project *)makeNewProject;
-(Worker *)makeNewWorker;
-(Task *)makeNewTask;

@end
```

Listing 10-52. *AppModel.m*

```
#import "AppModel.h"

@implementation AppModel
NSManagedObjectModel *_managedObjectModel;
NSPersistentStoreCoordinator *_persistentStoreCoordinator;
NSManagedObjectContext *_managedObjectContext;

-(Project *)makeNewProject{

    Project *managedProject = (Project *)[NSEntityDescription ↵
insertNewObjectForEntityForName:@"Project" ↵
inManagedObjectContext:[self managedObjectContext]];

    managedProject.name = @"New Project";
    managedProject.descrip = @"This is a new project";
    managedProject.dueDate = [NSDate date];

    managedProject.personInCharge = [self makeNewWorker];

    return managedProject;

}

-(Worker *)makeNewWorker{
    Worker *managedWorker = (Worker *)[NSEntityDescription ↵
insertNewObjectForEntityForName:@"Worker" ↵
inManagedObjectContext:[self managedObjectContext]];

    managedWorker.name = @"New Worker";
    managedWorker.Role = @"Works on projects";

    return managedWorker;
}

-(Task *)makeNewTask{
    Task *managedTask = (Task *)[NSEntityDescription ↵
insertNewObjectForEntityForName:@"Task" ↵
inManagedObjectContext:[self managedObjectContext]];

    managedTask.name = @"New Task";
    managedTask.details = @"Task details";
```

```
    managedTask.dueDate = [NSDate date];
    managedTask.priority = [NSNumber numberWithInt:1];

    return managedTask;
}

- (NSURL *)dataStoreURL {

    NSString *docDir = [NSSearchPathForDirectoriesInDomains(NSDocumentDirectory, ↩
NSUserDomainMask, YES) lastObject];

    return [NSURL fileURLWithPath:[docDir ↩
stringByAppendingPathComponent:@"DataStore.sql"]];
}

- (NSManagedObjectModel *)managedObjectModel {
    if (_managedObjectModel) {
        return _managedObjectModel;
    }
    _managedObjectModel = [NSManagedObjectModel mergedModelFromBundles:nil];
    return _managedObjectModel;
}

- (NSPersistentStoreCoordinator *)persistentStoreCoordinator {
    if (_persistentStoreCoordinator) {
        return _persistentStoreCoordinator;
    }

    NSError *error = nil;
    NSDictionary *options = [NSDictionary dictionaryWithObjectsAndKeys: ↩
[NSNumber numberWithBool:YES], NSMigratePersistentStoresAutomaticallyOption, ↩
[NSNumber numberWithBool:YES], NSInferMappingModelAutomaticallyOption, nil];

_persistentStoreCoordinator = [[NSPersistentStoreCoordinator alloc] ↩
initWithManagedObjectModel:[self managedObjectModel]];

if (![_persistentStoreCoordinator addPersistentStoreWithType:NSSQLiteStoreType
                                        configuration:nil
                                                URL:[self dataStoreURL]
                                            options:options
                                              error:&error]) {
    NSLog(@"Unresolved Core Data error with persistentStoreCoordinator: %@, %@", ↩
error, [error userInfo]);
}
    return _persistentStoreCoordinator;
}

- (NSManagedObjectContext *)managedObjectContext {
    if (_managedObjectContext) {
        return _managedObjectContext;
```

```
        }

        if ([self persistentStoreCoordinator]) {
            _managedObjectContext = [[NSManagedObjectContext alloc] init];
            [_managedObjectContext setPersistentStoreCoordinator:[self ↵
persistentStoreCoordinator]];
        }

        return _managedObjectContext;
}

@end
```

Listing 10-53. *Project.h*

```
#import <Foundation/Foundation.h>
#import <CoreData/CoreData.h>

@class Worker;

@interface Project : NSManagedObject

@property (nonatomic, retain) NSString * descrip;
@property (nonatomic, retain) NSDate * dueDate;
@property (nonatomic, retain) NSString * name;
@property (nonatomic, retain) Worker *personInCharge;
@property (nonatomic, retain) NSSet *listOfTasks;
@end

@interface Project (CoreDataGeneratedAccessors)

- (void)addListOfTasksObject:(NSManagedObject *)value;
- (void)removeListOfTasksObject:(NSManagedObject *)value;
- (void)addListOfTasks:(NSSet *)values;
- (void)removeListOfTasks:(NSSet *)values;

@end
```

Listing 10-54. *Project.m*

```
#import "Project.h"
#import "Worker.h"


@implementation Project

@dynamic descrip;
@dynamic dueDate;
@dynamic name;
@dynamic personInCharge;
```

```
@dynamic listOfTasks;

@end
```

Listing 10-55. *Task.h*

```
#import <Foundation/Foundation.h>
#import <CoreData/CoreData.h>

@class Project, Worker;

@interface Task : NSManagedObject

@property (nonatomic, retain) NSString * details;
@property (nonatomic, retain) NSDate * dueDate;
@property (nonatomic, retain) NSString * name;
@property (nonatomic, retain) NSNumber * priority;
@property (nonatomic, retain) Project *project;
@property (nonatomic, retain) Worker *assignedTo;

@end
```

Listing 10-56. *Task.m*

```
#import "Task.h"
#import "Project.h"
#import "Worker.h"


@implementation Task

@dynamic details;
@dynamic dueDate;
@dynamic name;
@dynamic priority;
@dynamic project;
@dynamic assignedTo;

@end
```

Listing 10-57. *Worker.h*

```
#import <Foundation/Foundation.h>
#import <CoreData/CoreData.h>

@class Project, Task;

@interface Worker : NSManagedObject

@property (nonatomic, retain) NSString * name;
```

```
@property (nonatomic, retain) NSString * role;
@property (nonatomic, retain) Project *project;
@property (nonatomic, retain) Task *task;

@end
```

Listing 10-58. *Worker.m*

```
#import "Worker.h"
#import "Project.h"
#import "Task.h"


@implementation Worker

@dynamic name;
@dynamic role;
@dynamic project;
@dynamic task;

@end
```

Usage

Versioning is a little tricky to test out. Start with the application from Recipe 10.8 and make sure to build it so that you can see the output in the console log. Then go through the process of following this recipe to see if you can update the data model gracefully. After you build and run this application you should see something like this appear in your console log:

```
-----
NEW PROJECTS IN CONTEXT
project.name = Proj1
  task.name = Task 1
  task.assignedTo = John
  task.name = Task 2
  task.assignedTo = (null)
```

11

Objective-C Beyond Mac and iOS

Objective-C is used almost exclusively with Mac and iOS, but it is possible to use Objective-C on other platforms. This chapter discusses how to write and compile Objective-C code on Windows 7 with GNUstep. This chapter also demonstrates Objective-J, a programming language based on Objective-C that is used to make web applications.

In this chapter, you will:

- Install GNUstep on Windows 7
- Write and compile a Hello World Objective-C program on Windows 7
- Download and install the Objective-J and Cappuccino Framework on Mac
- Create a Hello World Objective-J web app for the Safari web browser

11.1 Installing GNUstep on Windows

Problem

You need to install GNUstep on your Windows 7 computer so you can write Objective-C code that will run on a Windows 7 computer.

Solution

Download and install the GNUstep tools, including Foundation and AppKit, on your Windows 7 computer in order to use Objective-C.

How It Works

The purpose of GNUstep is to make Objective-C, Foundation, and AppKit a cross-platform development environment. GNUstep allows you to use the type of code covered in this book on many different systems, including Windows.

But first you need to install GNUstep on your Windows computer. You can do this by going to GNUstep's Windows Installer page at www.gnustep.org/experience/Windows.html.

You must download and install the following three packages in this order:

1. GNUstep MSYS System

2. GNUstep Core

3. GNUstep Devel

Leave all of the installation settings as the defaults. Upon completion, you will see a new folder on your Windows drive, C:\GNUstep. This is where the GNUstep development environment is located.

When you work with GNUstep, you will use a text editor to write code and a command-line Shell (Shell is like the Mac Terminal) to compile code. The text editor can be any program (like Notepad) that can save files as plain text. You can open your Shell window by going to the Windows Start Menu ➤ All Programs ➤ GNUstep ➤ Shell.

When you open the Shell, you will see a black window with a prompt. You will be located in the home directory of your GNUstep environment (not the Windows root directory). See Figure 11-1 for an example of what the Shell looks like.

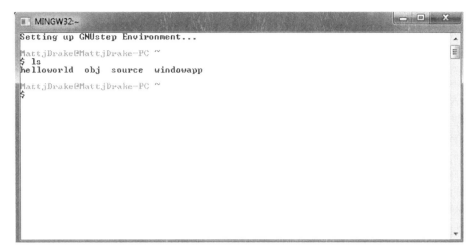

Figure 11-1. *GNUstep Shell*

> **NOTE:** Your screen may not list the files you see in Figure 11-1. The `ls` command will list the files and folders located in the folder you are currently in.

The GNUstep home directory is located at `C:\GNUstep\msys\1.0\home\[USER-NAME]`. Note that `[USER-NAME]` is your Windows username. This is where you will put the code files that you want to compile.

> **NOTE:** The GNUstep Shell is like a mini Mac, Unix, or Linux command-line utility, so those types of commands will work with the GNUstep Shell. For instance, Figure 11-1 shows the use of the command `ls` to show a listing of the folders in my GNUstep home directory. You can also use commands like `cd` to change your current directory and `mkdir` to make a new directory.

If you can open your GNUstep Shell and have installed all three of the packages from the GNUstep web site, you are ready to move on to the Hello World example shown in Recipe 11.2.

11.2 Objective-C Hello World on Windows

Problem

You want to write and compile a simple Objective-C program on Windows using GNUstep.

Solution

You will need two files to do this on Windows: a text file with the source code and a special text file called a **make file**. Make files are used to list the settings that compilers need to turn your code into a compiled program.

How It Works

Use a text editor (Notepad is fine) to create a new text file and put this code into the file:

```
#import <Foundation/Foundation.h>

int main (int argc, const char * argv[]){

        NSAutoreleasePool *pool = [[NSAutoreleasePool alloc] init];

        NSString *helloString = @"Hello World";
        NSLog(@"%@", helloString);

        [pool drain];
        [pool release];

        return 0;
}
```

This code is very similar to the code you've used in previous Hello World Objective-C recipes with one exception. You can see that you are using pre-ARC memory management here. The `@autoreleasepool{}` block is not supported in GNUstep right now.

Save the file into the GNUstep home directory and make sure to name the file `main.m`.

> **NOTE:** If you're using Notepad to edit your text files, take extra care to make sure that Notepad is not appending the txt file extension to your filename. Use the ls command from the GNUstep Shell to see the "real" filename if your Windows file explorer automatically hides file extensions.

Next, you need to write a make file. These files are used by the GNUstep environment to compile your code into a program. Create a new text file and include this text in the file:

```
include $(GNUSTEP_MAKEFILES)/common.make

TOOL_NAME = main
main_OBJC_FILES = main.m

include $(GNUSTEP_MAKEFILES)/tool.make
```

The parts of the make file that you will have to change for each program that you want to compile are highlighted in bold. The very first (after TOOL_Name) is the filename that your compiled program will have. This must match the second line (right before the _OBJC_FILES). The last area in bold must match the file name of the file that has the code that you want to compile.

Save the file with the name of GNUmakefile in GNUstep home directory. The file should have no file extension. Open the GNUstep Shell by going to the Windows Start Menu ➤ All Programs ➤ GNUstep ➤ Shell. Make sure that you are in the same location as your two files by typing in the ls command. You should see your two files listed with the file extensions that you expect.

```
$ ls
GNUmakefile main.m
```

Now all you have to do is type in the word make and press return. You will see a build log appear in your GNUstep Shell. If there are any errors, they will be reported in here as well. See Figure 11-2 for an example of how this should look.

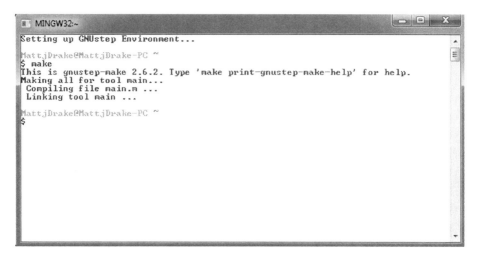

Figure 11-2. *Build log from make command*

You can test your Objective-C application by typing the name of the program into the GNUstep Shell. The compiled program will be saved in a sub-directory named obj so you will have to type in something like this:

./obj/main

See Figure 11-3 for an example and Listings 11-1 and 11-2 for the code.

Figure 11-3. *GNUstep Hello World output*

The Code

Listing 11-1. *main.m*

```
#import <Foundation/Foundation.h>

int main (int argc, const char * argv[]){

        NSAutoreleasePool *pool = [[NSAutoreleasePool alloc] init];

        NSString *helloString = @"Hello World";
        NSLog(@"%@", helloString);

        [pool drain];
        [pool release];

        return 0;
}
```

Listing 11-2. *GNUmakefile*

```
include $(GNUSTEP_MAKEFILES)/common.make

TOOL_NAME = main
main_OBJC_FILES = main.m

include $(GNUSTEP_MAKEFILES)/tool.make
```

Usage

You can use this code as described in the "How It Works" section. You can also try to add some other Objective-C objects to the main.m file to see how they work in your Windows development environment. For example, to see how an array would work, you can change main.m to look like this:

```
#import <Foundation/Foundation.h>

int main (int argc, const char * argv[]){

        NSAutoreleasePool *pool = [[NSAutoreleasePool alloc] init];

        NSString *helloString = @"Hello World";
        NSLog(@"%@", helloString);

        NSArray *listOfLetters1 = [NSArray arrayWithObjects:@"A", @"B", @"C", nil];
        NSLog(@"listOfLetters1 = %@", listOfLetters1);

        [pool drain];
```

```
        [pool release];

        return 0;
}
```

You would compile this again using the make command from the GNUstep Shell. To see the new results, you can simply open the program by typing ./obj/main again. This will give you output like this:

```
Hello World
listOfLetters1 = (A, B, C)
```

You can experiment with other Foundation classes here as well. Keep in mind that even though GNUstep is an open source project and has a goal of supporting all the Foundation components, there are really no guarantees that everything will work as you expect. Obviously, the development environment that you get on Windows is not the same as you are used to with Mac.

GNUstep provides similar functionality as Apple's Objective-C, but these two things are not identical. If you would like to learn more about this rich framework, go to www.gnustep.org/ to get the current details, tutorials, and documentation.

11.3 Downloading Objective-J for Web Apps

Problem

You want to be able to develop web apps with Objective-J using the same coding patterns used for Mac and iOS apps with Objective-C.

Solution

Download the Starter Package from http://cappuccino.org/download/ to get the frameworks that you need to develop apps using Objective-J.

How It Works

Objective-J brings Objective-C—like code to web apps. Web apps are different than Mac or iOS apps in that they run inside of a browser like Safari. Instead of being deployed to a user's Mac or iPhone, web apps are deployed to a web server and users get the apps by pointing their browser to the web server. Web apps have been around awhile, but what is neat about Objective-J is that you can use the sophisticated patterns and code used for desktop apps for your web apps. Objective-J was built to closely mimic how Objective-C works and so you will see very similar (but not identical) classes in Objective-J as you do in Objective-C.

The "J" in Objective-J stands for JavaScript, and this underlies the key difference between Objective-J and Objective-C. While Objective-C is an extension of C, Objective-J is an extension of JavaScript (a web app language). You will also see the name "Cappuccino" associated with Objective-J. Cappuccino is the Objective-J equivalent of Objective-C Cocoa. Both words refer to the application frameworks (as opposed to the pure programming languages).

To get started with Objective-J, you will need a text editor like TextEdit on Mac, a web browser like Safari on Mac, and you will need to download the Starter Package from `http://cappuccino.org/download/`.

The Starter Package comes with a Hello World application already set up. Once you've downloaded the Starter Package, just navigate to the folder `New Application` and open the file named `index.html` in Safari. You'll see a web page pop up with the words "Hello World" on a label.

> **NOTE:** This app will not work with Chrome unless you have the Objective-J application deployed to a web server. This is due to Chrome's security settings.

Usage

In the next recipe, you'll set up your own Hello World app along with some user controls so you can see how Objective-J is used. When making your own apps, you will generally use the example application provided in the Cappuccino Starter Package as a template.

11.4 Coding a Hello World Objective-J Application

Problem

You want to set up a simple Objective-J application that says Hello World.

Solution

Create a folder for your Objective-J application that includes the Objective-J frameworks that you downloaded with the Starter Package. You will also need these files: `Info.plist`, `index.html`, `main.j`, and `AppController.j` in the Objective-J application folder.

How It Works

Objective-J applications are not compiled like Objective-C Mac and iOS applications. Instead, you house the files either locally on your desktop while you are developing the application or on a web server when the application is released. When a user points to an Objective-J file, the browser interprets the code in the file and presents the results inside the browser window.

The first thing that you need to make is a new folder named `helloworldapp` that will house your Objective-J application. You can simply use Finder on the Mac to do this right on your desktop.

> **NOTE:** You can develop these types of applications on any system with any text editor and web browser, but I'll be using the standard Mac setup for this example.

Next, you need the Objective-J frameworks. Go to the Starter Package that you downloaded in Recipe 11.3 and go into the `NewApplication` folder and locate the folder labeled `Frameworks`. Copy the `Frameworks` folder. Go back into your Objective-J app's folder and paste the Frameworks folder in.

Info.plist

Now you need an `Info.plist` file. This file serves the same purpose as the file of the same name does in Mac and iOS applications: it lists parameters that the Objective-J application will need to function.

Add a new text file to your folder named `Info.plist` and add this code to the file:

```
<?xml version="1.0" encoding="UTF-8"?>
<plist version="1.0">
<dict>
        <key>CPApplicationDelegateClass</key>
        <string>AppController</string>
</dict>
</plist>
```

This is XML file that tells the application that the app delegate class name is `AppController`. This is a simple example. More complicated applications will likely include additional settings in the `info.plist` file.

index.html

The `index.html` file is the web page that houses the Objective-J application, so the code will be in HTML. The main purpose of this page is to load up the code files that you are going to set up in the next two files. Like the `Info.plist` file, add the `index.html` file to the app's folder. It should contain this HTML code:

```
<!DOCTYPE html
    PUBLIC "-//W3C//DTD XHTML 1.0 Strict//EN"
    "http://www.w3.org/TR/xhtml1/DTD/xhtml1-strict.dtd">
<html xmlns="http://www.w3.org/1999/xhtml" xml:lang="en" lang="en">     <head>
        <script type="text/javascript">
            OBJJ_MAIN_FILE = "main.j";
        </script>
        <script type="text/javascript" src="Frameworks/Objective-J/Objective-↵
J.js"></script>
    <title></title>
    </head>
</html>
```

This file is doing two major things: specifying the code file where the main Objective-J program is located and pointing to the Objective-J frameworks.

main.j

The `main.j` file is where the main function is located. This serves the same purpose as the `main.m` file does in an Objective-C Mac or iOS application, namely `main.j` launches the application object (which in Objective-J is a `CPApplicationMain` object).

Create a text file named `main.j` in your application folder and input this code:

```
@import <Foundation/Foundation.j>
@import <AppKit/AppKit.j>

@import "AppController.j"

function main(args, namedArgs){
    CPApplicationMain(args, namedArgs);
}
```

AppController.j

`AppController` acts as the app delegate for the web app, and like a Mac or iOS application, this is where most of the initial application setup will take place.

> **NOTE:** The app delegate class is specified in the `Info.plist` file.

Add a text file named `AppController.j` with this code into your application folder:

```
@import <Foundation/CPObject.j>

@implementation AppController : CPObject{
}

- (void)applicationDidFinishLaunching:(CPNotification)aNotification{

}

@end
```

This code probably looks a bit familiar to you since it's like the app delegate code used in both iOS and Mac applications. In the `applicationDidFinishLaunching:` method, you put the code that sets up the app user interface.

Add this code to set up an app window and content view:

```
@import <Foundation/CPObject.j>

@implementation AppController : CPObject{
}

- (void)applicationDidFinishLaunching:(CPNotification)aNotification{

    var theWindow = [[CPWindow alloc] initWithContentRect:CGRectMakeZero()
                                           styleMask:CPBorderlessBridgeWindowMask];

    var contentView = [theWindow contentView];

}

@end
```

Now that you have a window and view, you can add a label to your web app.

```
@import <Foundation/CPObject.j>

@implementation AppController : CPObject{
}

- (void)applicationDidFinishLaunching:(CPNotification)aNotification{

    var theWindow = [[CPWindow alloc] initWithContentRect:CGRectMakeZero()
                                           styleMask:CPBorderlessBridgeWindowMask];

    var contentView = [theWindow contentView];

    var label = [[CPTextField alloc] initWithFrame:CGRectMakeZero()];
    [label setStringValue:@"Hello World!"];
    [label setFont:[CPFont boldSystemFontOfSize:24.0]];
    [label sizeToFit];
    [label setCenter:[contentView center]];
    [contentView addSubview:label];

    [theWindow orderFront:self];

}

@end
```

Use the CPTextField class to create a label here. To display the object, you must add the label to the contentView subview collection with the addSubView: message. This is where you'll be saying Hello World. You will also notice that you send the orderFront: message to the window. This essentially presents the window in the browser. See Listings 11-3 through 11-6 for the code.

The Code

Listing 11-3. *Info.plist*

```
<?xml version="1.0" encoding="UTF-8"?>
<!DOCTYPE plist PUBLIC "-//Apple//DTD PLIST 1.0//EN"
"http://www.apple.com/DTDs/PropertyList-1.0.dtd">
<plist version="1.0"><dict>
        <key>CPApplicationDelegateClass</key>
        <string>AppController</string>
</dict>
</plist>
```

Listing 11-4. *index.html*

```
<!DOCTYPE html
    PUBLIC "-//W3C//DTD XHTML 1.0 Strict//EN"
    "http://www.w3.org/TR/xhtml1/DTD/xhtml1-strict.dtd">
<html xmlns="http://www.w3.org/1999/xhtml" xml:lang="en" lang="en">    <head>
        <script type="text/javascript">
            OBJJ_MAIN_FILE = "main.j";
        </script>
        <script type="text/javascript" src="Frameworks/Objective-J/Objective-↵
J.js"></script>
    <title></title></head> </html>
```

Listing 11-5. *main.j*

```
@import <Foundation/Foundation.j>
@import <AppKit/AppKit.j>

@import "AppController.j"

function main(args, namedArgs){
    CPApplicationMain(args, namedArgs);
}
```

Listing 11-6. *AppController.j*

```
@import <Foundation/CPObject.j>

@implementation AppController : CPObject{
}

- (void)applicationDidFinishLaunching:(CPNotification)aNotification{

    var theWindow = [[CPWindow alloc] initWithContentRect:CGRectMakeZero()
                                        styleMask:CPBorderlessBridgeWindowMask];
```

```
    var contentView = [theWindow contentView];

    var label = [[CPTextField alloc] initWithFrame:CGRectMakeZero()];

    [label setStringValue:@"Hello World!"];
    [label setFont:[CPFont boldSystemFontOfSize:24.0]];
    [label sizeToFit];
    [label setCenter:[contentView center]];

    [contentView addSubview:label];

    [theWindow orderFront:self];
}

@end
```

Usage

Use this app by opening index.html in the Safari browser. You may use the
Safari File menu to open index.html or you can just drag the index.html file into
the Safari icon to open the app. You will see the Hello World message presented
in your browser window. See Figure 11-4 for an example of what it should look
like.

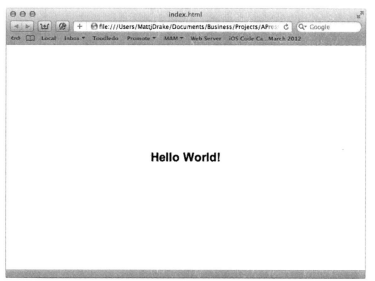

Figure 11-4. *Hello World Objective-J application*

If you want to deploy an application like this to users, you must provide the entire folder on a web site. Users will just go to your web site to use the application. You can use this app in any modern browser, including Microsoft Internet Explorer. However, if you are using Chrome, you will not be able to test Objective-J programs locally unless you have a web server running locally on your Mac.

Objective-J is a rich platform in its own right and thus can't be covered in detail here. If you want to learn more about Objective-J, head over to `http://cappuccino.org/` to get tutorials and documentation.

11.5 Adding a Button to an Objective-J Application

Problem

You want to add user controls like buttons to your web application.

Solution

Follow the same template that you used for the Hello World application to set up the web app itself. To create a button in your web app, use the `CPButton` class in the app controller.

How It Works

Set up the web application user controls in the `AppController.j` file. If there are any controls that you want to keep a reference to, make sure that you declare the object variables outside of a method so that the object variables will stay in scope while the app is active.

Set up the app controller in the file `AppController.j`.

```
@import <Foundation/CPObject.j>

@implementation AppController : CPObject{
}

var label;
var contentView;
```

```
- (void)applicationDidFinishLaunching:(CPNotification)aNotification{

    var theWindow = [[CPWindow alloc] initWithContentRect:CGRectMakeZero()↵
styleMask:CPBorderlessBridgeWindowMask];

    contentView = [theWindow contentView];

    var frame = CGRectMake(0, 13.0, 150.0, 24.0);

    label = [[CPTextField alloc] initWithFrame:frame];

    [label setStringValue:@"Press the Button"];
    [label setFont:[CPFont boldSystemFontOfSize:24.0]];
    [label sizeToFit];
    [label setCenter:[contentView center]];
    [contentView addSubview:label];


}

@end
```

This code is a modified version of the Hello World app in Recipe 11.4. The major difference is that the contentView and label objects are declared outside the function so that they will stay in scope.

To create the button, use the CPButton class and set the button's properties. CPButton works much like UIButton for iOS, and the pattern of use is about the same. Here is how you add it to applicationDidFinishLaunching: method:

```
frame = CGRectMake(CGRectGetWidth([contentView bounds])/2.0 - 40, ↵
CGRectGetMaxY([label frame]) + 10, 80, 24)
var button = [[CPButton alloc] initWithFrame: frame];
[button setAutoresizingMask:CPViewMinXMargin |
                            CPViewMaxXMargin |
                            CPViewMinYMargin |
                            CPViewMaxYMargin];
[button setTitle:"Make Gray"];
[button setTarget:self];
[button setAction:@selector(changeBackground:)];
[contentView addSubview:button];
```

This follows the **target-action** design pattern. You can see that the app controller here is the target and the action is called changeBackground:.

Here's the code for changeBackground: method to change the background color of the app and add content to the label:

```
- (void)changeBackground:(id)aSender{
    var c = [CPColor lightGrayColor];
```

```
    [contentView setBackgroundColor:c];
    [label setStringValue:@"Color Changed!"];
}
```

That's all you need to do to add a button to this web app! See Listing 11-7 for the code.

The Code

Listing 11-7. *AppController.j*

```
@import <Foundation/CPObject.j>

@implementation AppController : CPObject{

}

var label;

var contentView;


- (void)applicationDidFinishLaunching:(CPNotification)aNotification{


    var theWindow = [[CPWindow alloc] initWithContentRect:CGRectMakeZero()↩
styleMask:CPBorderlessBridgeWindowMask];
    contentView = [theWindow contentView];
    var frame = CGRectMake(0, 13.0, 150.0, 24.0);
    label = [[CPTextField alloc] initWithFrame:frame];
     [label setStringValue:@"Press the Button"];
     [label setFont:[CPFont boldSystemFontOfSize:24.0]];
     [label sizeToFit];
     [label setCenter:[contentView center]];
     [contentView addSubview:label];


    frame = CGRectMake(CGRectGetWidth([contentView bounds])/2.0 - 40,  ↩
CGRectGetMaxY([label frame]) + 10, 80, 24);
    var button = [[CPButton alloc] initWithFrame: frame];
     [button setAutoresizingMask:CPViewMinXMargin |
```

```
                                    CPViewMaxXMargin |
                                    CPViewMinYMargin |
                                    CPViewMaxYMargin];
    [button setTitle:"Make Gray"];
    [button setTarget:self];
    [button setAction:@selector(changeBackground:)];
    [contentView addSubview:button];
    [theWindow orderFront:self];
}


- (void)changeBackground:(id)aSender{
    var c = [CPColor lightGrayColor];
    [contentView setBackgroundColor:c];
    [label setStringValue:@"Color Changed!"];
}

@end
```

Usage

To use this app, re-use the template that you set up with the Hello World example in Recipe 11.4. Replace the code in the file `AppController.j` with the code from Listing 11.7.

Run this app by opening `index.html` in the Safari web browser. You may use the Safari File menu to open `index.html` file or you can just drag `index.html` into the Safari icon to open the app. You will see a button and a label in the browser window. Click the button and see how the label content changes and the background color turns to light gray.

Index

CPSIA information can be obtained at www.ICGtesting.com
Printed in the USA
LVOW111802190712

290770LV00002BA/1/P